NEW EXHIBITION STANDS

New Exhibition Stands

Author: Arian Mostaedi

Publisher: Carles Broto

Graphic Design: Federico Orozco

Production: Jorge Carmona

Editorial Coordinator: Jacobo Krauel

Architectural Adviser: Pilar Chueca

Text: Contributed by the architects, edited by Jacobo Krauel and Núria Rodríguez

Photo cover: © HG Esch

© Carles Broto i Comerma
Jonqueres, 10, 1-5
08003 Barcelona, Spain
Tel.: +34 93 301 21 99 Fax: +34-93-301 00 21
E-mail: info@linksbooks.net

Printed in Barcelona, Spain

NEW EXHIBITION STANDS

Index

07 **Introduction**

08 **Fractal Building Systems + Rotor**
fractal building systems

10 **Imagination** orange

12 **Ferruccio Laviani** kartell

14 **Cino Zucchi Architetti** boho light trap

18 **Stefan Zwicky** gt

20 **Jürgen Mayer H.** stylepark lounge

22 **Stefano Colli** design hotels

24 **Arno Design** sto

28 **Lorenc + Yoo** sony ericsson

34 **Burkhardt Leitner constructiv**
deutscher volkshochschul-verband

36 **Imagination** mazda

38 **Sieger Design** blome

42 **Artek** Alvar Aalto furniture

44 **Francesc Rifé** midi

46 **Design Company** sony

50 **Peter Bottazzi** desalto

52 **Schmidhuber + Partner / KMS** O_2

58 **Matali Crasset** casaderme

60 **Ramón Pico + Javier López** pensar la casa

62 **Arno Design** speedo

66 **Stefano Colli** husa hoteles

68 **Burkhardt Leitner constructiv**
helmut jacoby

70 **Deu i Deu** tafesa

72 **Burkhardt Leitner constructiv**
design prize switzerland

76 **Atelier Markgraph**
+ Kauffman Thelig & Partner eads

80 **The GCGroup AG** orange

84 **Atelier Markgraph** daimler chrysler

86 **Artekstands** gas natural

88 **General Graphics Exhibits**
monterrey design systems

90 **Atelier Brückner** kodak

94 **Stefano Colli** tombow

96 **Formpol AG** century

98 **Kaufmann Theilig & Partner**
mercedes-benz & maybach

104 **Stefan Zwicky** legero

106 **D'Art Design Gruppe** horst

110 **Traast & Gruson** hidden

112 **Sieger design** kaldewei

114 **Matteo Thun** zucchetti

116 **Sevil Peach Gence Associates** visplay & vizona

120 **Schmidhuber + Partner** audi

126 **Form 3** blend of america

128 **Rotor + Fractal Building Systems**
under water vessel

130 **Vicente Sarrablo, Jordi Roviras & Cristina García** dcpal

132 **Francesc Rifé** cerámicas diago

136 **Droog Design + Traast & Gruson** bang & olufsen

138 **D'Art Design Gruppe** zack

140 **Rotor + Fractal Building Systems**
modular (freep deez)

144 **Athanasios Megarisiotis & Matthias Siegert** :fepcon

146 **Atelier Brückner** panasonic

152 **D'Art Design Gruppe** mono

154 **Peter Maly** ligne roset + cor

158 **Arno Design** hoechst marion

160 **Mariona Benaín, Patricia de Muga & Laura García Hintze**
cemex-españa

164 **Traast & Gruson** droog design

166 **Dieter Thiel** ansorg

168 **Gert M. Mayr-Keber** perlen pöll

170 **Zeeh Bahls & Partner Design** siemens

178 **KMS / Schmidhuber + Partner** lamborghini

Introduction

In today's media-saturated and design-savy marketplace, a company's image is just as important to its success as the quality of the product or service it provides. Top companies dedicate a considerable part of their resources to creating a strong corporate image that sets them apart from competitors. Increasingly, this includes developing a strong presence at industry trade fairs, which play an important role in attracting potential clients. This situation has led many companies to engage the services of some of the leading names in architecture and design when planning their stands, and to the birth of a new hybrid discipline combining cutting-edge elements of both marketing and spatial design.

Designing a stand is a new kind of challenge for architects and designers. It requires them to transmit the essence of a company in a much smaller scale and time frame than traditional architecture, allowing them to experiment and propose unusual and innovative solutions. In order to be successful, a stand must balance a striking and eye-catching design with perfectly reflecting the company's products and image. The nearly 60 stands in this collection have been selected according to this criteria. Some of the most innovative architectural work being done today is illustrated here, with designers using unusual materials and the latest technology to differentiate their designs and create a lasting impression in a short time.

Ranging from modest one-room stalls to sprawling, multi-story stands and representing industries as diverse as jewelry, automobiles, construction materials and furniture, this collection surveys the spectrum of stand styles, from the simple and classy to high-tech or experimental designs. It includes the work of some of the most respected and brilliant professionals and design groups, such as Cino Zucchi, Traast & Gruson, Jürgen Mayer H., Ferrucio Laviani and Matali Crasset. We hope this overview of the most interesting work being done in this rapidly evolving field will be a source of insight and inspiration for the reader.

Fractal Building Systems + Rotor
fractal building systems

Fractal derives its name from a fractal, a random computer drawing based on mathematical formulas resulting in endless unpredictable forms.

Being trendsetters in the world of design, Fractal Building Systems wanted a stand with aesthetic appearance, and ended up creating the now famous perforated profile called Fractal. At popular demand of architects and designers, Fractal continued to manufacture and sell new profiles. Since then Fractal has never stopped developing original designer materials.

This stand for the 100% Design trade fair in London was a simple and striking demonstration of Blobb-profile and acrylic plates as construction materials. The "wobbly" stand made maximum use of the sculptural and colour possibilities of the materials, in a vibrant red, rounded space that was womb-like and high-tech at the same time.

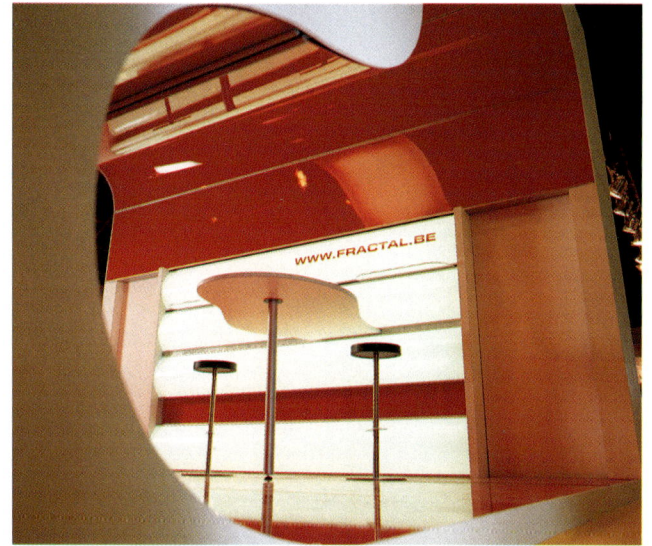

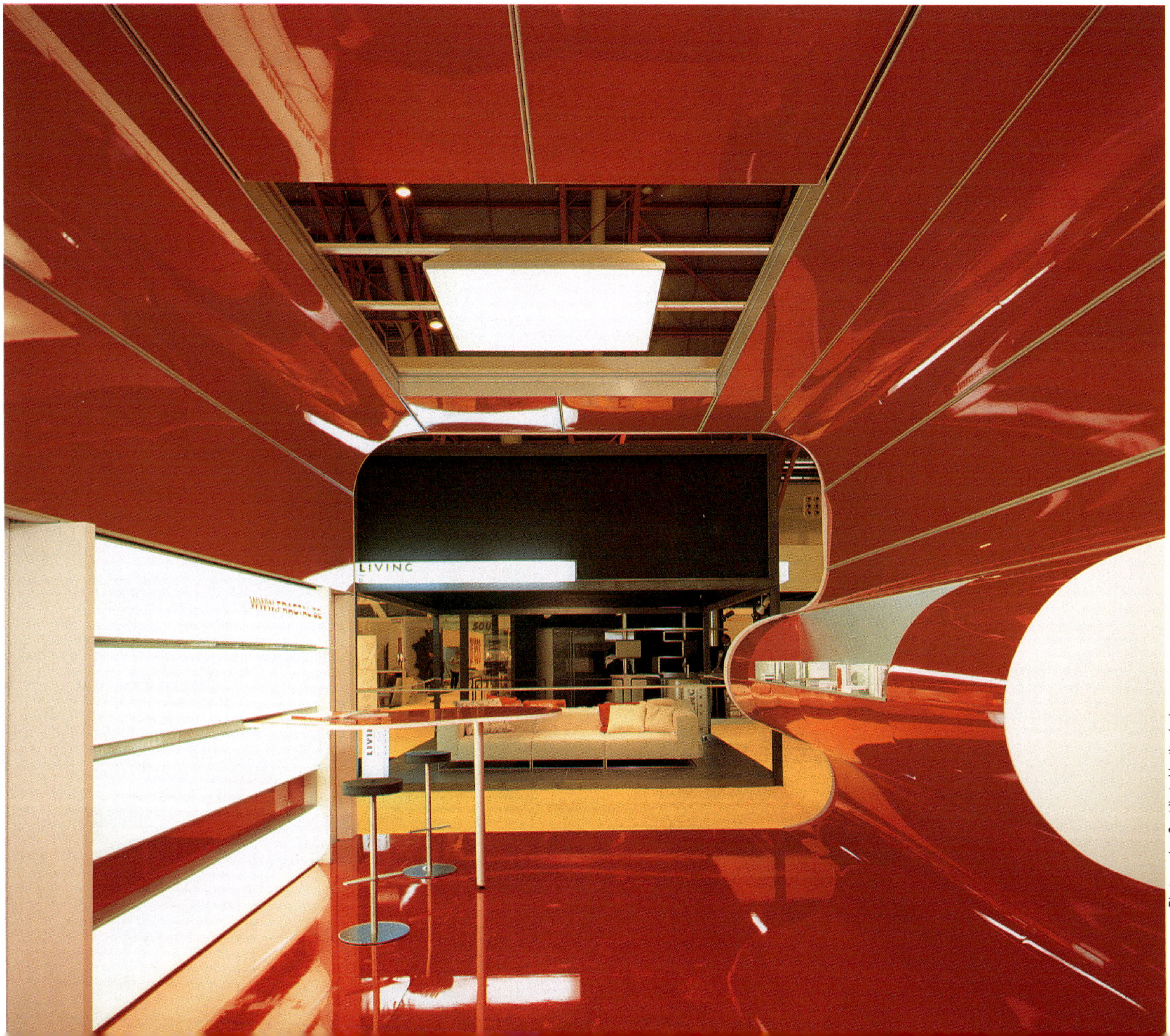

Photographs: Contributed by the designers

Imagination
orange

The objective of this presentation was to create an experiential zone from an empty space. Imagination developed an interactive learning environment in which the wireless technology 'experience' was explained from a child's perspective in simple, fun, surprising and stimulating ways. The idea was to engage the imagination of a child on a multi-sensory level.

The experience was a fully immersive one where the senses and the environment connected and interacted, helping children to understand that both now and in the future, their voices, hearing - or mere presence - will connect them to the world around them, and allow them to control various aspects of their lives.

The Orange Imaginarium experience is divided up to 3 different areas:

Say Your Name demonstrates that machines will respond like people. Children interact with directional speakers which play back their voices at different pitches and which the children find fun and interactive.

Photographs: Contributed by the designers

Tell Me a Joke is the zone in which voice activation technology has been developed to recognise children's individual voices and interacts with them by telling them jokes at their request. Chase the Rainbow allows children to move through clusters of touch sensitive fibre optics turning them from white to orange in a representation of how technology can personalise their space.

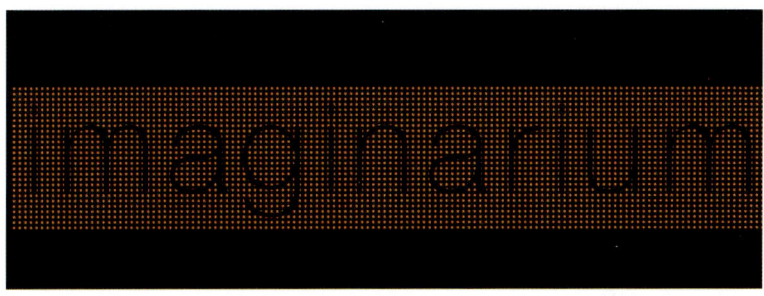

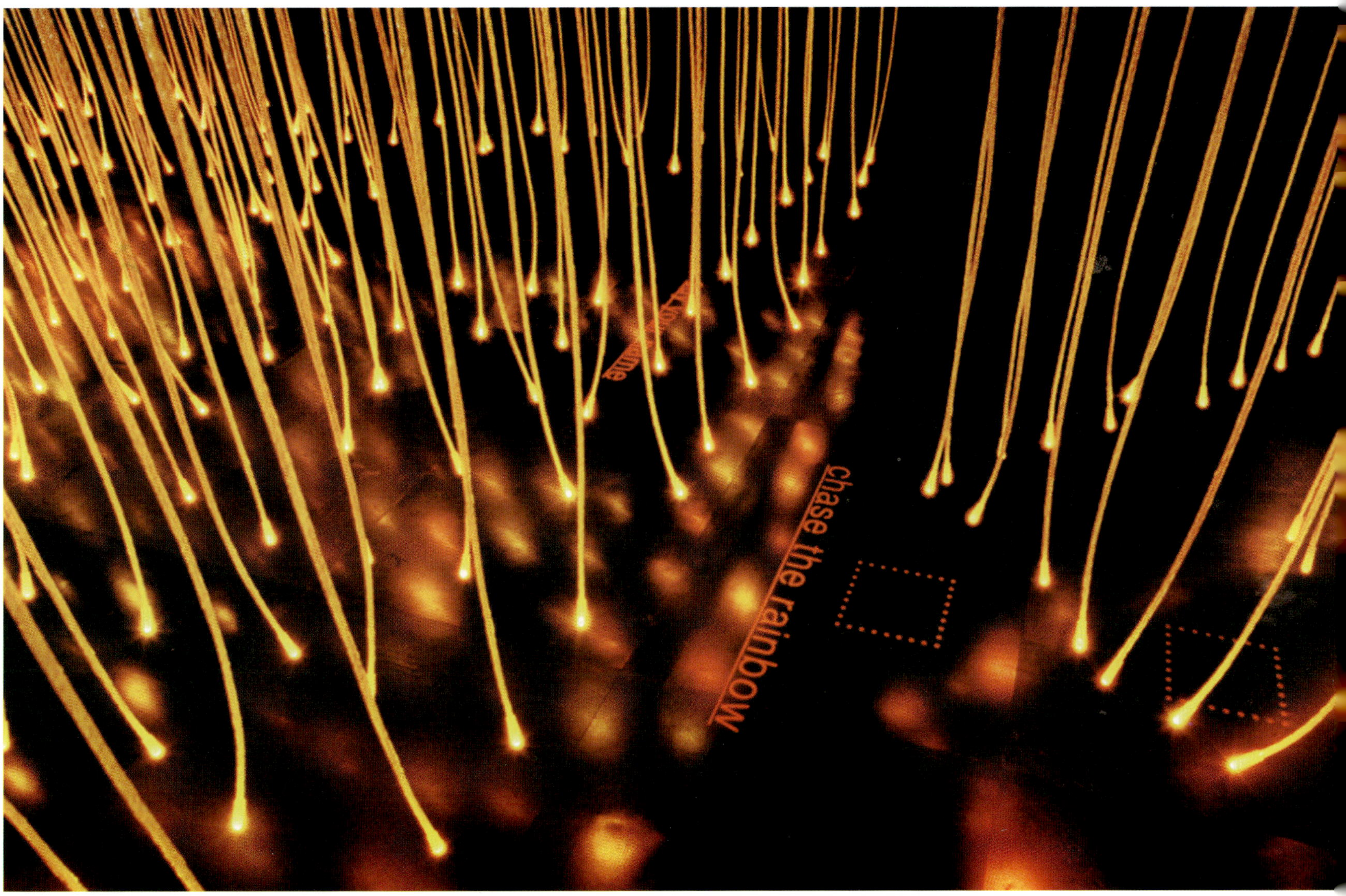

Ferruccio Laviani

kartell

The aim of the Kartell stand at the 2003 Furniture Fair was to bring together all the best-known Kartell products and allow them to interact in a feast of colors, images and designs. Ferrucio Laviani once again abandoned all preconceived ideas to transform the space into a fantasy world that expressed the spirit of the Kartell brand, the perfect showcase for its products.

The image of an infinite rainbow was used as the main design element, capturing the brand's free, happy, ironic and unconventional style. The stand was an open container crossed with rainbows, luminous colored platforms and words, with a background of palm trees, horses and a seaside town against a blue sky. The central area was populated by larger-than-life cut outs of anonymous people on their individual journeys around the world.

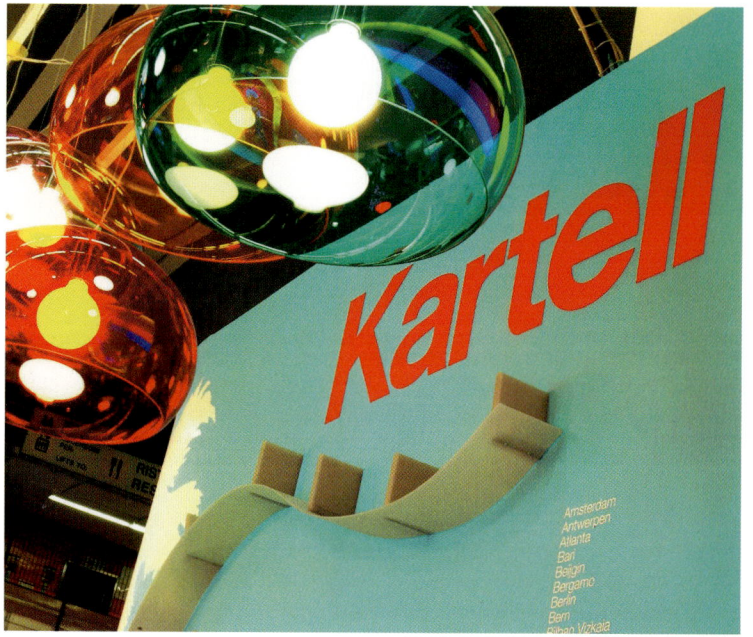

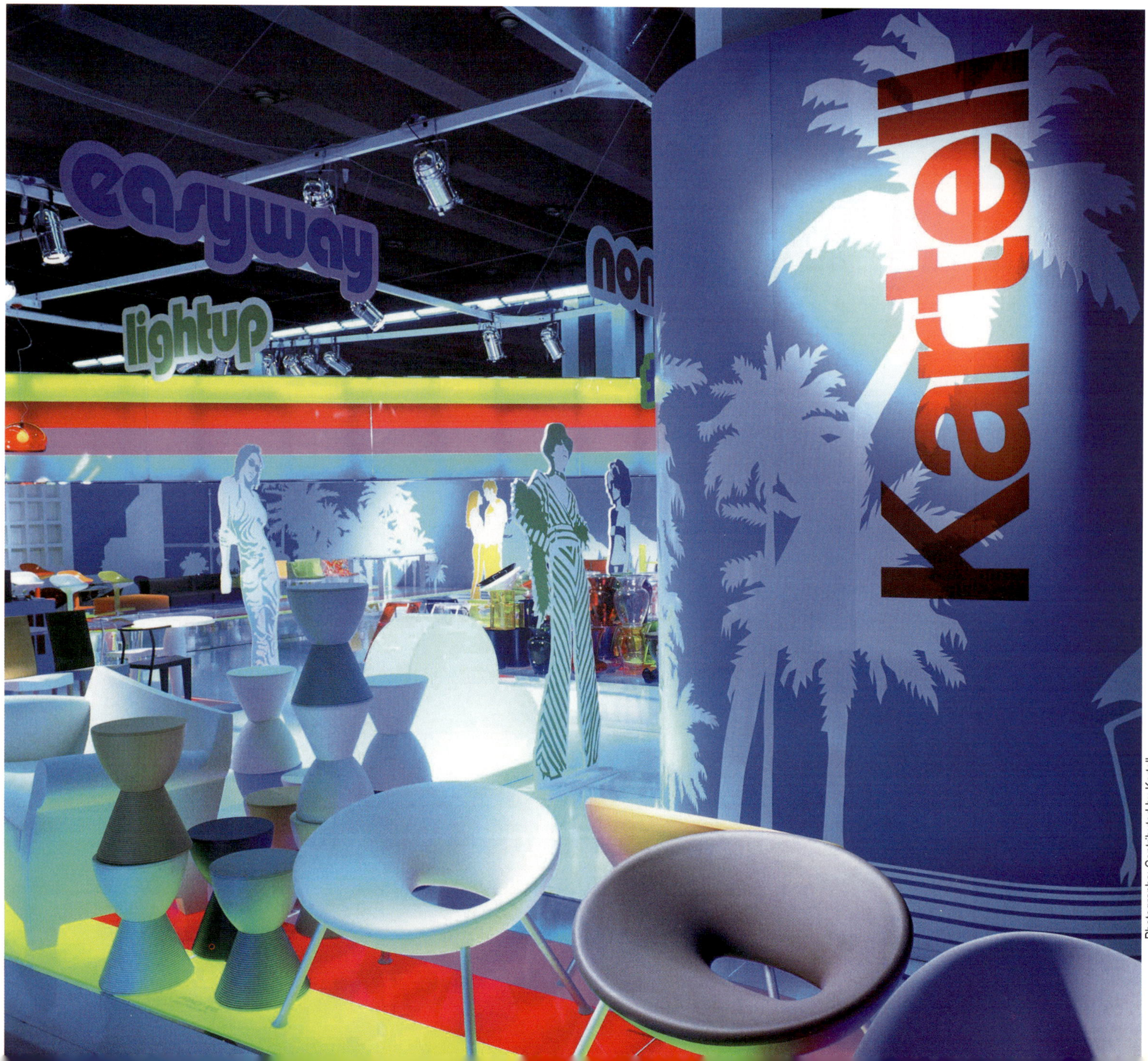

Photographs: Contributed by Kartell

Cut-out figures of young people populated the stand, transmitting the brand's fun, free image. Visitors could wonder through this bright, happy world that showcased the company´s products.

Cino Zucchi Architetti
boho light trap

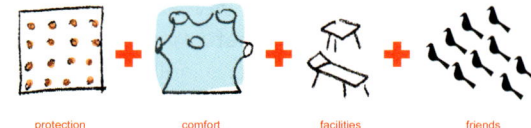

protection   comfort   facilities   friends

"Lonely Living" is an event that explores the private and public spheres of today's "extended cities", where different lifestyles merge in a new and changing social landscape. The "urban nomad" is the new type of citizen that best defines this new condition, where the traditional private domain is being replaced by new ways of organizing individual space. The client-dweller for the Lonely Living pavilion was Gustavo Gandini, an environmentalist involved in battles to save endangered environments, the prototype involved scientist who frequently moves between an urban, academic environment, and a wild, primary one.

The (con)temporary shelter took the form of a double shell that evoked tropical climates and environments. It consisted of an outer layer in the shape of an abstract cubic volume 4x4x4 meters made of recycled wood panels, and a tent-like interior. The use of natural materials and irregular shapes provoked an imaginative and emotional response to the structure and the environment.

The external wooden cube was pierced at regular intervals by small holes and interrupted by larger round "windows" of different dimensions. The interior of the cube contained a few basic pieces of furniture - a bed, a bucket, a camp chair and a table. These were protected by a large tent made of stretch fabric, which articulated the single space into a series of smaller areas according to function. The rays of sunlight that passed through the smaller holes were filtered through this inner skin, creating fluctuating optical effects.

The pavilion was a homage to life in the open, to the concept of nomadism and architecture conceived as an amplifier of natural phenomena. The exterior resembled an aerated box for the transportation of animals rather than a pavilion (in this case, a shy and savage King Kong - Gustavo Gandini being transported to the city and the Biennale spotlights).

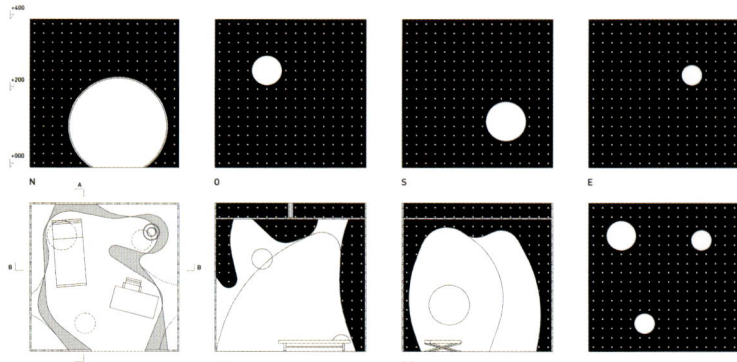

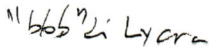

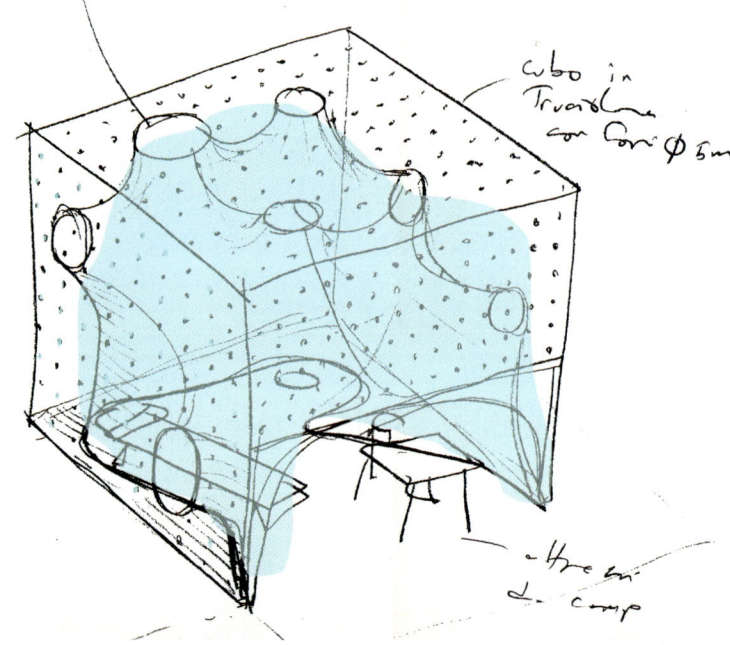

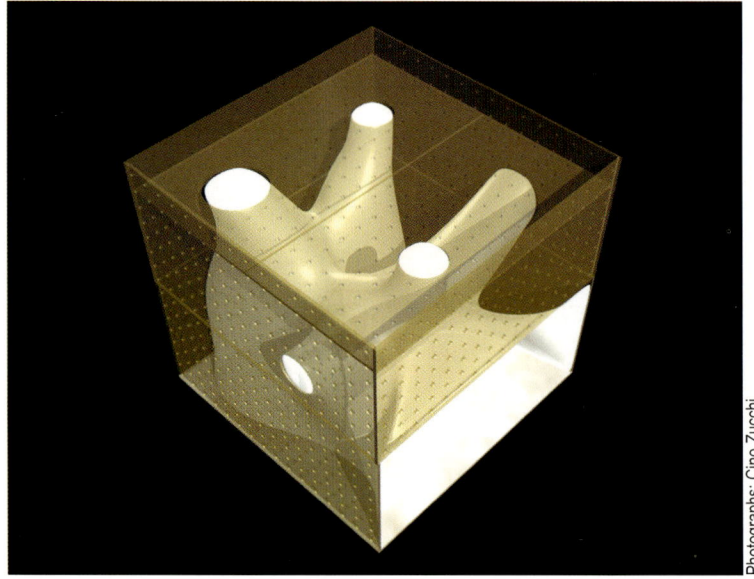

Photographs: Cino Zucchi

14

The warped geometry of the interior space resonates with cultural and natural references: a heart ready for transplant; a hollow baobab tree; the sensual stage set for the movie Barbarella; the innocent utopian experiments of 1960's and 70's "radical architecture" for a future that never arrived.

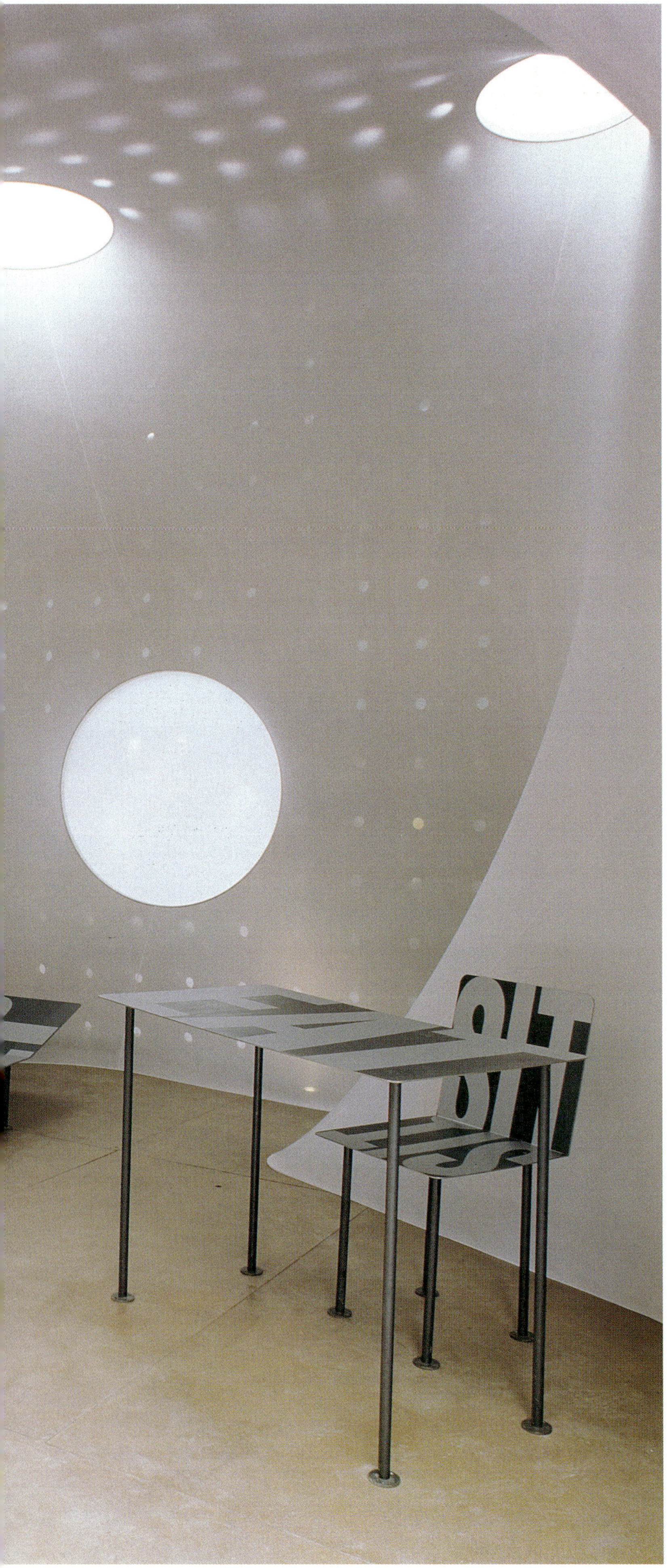

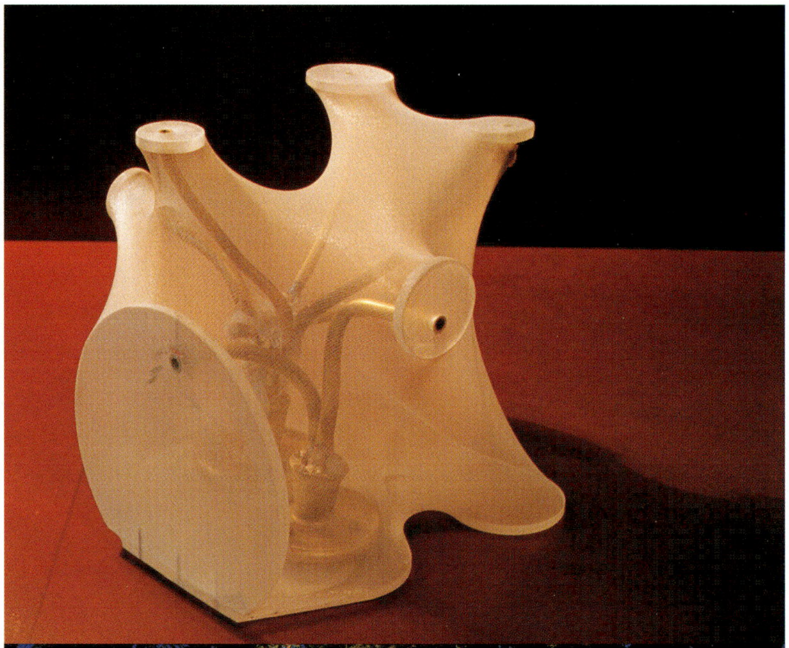

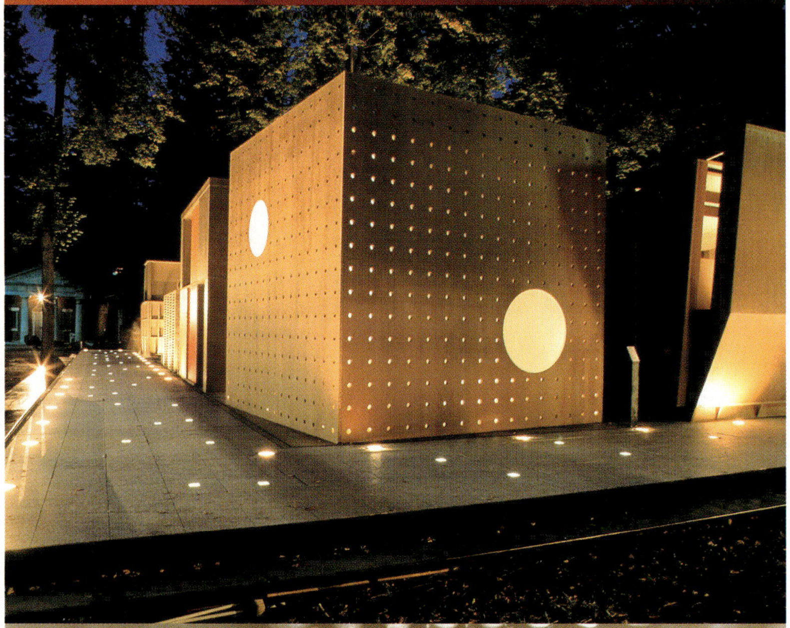

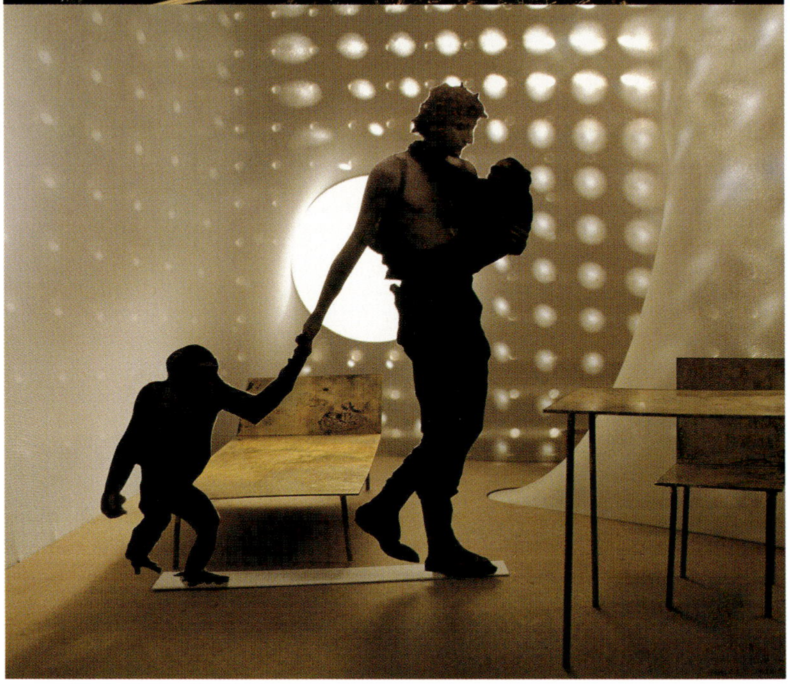

Stefan Zwicky

gt

The aim of the CTC (Cycle Trading Company) stand at the 2-Rad 2000 trade fair in Zurich was to create a new image for the bicycle brand GT. The design was based on the rotating arms of a windmill, which evoked the idea of a bicycle and worked well within the "island" characteristics of the stand. This concept translated into four enormous, brightly colored walls placed on a wooden podium in a rotating configuration. From the outside, these walls were a striking point of reference for the stand, while creating an intimate internal courtyard space. The spaces between the walls allowed visitors glimpses into the center of the stand from any angle, and invited them to approach and enter. The bicycles were arranged along the walls, while the inner patio featured the newest or star products.

Photographs: Contributrd by the designer

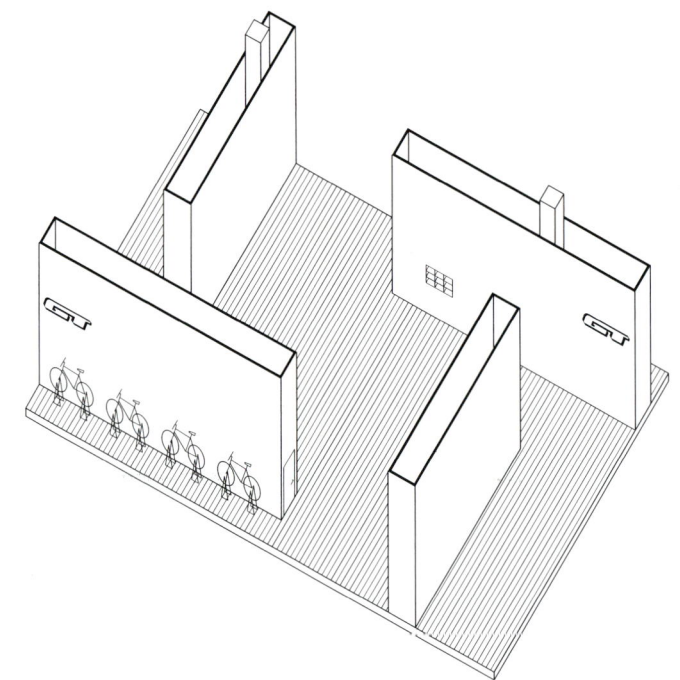

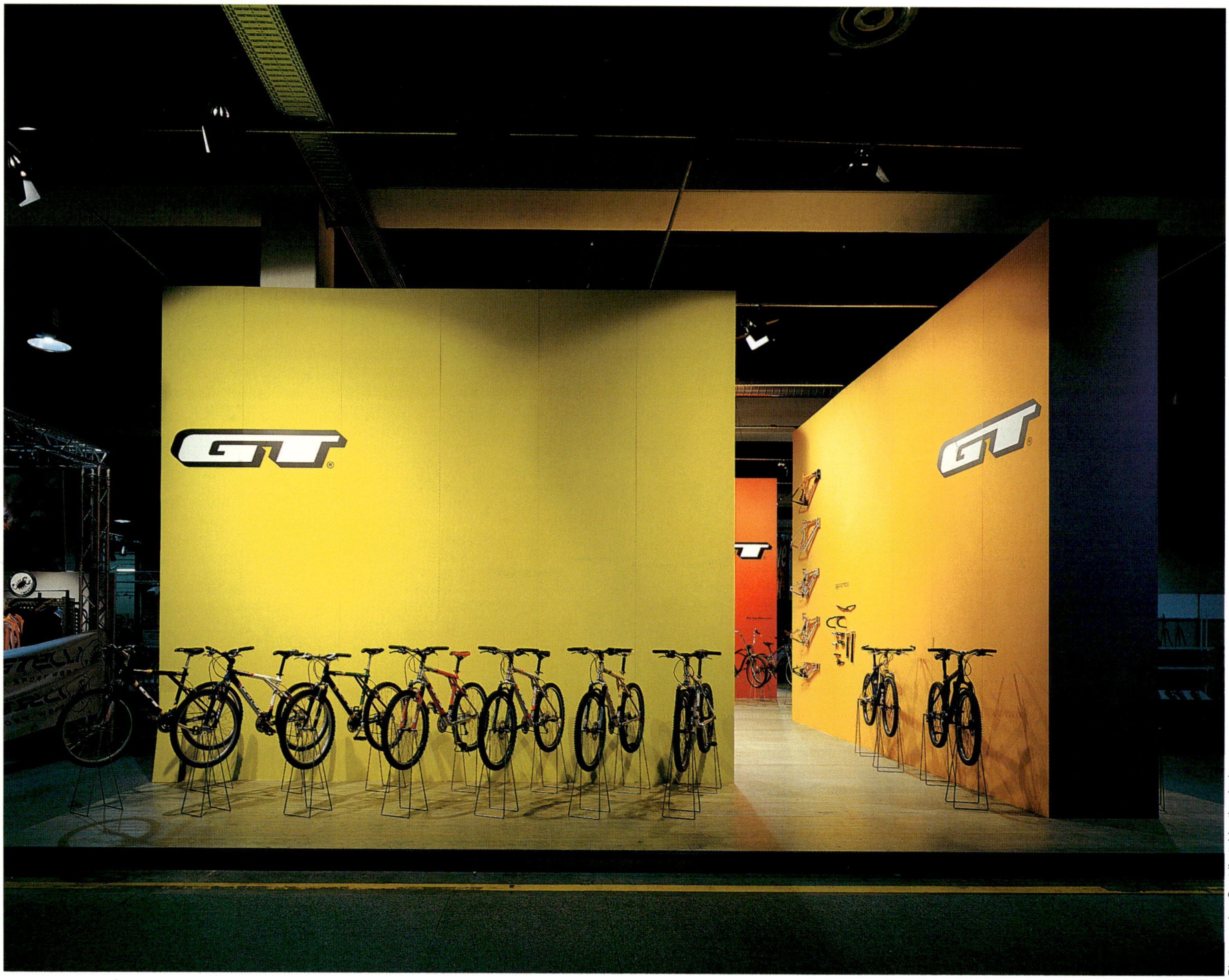

Jürgen Mayer H.
stylepark lounge

Stylepark AG presented its latest Case Study project within the framework of the XXI UIA Congress and PlanCom 2002 trade fair, events aimed at planning professionals in the construction industry. Stylepark asked Berlin-based architect J. Mayer H. to design an interactive lounge to be used by visiting professionals. The idea of the project was to create an attractive and comfortable lounge space that would allow visitors to explore and interact with computer terminals. The main feature of the lounge were the terminals displaying a new software tool for creative processes, a cooperatively designed project that aims to generate new perceptions though emotional interaction and engaging users in a playful process.

The design of the lounge reflected the playful and creative character of the new tool. It was based around the idea of transforming the linoleum floor surface into an undulating topography that separated the different functional requirements. Communication areas, lounge zones, video projections and interactive elements fused into each other, connecting all the different elements into a homogeneous but structured configuration. Active and passive information suggested privacy and openness. The conventional categories of furniture, wall and multimedia display were transformed into a communications landscape that incorporated and provided all these elements, creating a close interaction between the space and the visitor.

This meeting lounge was specifically designed to be used at the UIA and PlanCom, but its modular system allows for various configurations and can therefore be adapted to other sites in future.

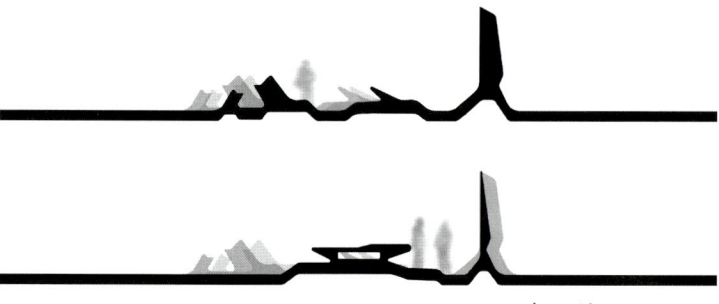

elevations

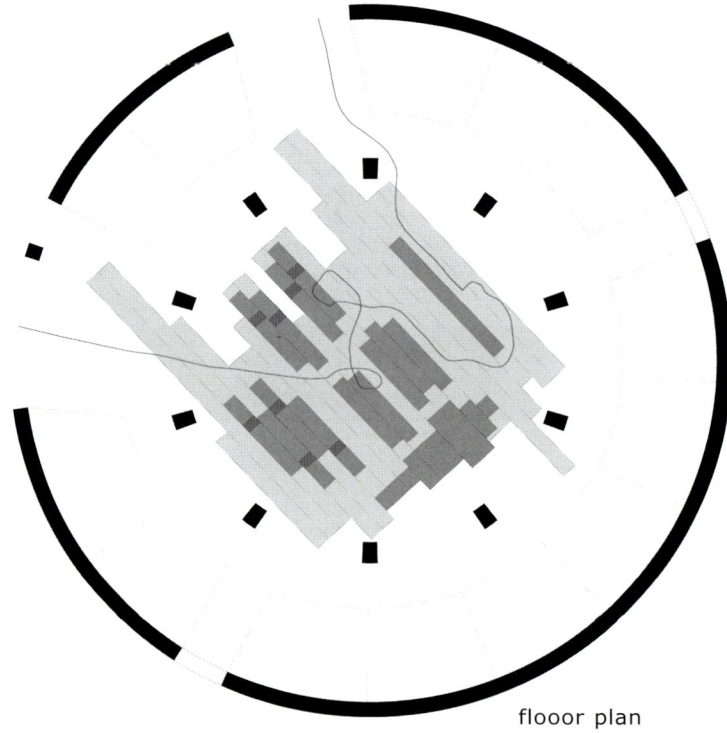

flooor plan

The playful, unusual elements blur the lines between hardware, furniture and architecture and encourage visitors to interact with each other and the displays. The design invites trade fair visitors to approach the terminals showcasing the new software tool with an open mind and a playful attitude. The open plan allows the relaxation and meeting areas, terminals and video projections to blend into a single space, while maintaining their separate functions.

Stefano Colli
design hotels

This stand was designed as recessed area that opened out to the corridor and contained a single, expressive furniture element that could be used for generating different situations, meetings, water tastings…

For the wall coverings, one of the most distinctive features of the stand, the designers chose to use white Styrofoam cubes of varying thickness. These pieces absorbed sound and provided soundproofing as well as contributing to the expressive quality of the stand.

The stand also included an adjacent storage area, separated from the rest of the stand by a PVC curtain that allowed visitors to glimpse its red interior.

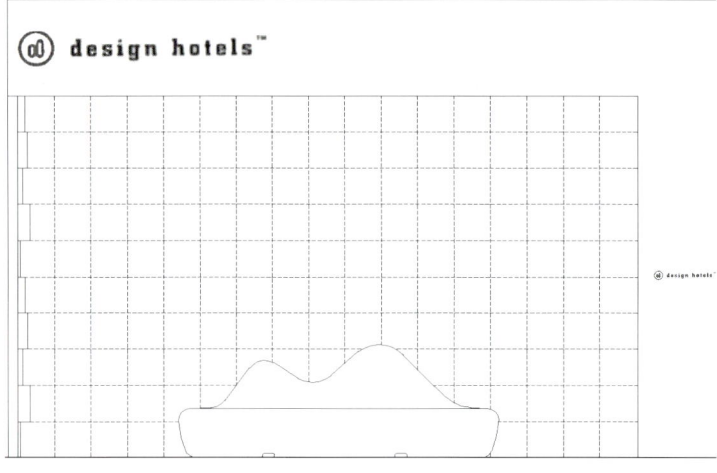

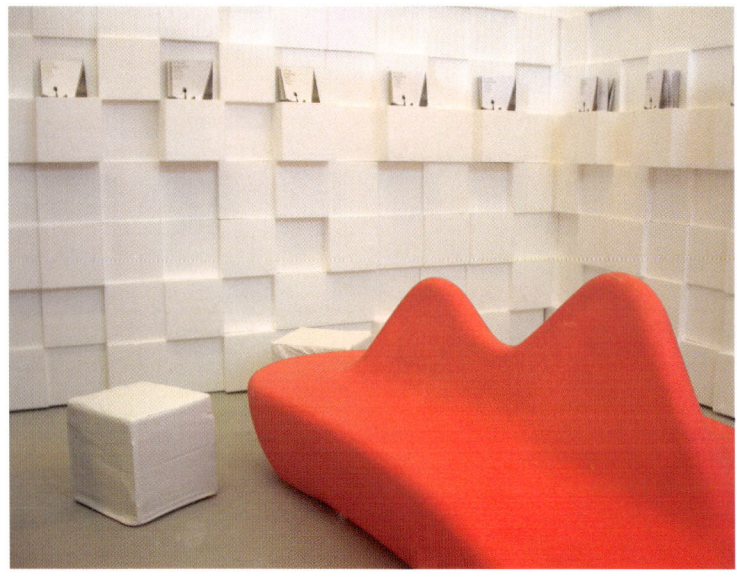

Photographs: Contributed by the architect

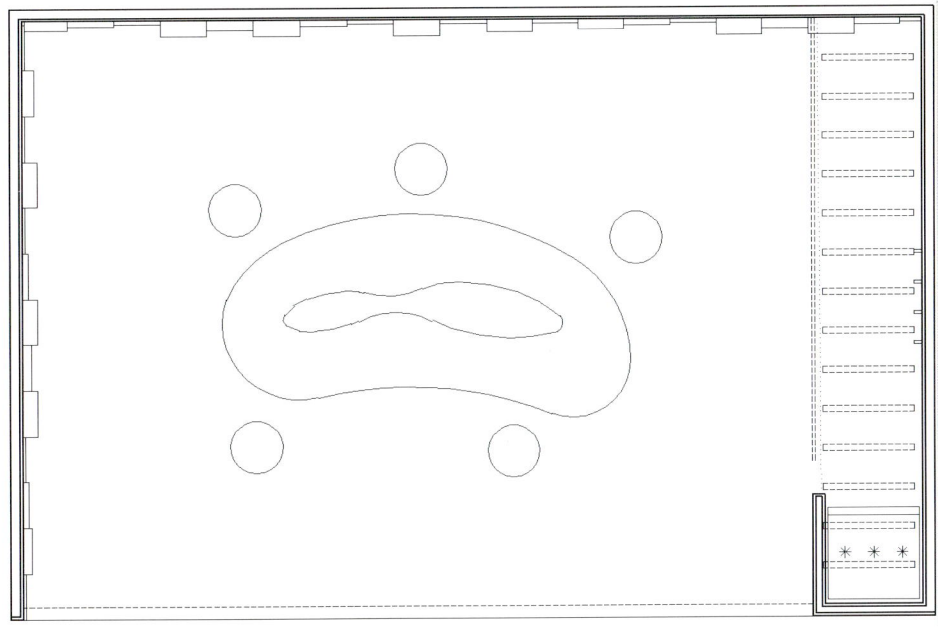

Arno Design
sto

Arno Design, the company that has designed Sto's trade fair presence for over 10 years, was once again entrusted to design the company's stand for the Farbe 2002 fair in Munich, at which the revolutionary new Sto Color Fan was to be launched. Their brief was to allow visitors to experience the new Sto Color Fan, to encourage communication with the public, to express the brand's self-confidence, and to represent Sto's vision.

The 700 m² area was designed to represent a town, the environment that best corresponds to the market for Sto products. "Building cubes" were used as rooms for visitors to visit and learn about the products, a "main square" with a pool provided a meeting point, and "advertising spaces" were projected on colored areas of the transparent walls. The stand was both open and intimate, a feature that was appreciated by many visitors to the fair. The real pool in the center was a calm place that encouraged conversation and also afforded an overview of the entire stand. Close by, visitors were encouraged to touch a large model representing Sto's entire world of colors and structures. The exterior of the stand was gray and, other than the yellow house color, there was nothing to hint at the colorful interior - a "gray giant" that only revealed its nature to curious and interested visitors. Inside, primary color theories formed the basis of the stand, and four colors from the Sto Color Fan range - orange, wine-red, pink and mustard-yellow - were used to convey different moods and impressions in each of the spaces.

The cube dedicated to the Color Fan included multi-media elements. Monitors on plain bases inside the cubes showed clips, collages and images full of light and color, and drawers in the bases contained items related to the corresponding color.

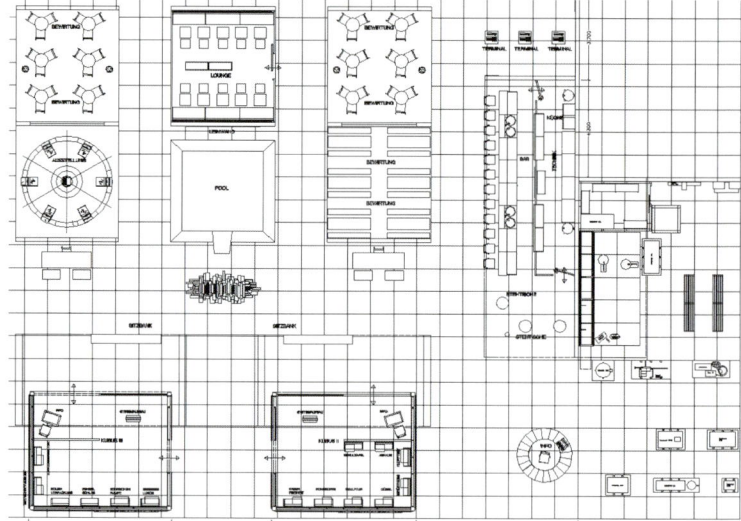

Photographs: Contributed by the designers

The Color Fan concept was used throughout the design, with the designers aiming to create a sensual experience in order to reach the hearts and minds of visitors to the stand. Their strategy was to use unexpected materials, projections, and, in particular, color. In the VIP lounge, for example, pink designer benches stood against bright orange walls, and a striking multicolored bar was created from individual lacquered layers. Throughout the stand, colors were used to separate different elements and at the same time create a sense of unity and a connection between product and emotion, information and experience.

Lorenc + Yoo
sony ericsson

Designed as a monument within the 2002 CTIA Orlando Convention center, the Sony Ericsson Exhibit stands in stark white contrast to the visually hyperactive booths nearby. Its sinuous planes bend gracefully, spelling out the two capital letters of the newly formed company it represents. Simultaneously weighty and massive yet ethereal and fluid, the undulating minimalist S+E letters visually symbolize the two industry titans' prominent positions of strength and futuristic outlook. The shared geometry of the letters allows for interlocking of their forms along the centerline of the exhibit, so the S+E reads properly from each exhibit aisle.

Practically, the sweep of the two-level design accommodates the dual program of the exhibit: product demonstration and reception on the first level, and private conference on the second. Raised almost two feet above the convention floor (like prominent architectural precedents), the elevated floor gives visitors the impression they are entering a significant event space. The linear slotted ceiling above tightens the sense of space, creating a focused environment for previewing small electronic devices.

Bound between the ethereal floating floor plane above and the curved sweep of the inside wall plane, visitors occupy a surreal environment of technology. Circular acrylic discs showcase high-tech devices against the curved wall behind, and bent planes with circular punches form demonstration counters. A white-green halo of light illuminates the space from the displays. A custom bent tubular rod "cellular wave" sculpture grows like a tree from a four-person circular ottoman below where visitors are encouraged to try phones out personally. Illuminated phone globes anchor the corners and 1960's styled Ball chairs allow visitors to retreat from the party inside.

Photographs: Contributed by the designers

Sony Ericsson
Sony Ericsson

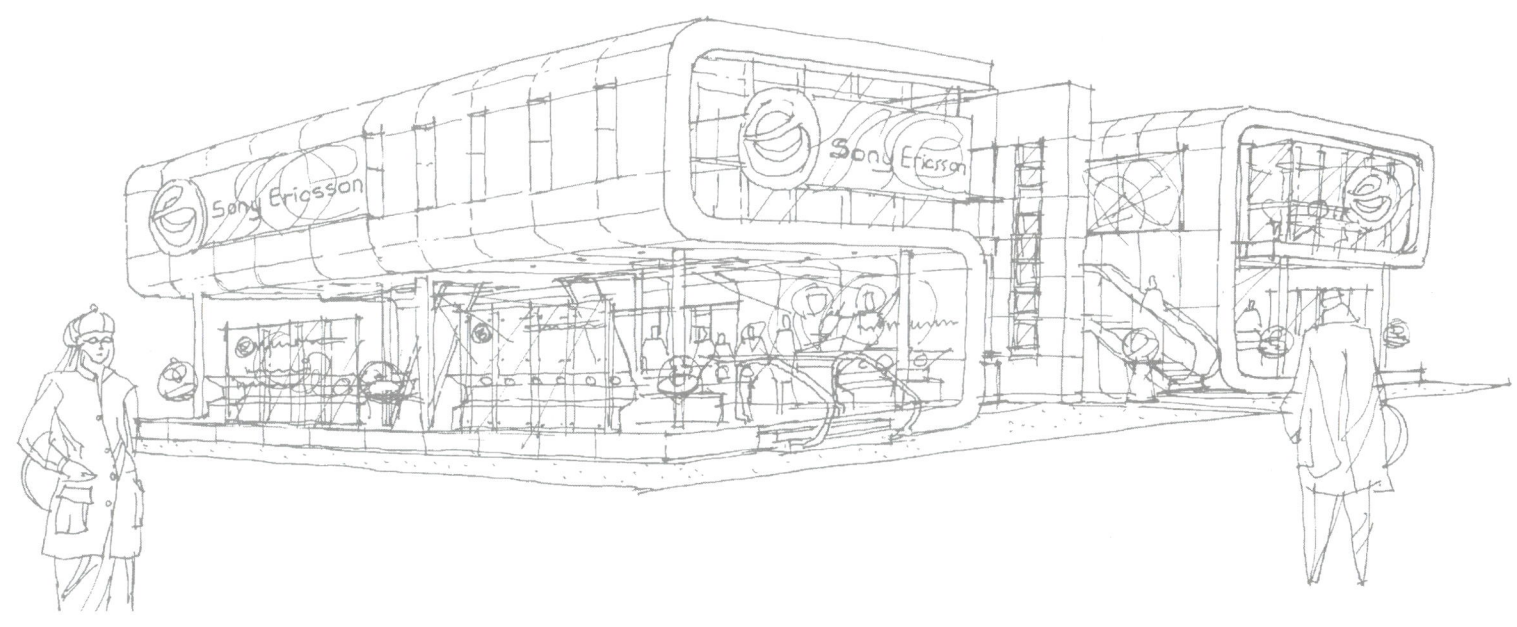

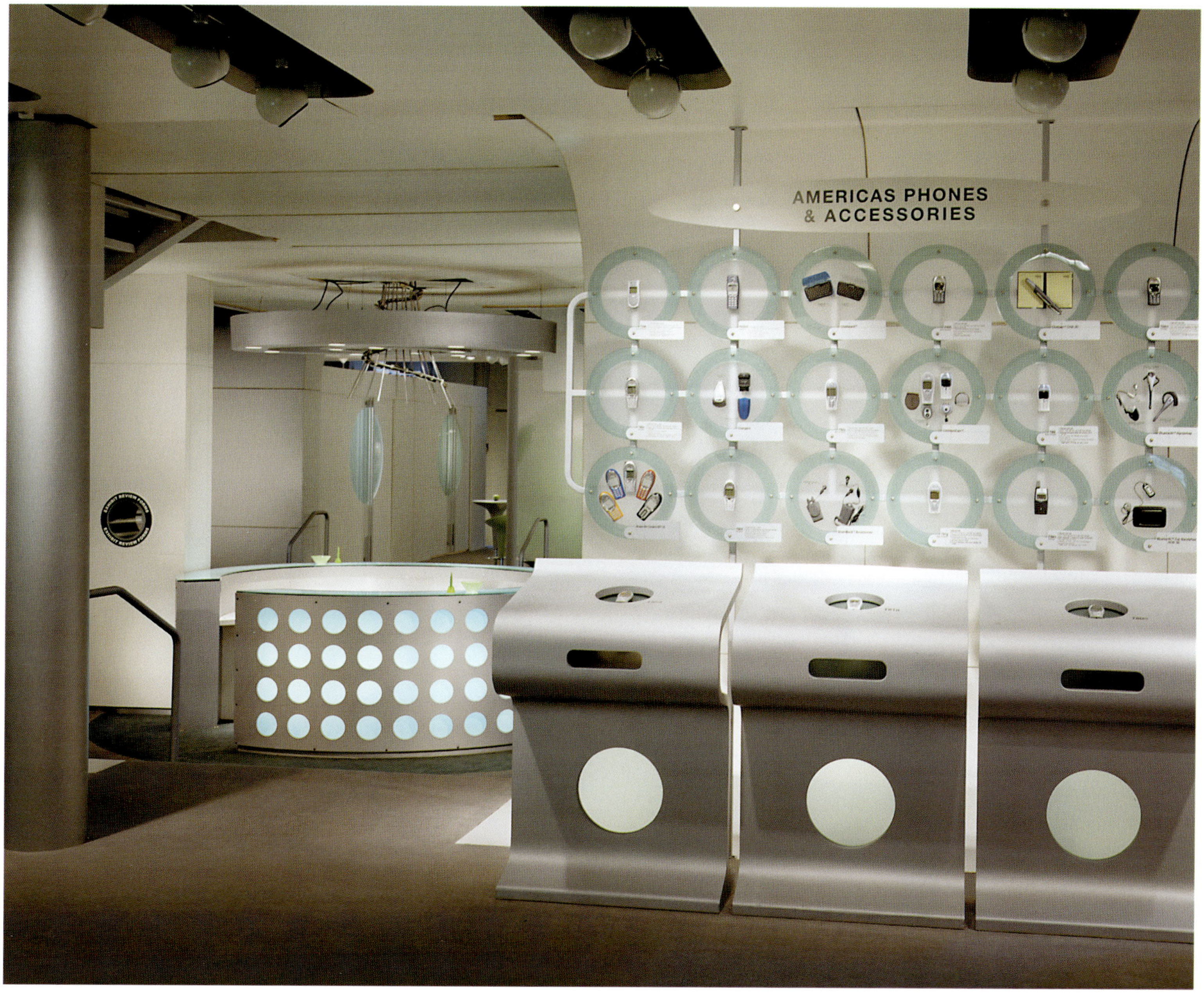
AMERICAS PHONES
& ACCESSORIES

ENTERTAINMENT
Fun on the go
GLOBAL PRODUCTS

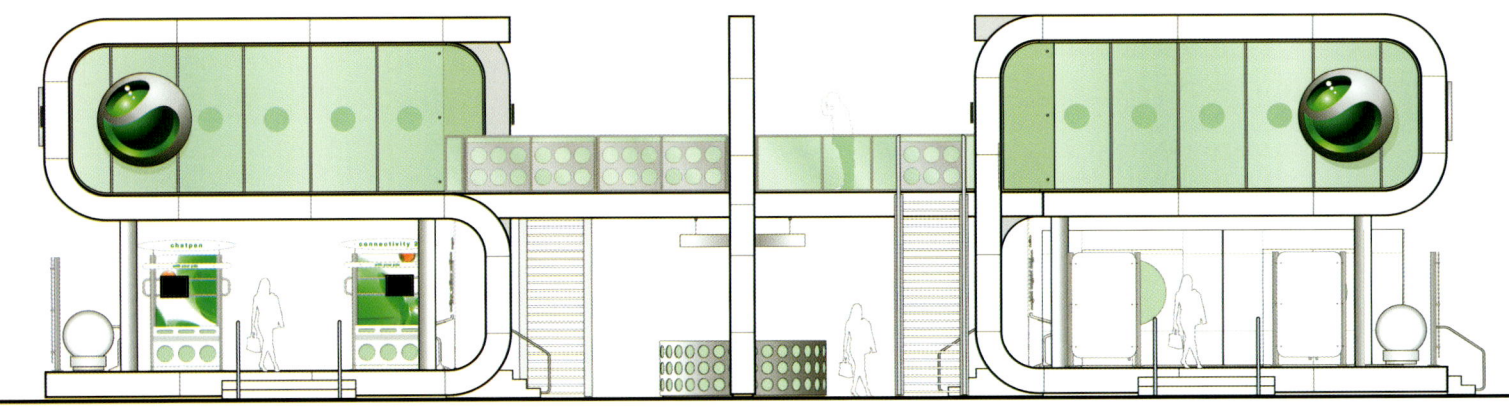

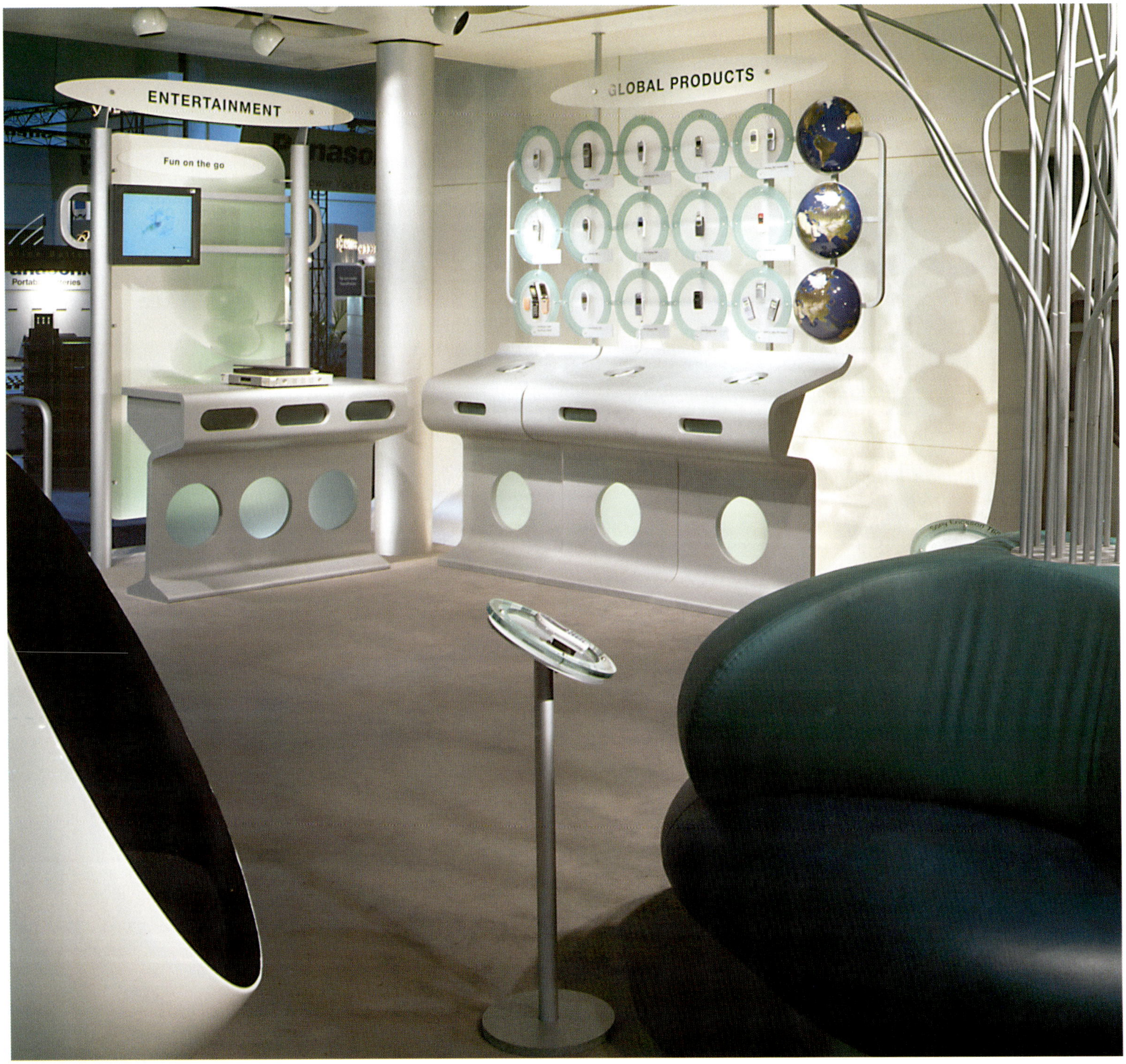

Hovering above, the second floor is designed for meetings, with one large conference room for sixteen persons and two smaller eight-person conference spaces. Connected by an upper reception bridge, the two-sided conference level was designed for private presentations. Each space maintains privacy by using exterior translucent plexiglass walls punctuated by a linear series of clear portholes to allow an overview of the surrounding convention floor. Inside a perforated aluminum wall, cellular devices are profiled and compliment the sweep of the outer white wall. Yellow "paper clip" credenzas with translucent doors float clear of outside curved wall panels. Overhead wide open slotted panels define the conference spaces while meeting fire code requirements. A 60's inspired breakout room is abstracted and simplified from old diner models and is complete with circular banquets and lava lamps.

medium/charcol grey carpet
Ball chair
silver pipe rail
white chairs
ELISE Floor lamp
Globus chair
green carpet strip
Ball chair:
silver or white ext.
green/greenblue interior
silver pipes
22'-0"
50'-0"
90'-0"

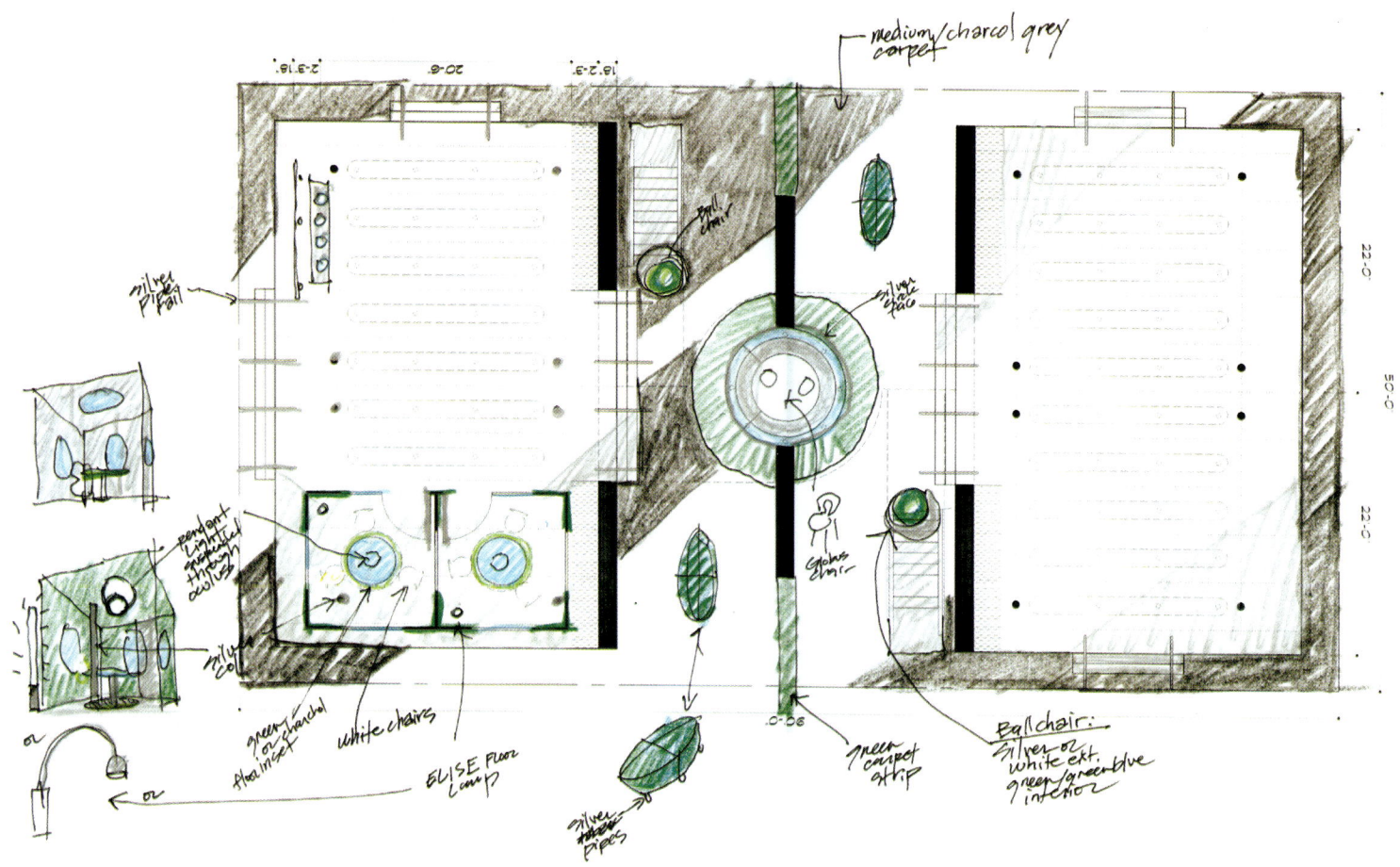

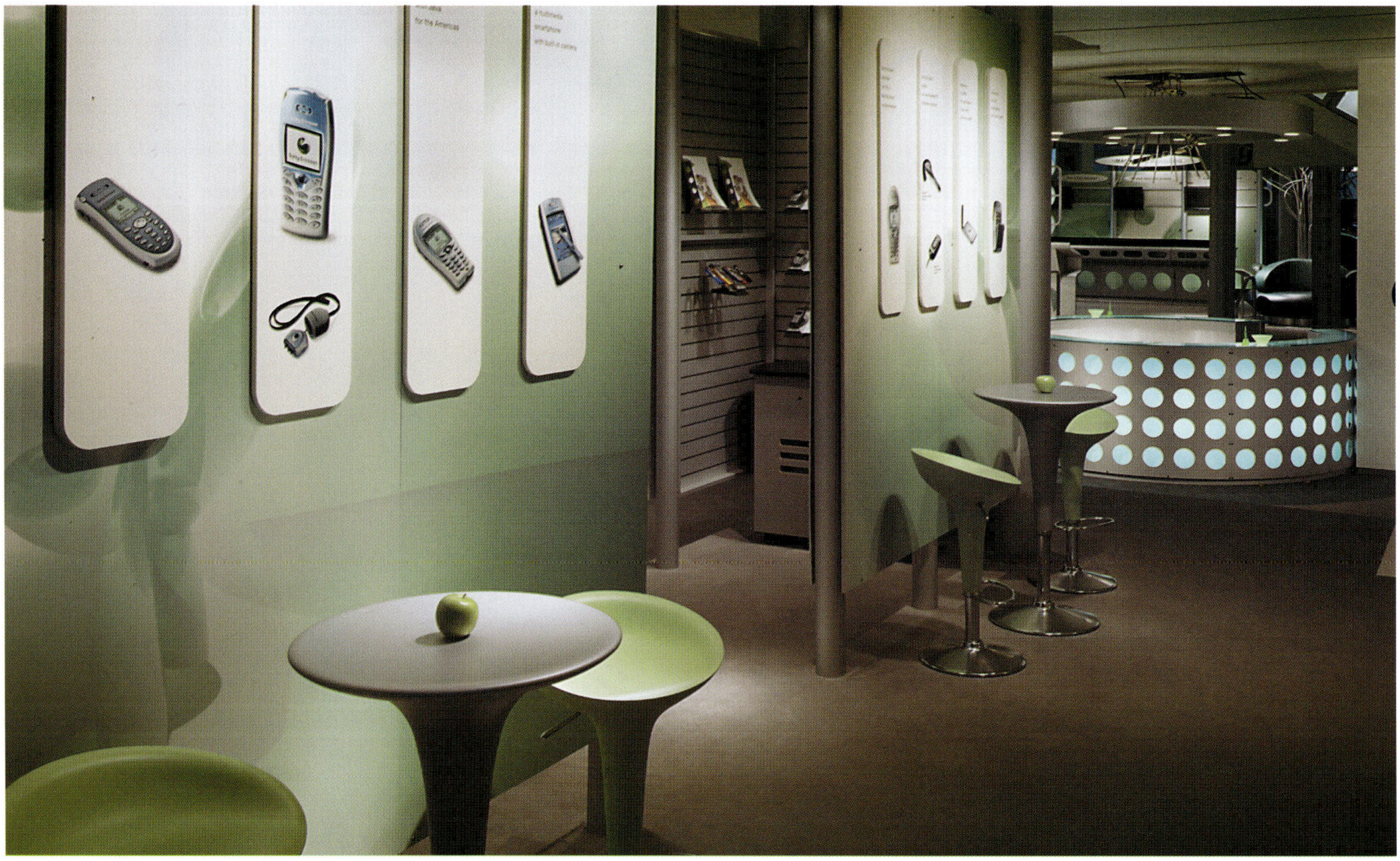

Burkhardt Leitner constructiv
Design: Ballweg & Ballweg, München + Häussler, Erbach
deutscher volkshochschul-verband

Whether designing for Ulm's "Kornhaus" or the "Altes Rathaus" stand, the touring exhibition about the "Weisse Rose" anti-Nazi group (shown on these pages), the designers of this stand had to contend with a variety of ever-changing spatial conditions, each one unique to each new venue.

For that reason, the exhibition walls were designed using the company's own "constructiv CLIC" system. This system uses modules that can be set up either singly or back to back, and in variable heights. Flexible and modular, it is particularly suitable for changing and travelling exhibitions that benefit from short assembly and dismantling times, and low transport volume and weight.

The uniform back lighting that forms part of the system means the modules are also independent of the frequently inadequate lighting conditions in many trade show venues. This modular-designed exhibition could be set up in new configurations each time, not only to fit flexibly into the allotted space, but also to explore different ways of communicating the theme. It was a good example of exhibition architecture as a dialogue between space and content.

Photographs: Frank Schubert

34

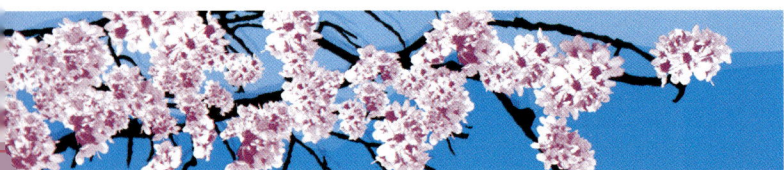

Imagination

mazda

The concept for the Mazda exhibition stand at the North American International Auto Show 2003, held in Detroit, was developed and delivered by Imagination, a global design and communications company with it's headquarters in London. The brief was to bring the Mazda brand to life, present key feature vehicles and create an engaging visitor experience. The stand also had to be capable of adapting easily to other global autoshows throughout the automotive exhibition calendar.

The Mazda brand DNA is epitomised by three words: stylish, insightful, spirited. As well as expressing those defining elements, the Mazda stand had to evoke the brand's Japanese heritage and the dynamic qualities of contemporary Japanese culture.

The design strategy to achieve this was appealing in its simplicity - the brand DNA inspired the creation of three related zones, each dedicated to one of the three core brand values. These Zones occupied a series of raised floors, creating a more stimulating experience for the visitor. Inside each Zone, visitors encountered vehicle displays relating to that particular brand element as well as graphic interactive multimedia installations communicating key messages. These Zones were clustered around the heart of the stand, which displayed a single star vehicle (the Mazda RX-8). The backdrop to this area was a large scale curving LED wall some 10 feet high and 70 feet long - a unique visitor attraction.

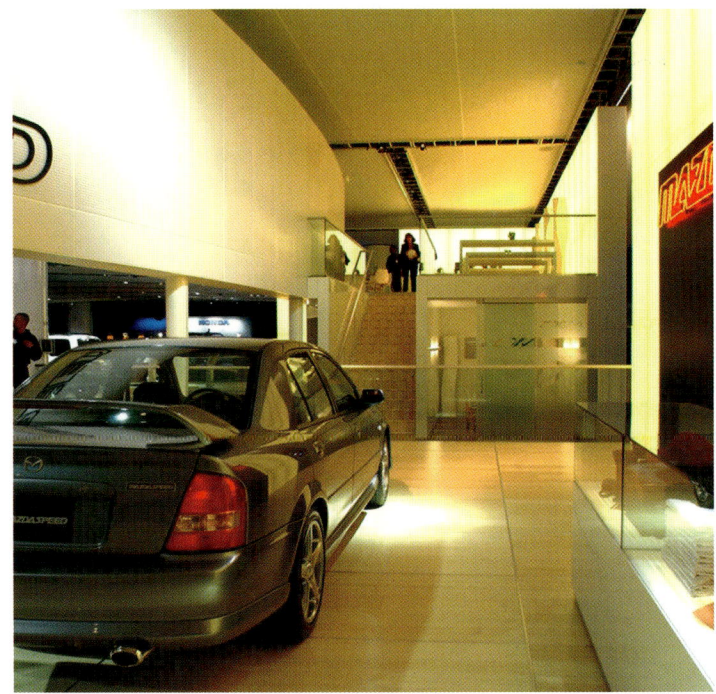

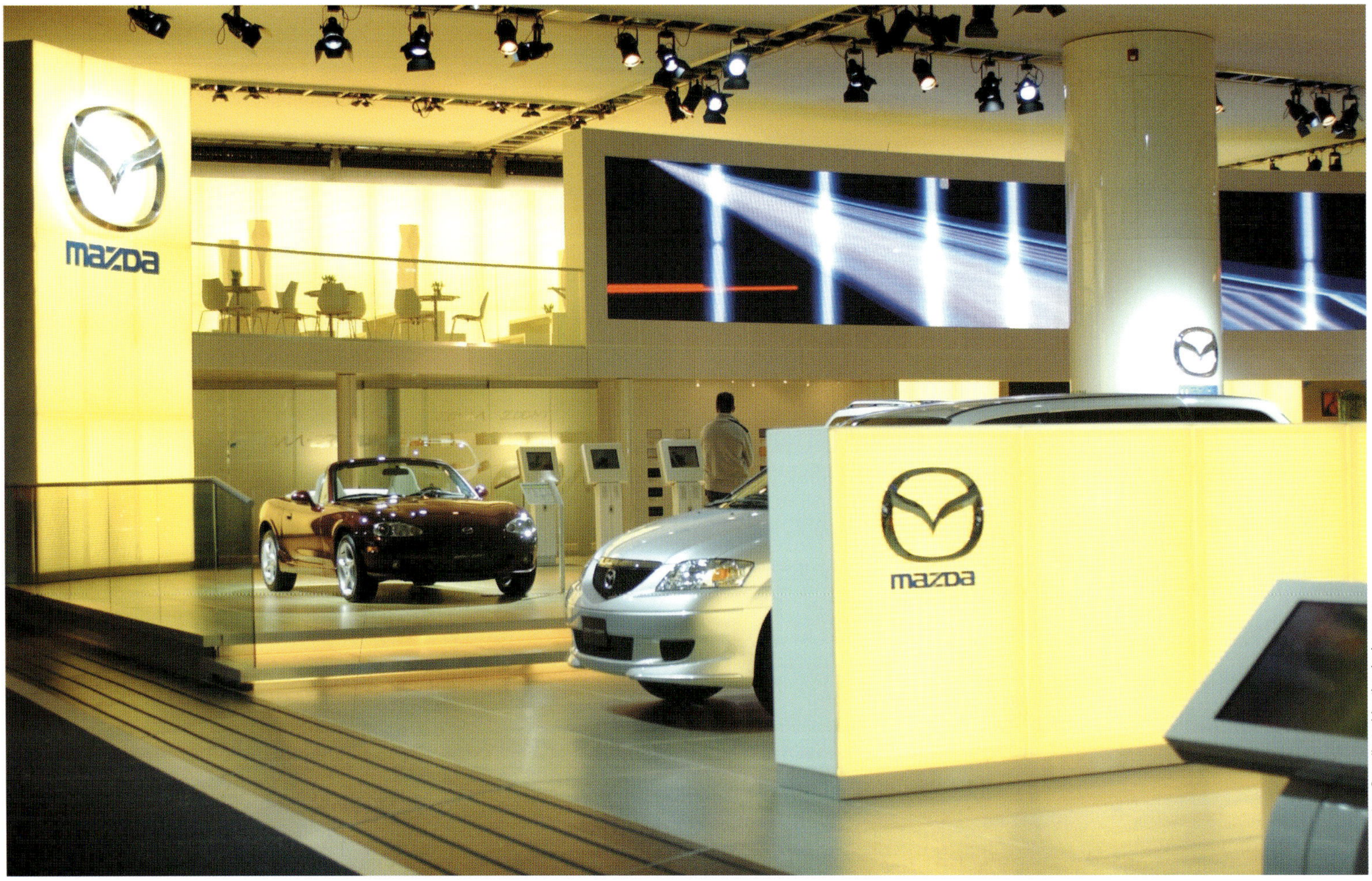

Photographs: Contributed by the designers

Across the exhibition stand, Japanese heritage and contemporary quality came to life through environmental design, materials, finishes and interactive content. The brand DNA Zones, for example, were defined by large glowing yellow walls, in a contemporary re-interpretation of traditional Japanese lanterns adding warmth and texture. These were complemented by bamboo finished floors, on a 6' x 3' grid that evoked the proportions of traditional Japanese tatami mats - again, a subtle reference to Japanese design language, but in a refreshingly contemporary idiom. The simplicity of the design concept was echoed in its execution.

Sieger Design
blome

The Blome stand at the Heimtextil 2002/03 trade fair in Frankfurt was defined by the brand's new profile. The display area used a reduced selection of materials and colours to create a noble backdrop for the stylish products. The lounge was designed as a communication area with violet upholstery to attract the attention of visitors. Four-metre high curtain flags produced an intimate atmosphere and also provided references to the textile theme. The style sets were displayed with selected home accessories, creating an association with visitors' own homes.
The timing constituted a special challenge: there were only three weeks between the commission and the opening of the trade fair. The designers' success in overcoming this obstacle was confirmed by the jury of the red dot award, which honoured the stand with an international design prize.

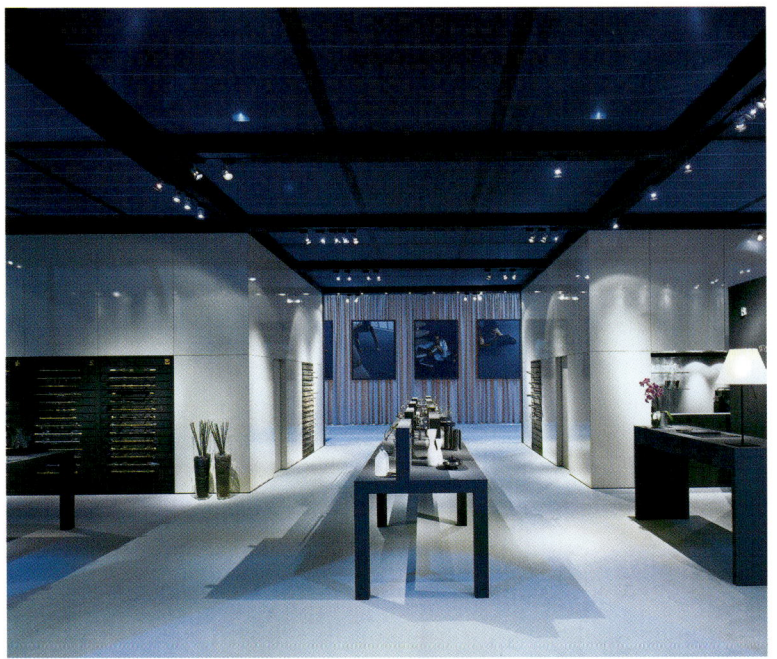

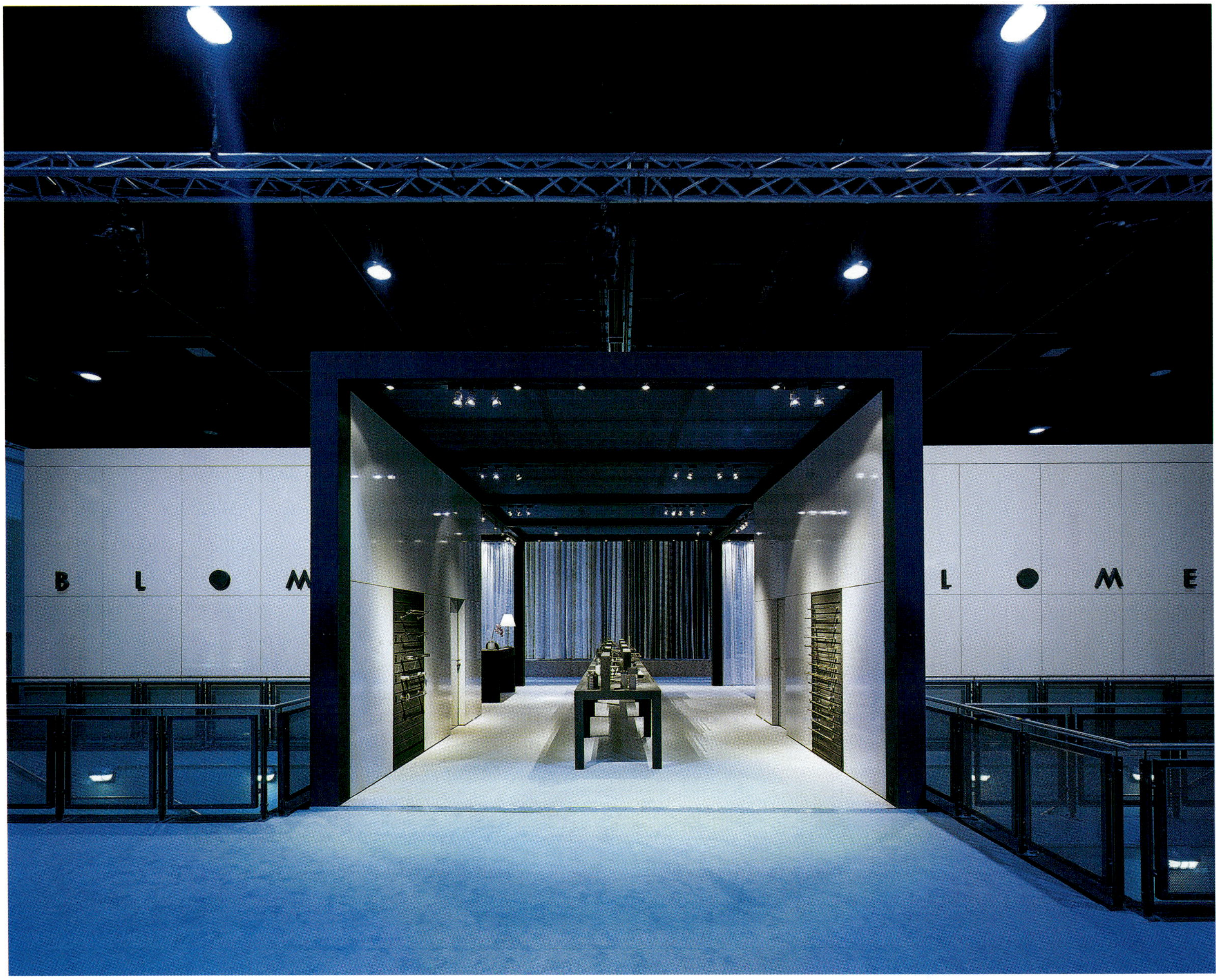

Photographs: Contributed by the designers

B L O M E
Willkommen ! Welcome ! Bienvenue !

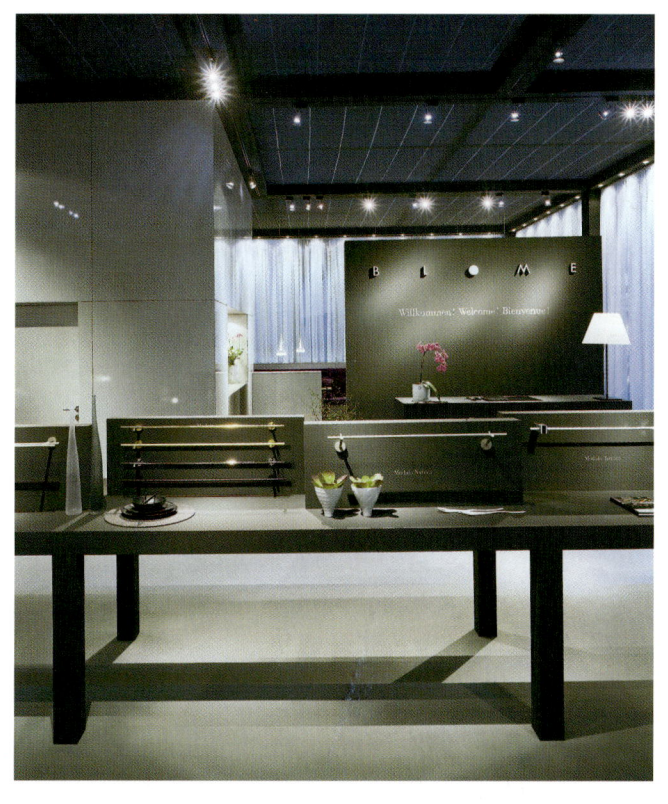

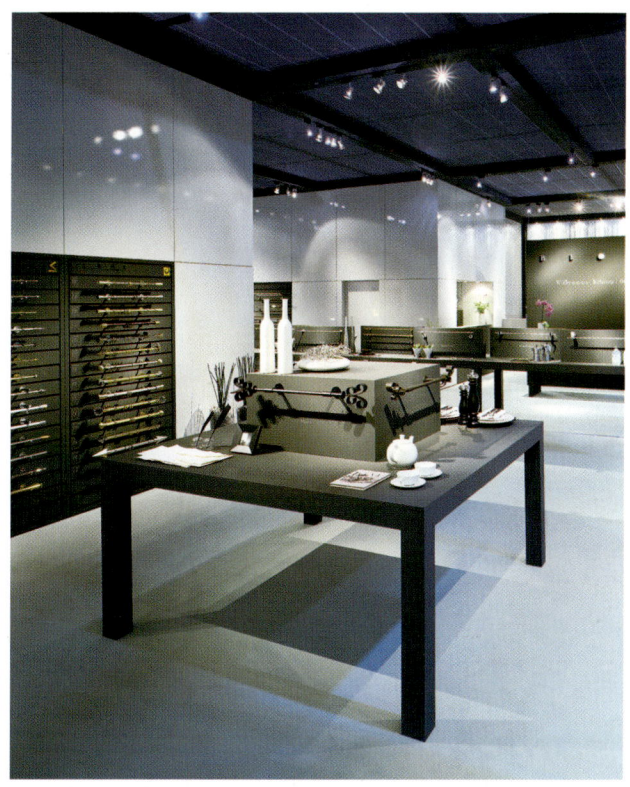

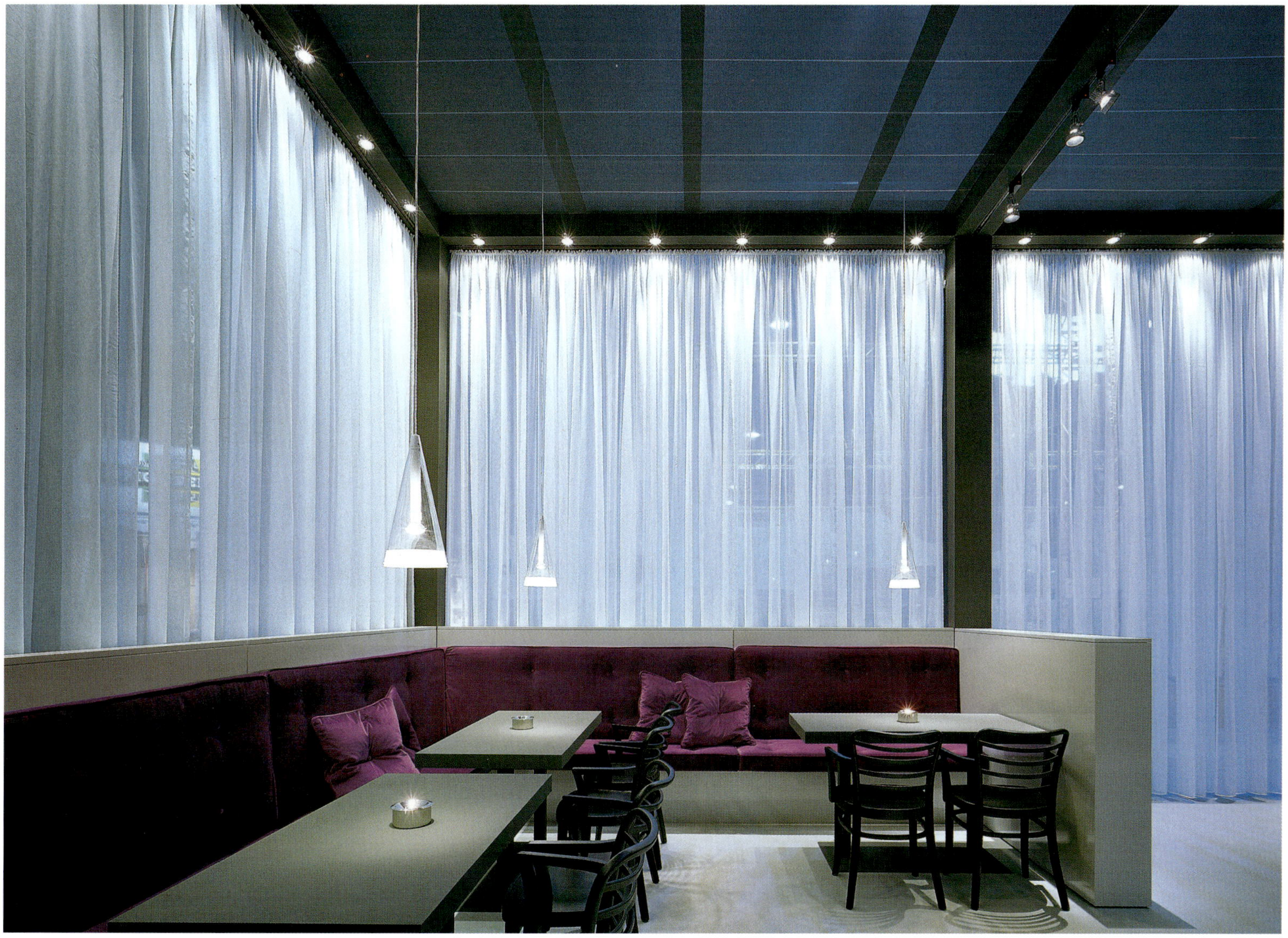

Artek
Alvar Aalto furniture

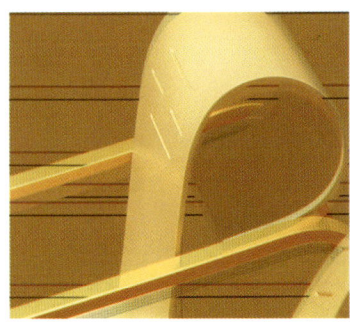

Presented in Milan for the first time in years, Artek brought a fresh vision to the iconic modern furniture designed by the great Finnish architect Alvar Aalto. A series of bold installations at superstudio Píu played on the striking combination of pure form and functionalism that make Artek as desirable and contemporary as ever.

Alvar Aalto (1898-1976) designed furniture as a natural extension of his architectural projects. In the 1930s he was influenced by the international modern style, but redefined this according to his own aesthetic and philosophical preferences for natural materials and organic forms. His revolutionary structural forms were based on new methods of bending and laminating birch. The simple beauty of Artek furniture is still astonishing today, bringing a human modernism and tactile warmth to contemporary interiors.

Photographs: Se/Di/Ci

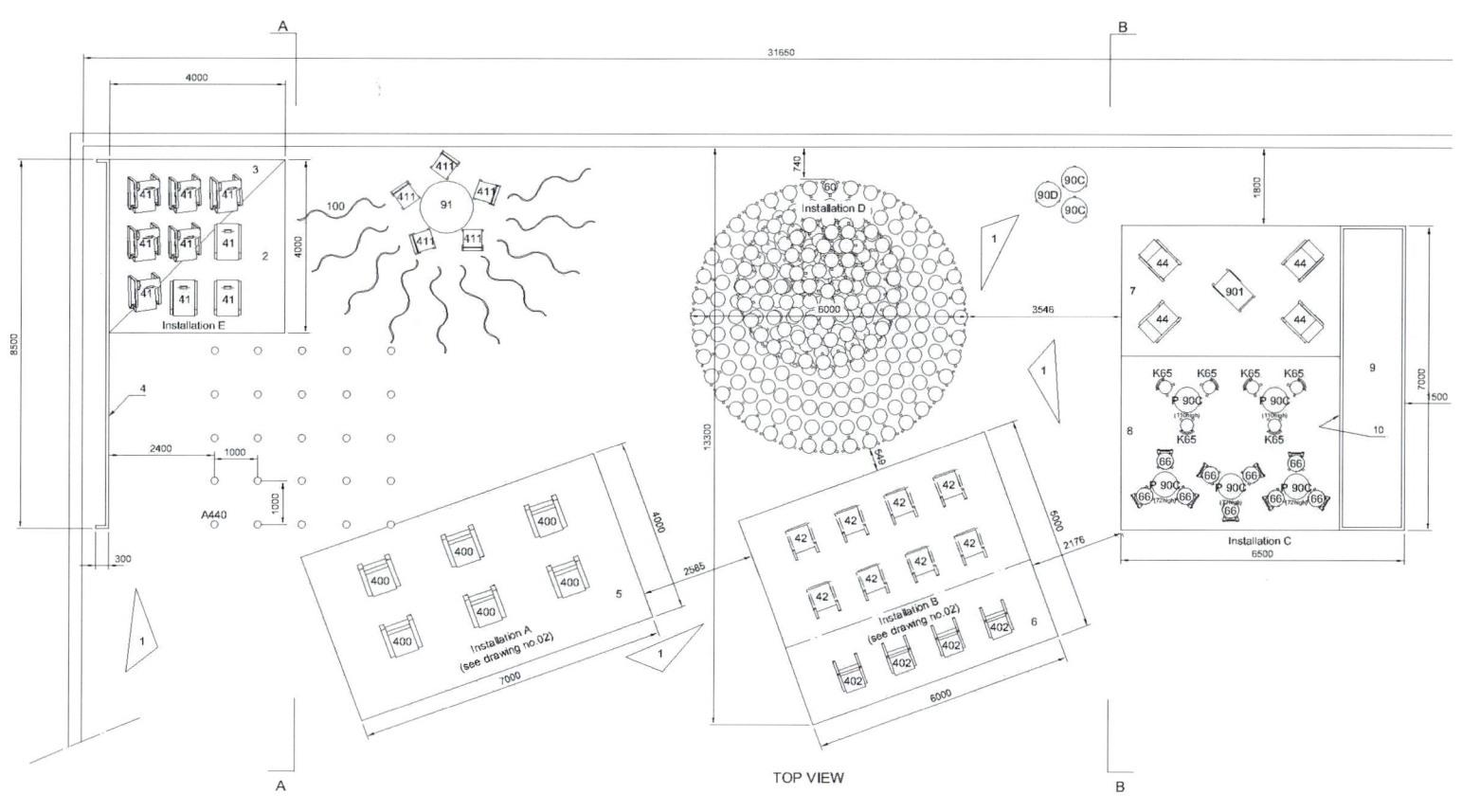

TOP VIEW

Francesc Rifé
midi

This stand was designed to display the latest collection of MIDI-Flat cupboards. The main feature of these cupboards is their aluminium structure that allows for a completely diaphanous interior, with no divisions, and glass shelving that takes the feeling of lightness even further. Their sliding doors use an innovative system that allows them to sit along a single plane when closed (Flat System).

The space created to display these and other MIDI products was basically a spectacular black box with display elements built into the structure. The playful lighting was the most distinctive element, reflecting the light and distinctive image of the company.

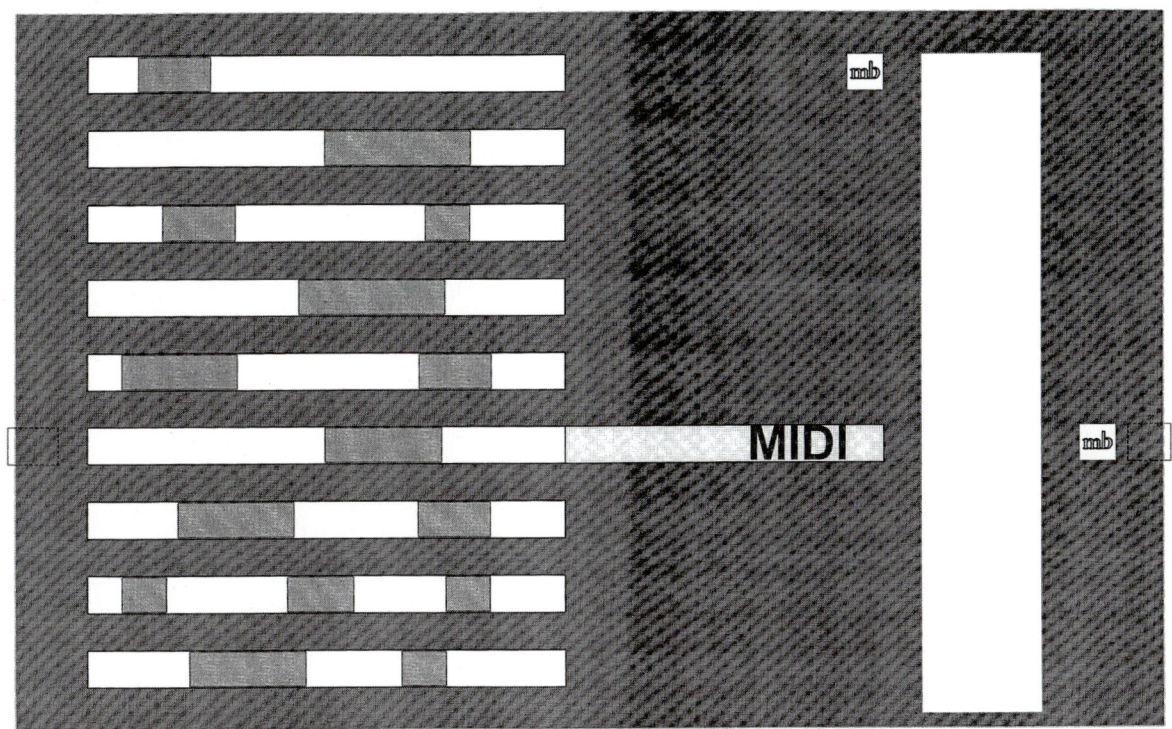

Design Company
sony

The Sony Electronic and Entertainment Products Group stand at Hannover CeBIT 2003, the world's largest IT trade fair, was called "Connectivity". Its central core contained a network of Sony Products.

Visitors to the stand entered through the "Highlight Gates", which provided the latest Sony news through colors and thematic groups illustrated on the exterior.

These doors were connected by a semicircular convex wall created specially for the occasion. The wall, made from mobile plexiglass panels that could either be arranged as a curve or a circle, was a symbol of the reticulation of Sony products: each product can stand alone, but together they create the Sony concept, the Sony World.

The central core of the stand contained a circular space open on three sides, which offered visitors complete and varied information about the key points of each theme. This was the "Connectivity Dome", a slightly sheltered space where the bustle of the trade fair was filtered through translucent acrylic panels. Three small stages were used as rest areas, so that visitors could take some time out and relax, and also as platforms for live events. The scale of the architectural elements and design was human-friendly, and in the "Connectivity Dome" visitors were surrounded by a calm atmosphere that allowed them to seek information in a completely relaxed manner.

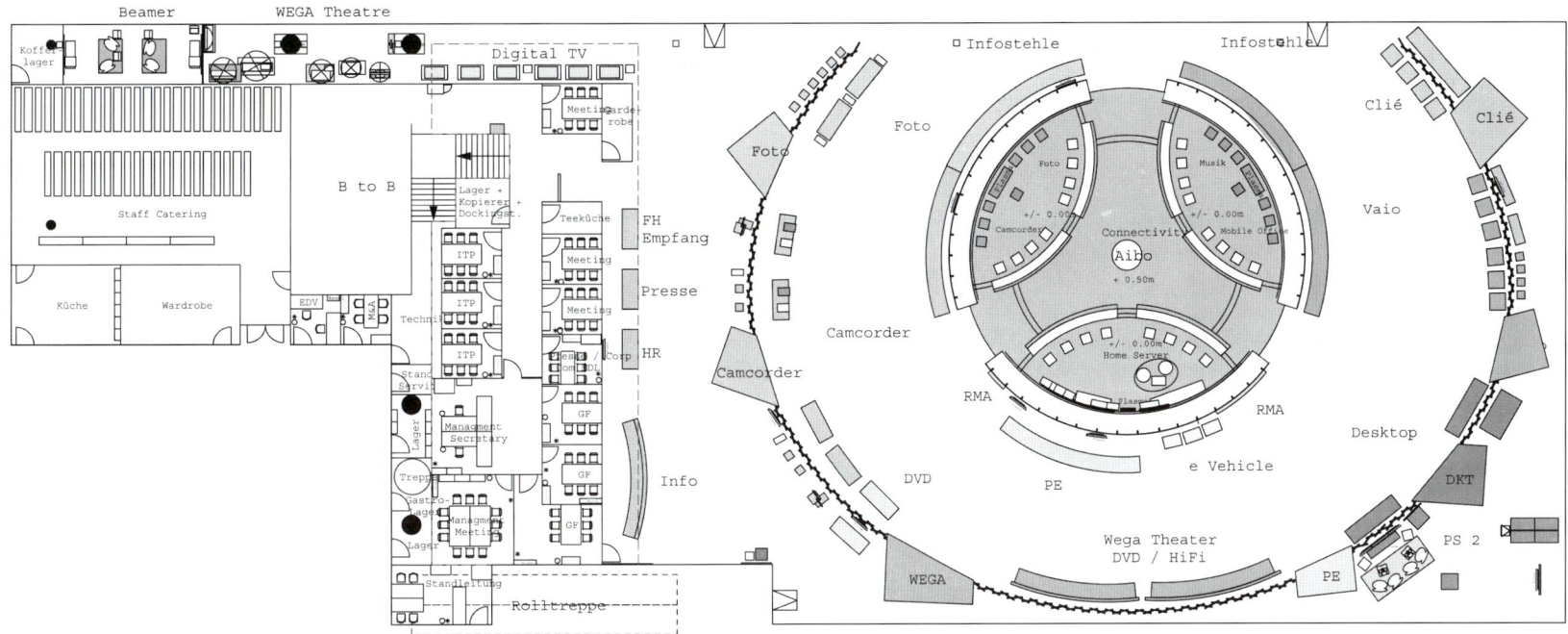

The look and architecture of the stand worked together to generate an unmistakable corporate image and a memorable experience for visitors. Easily identifiable scenography and the combination of materials such as illuminated acrylic panels and plexiglass left a lasting impression. The graphic design concept, based on the company's corporate colors and products, was seemlessly integrated with the general design concept.

Sony's "Connectivity" stand was granted the "ADAM" prize, the most prestigious German trade fair award, by the Münchner Design Company.

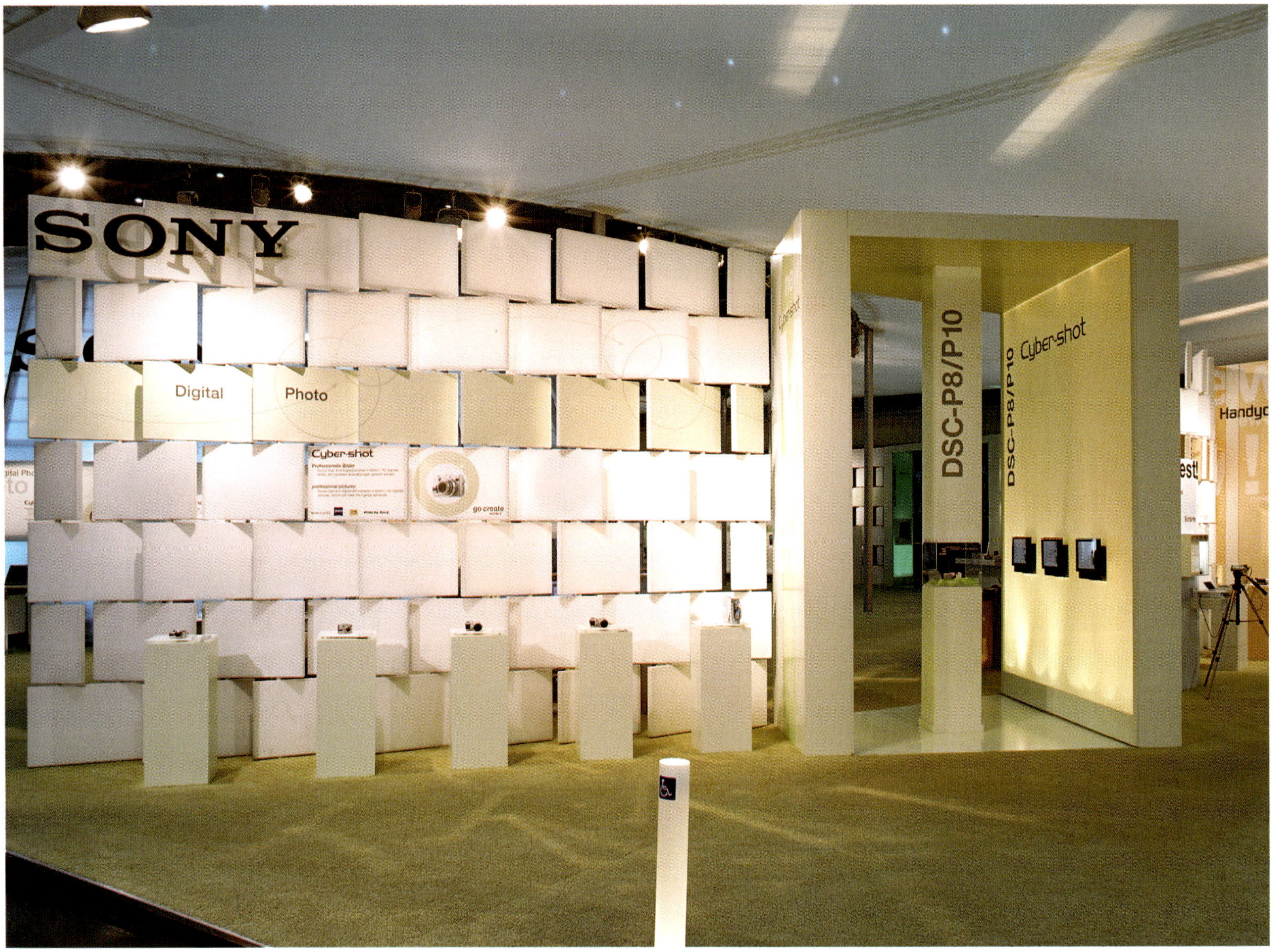
SONY
Digital
Photo
Cyber-shot
go create
DSC-P8/P10
DSC-P8/P10
Cyber-shot
Handyc

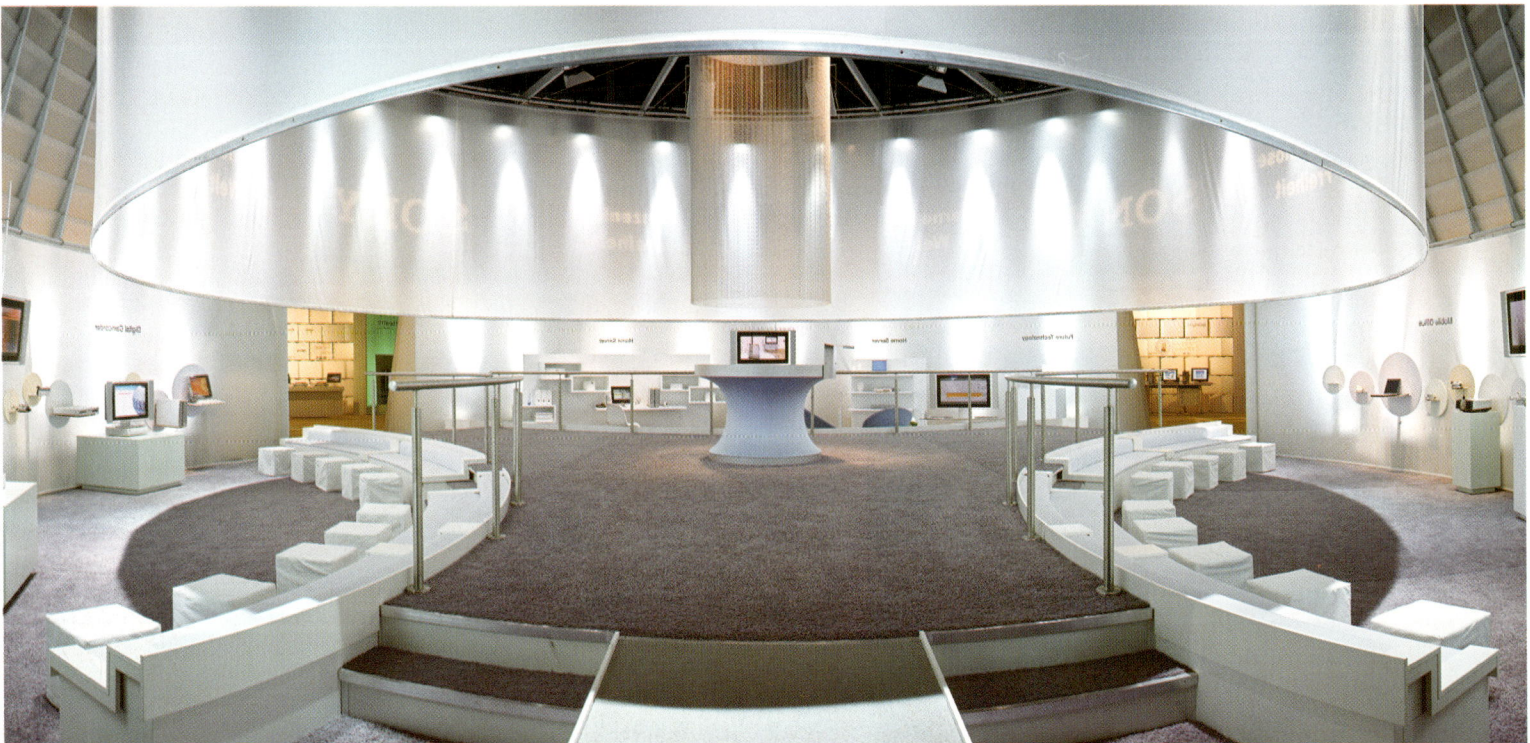

Peter Bottazzi
desalto

Desalto entrusted the design of its new stand to a stage director, Peter Bottazzi, in order to go beyond the concept of simply displaying its range - the company wanted a stand that would not just display, but also represent their products and philosophy. The difference between these two concepts is the capacity to transmit emotion and communicative power to the product, and the company was looking for a way to communicate its attitude of constant innovation and associate this with its products. The stand, open on two sides and closed on the longest one, appeared somewhat like the back of a movie set. Inside, visitors found an indoor non-place, a neutral, bare space that resembled a big black box, with black carpet, black ceiling, black walls. The only light reached visitors through a set of soft, transparent PVC sheet cylinders, inside which the products were displayed. These sky-light lanterns guided visitors through the semidarkness. The sheets had a light, almost aqueous texture and stirred with the disturbances to the air caused by visitors. The designer wanted to create a dark and almost inhospitable environment with magic lanterns to highlight and show the way, and surprise visitors as they were brought face-to-face with different objects.

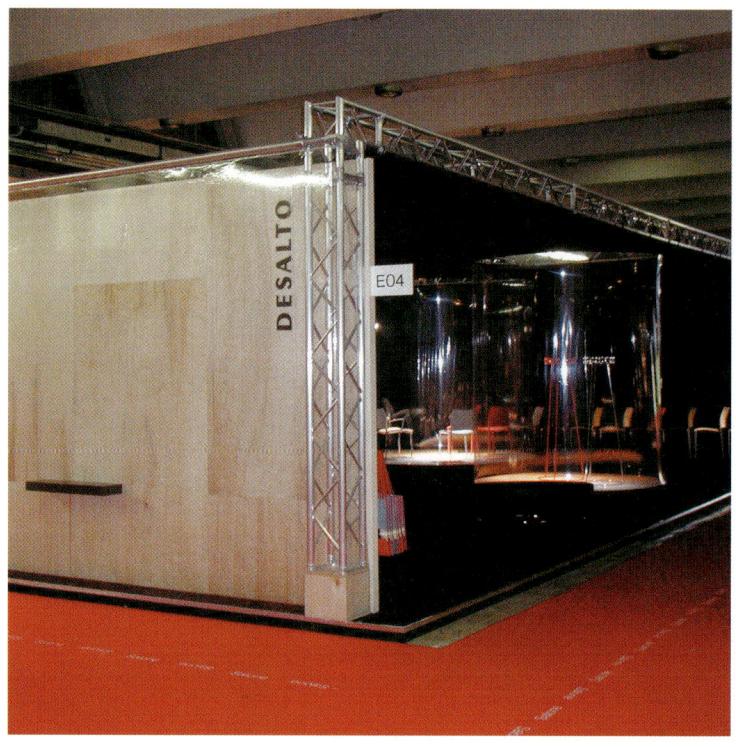

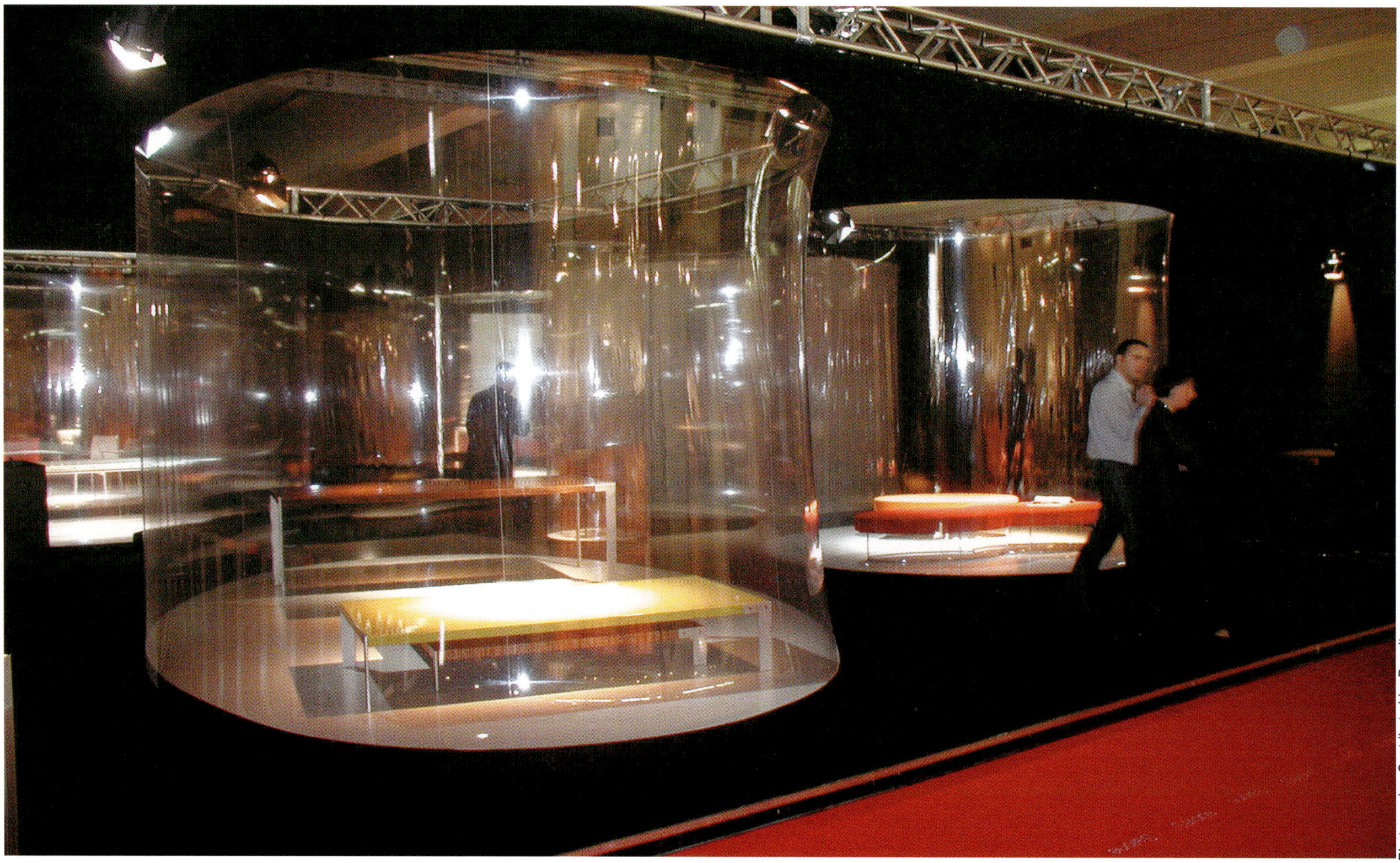

Photographs: Contributed by Desalto

The stand emerged around a central pillar that brought together products and general services for the public. Inside, people could be glimpsed as shadow-play figures through a thin white fabric. The few products displayed were theatrically isolated and lit within the PVC membrane.

In order to describe the different finishes of products like the Liko table or the Sand chair, Bottazzi anchored table and chair halves to the wall so that they hung in mid-air, reminiscent of a stage set.

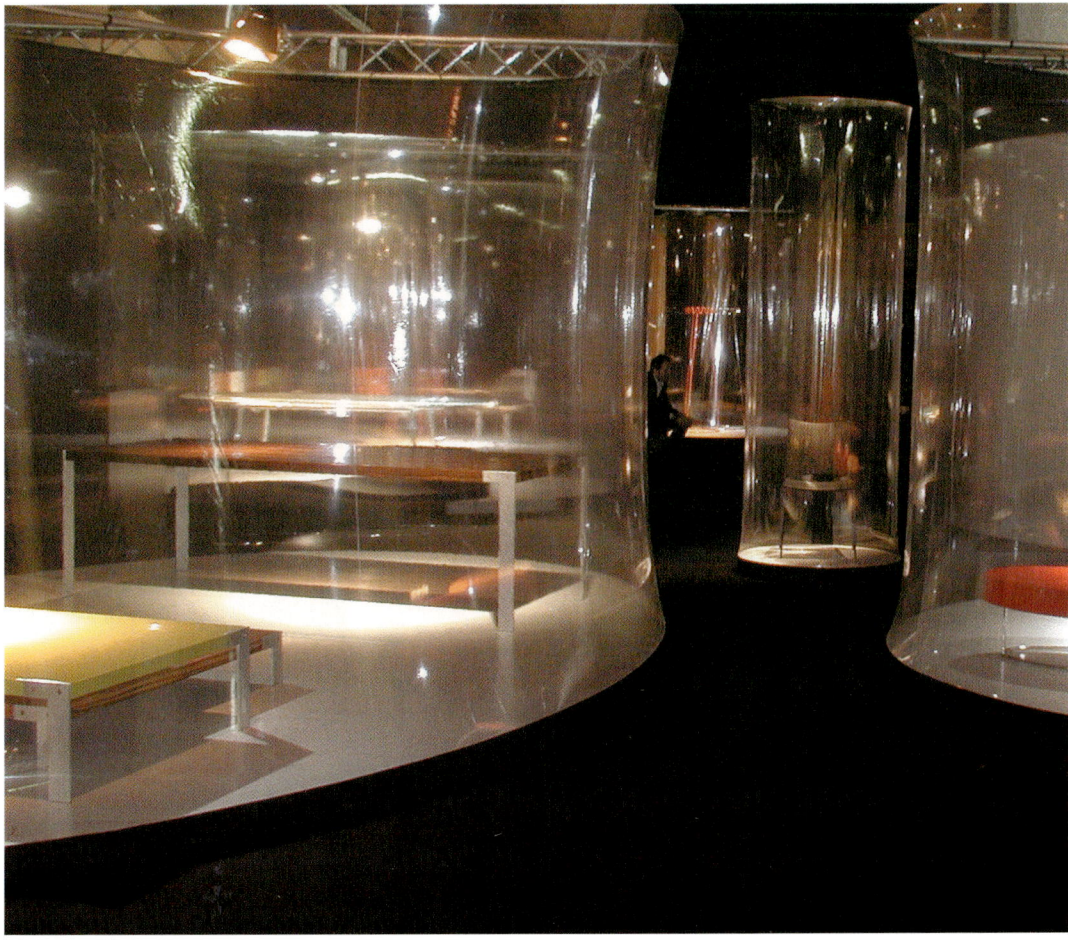

Schmidhuber + Partner / KMS

O$_2$

The stand of mobile telephone provider O$_2$ at the CeBIT 2003 trade fair was based on the motto "O$_2$ can do". The brand had been successfully launched the previous year, and the company wanted to use the opportunity to show the results generated by the expectations during its first year. This translated into a design based around a 20 m long counter representing a street in a shopping district. The different areas of everyday life in which O$_2$ can provide useful services were displayed along this counter, so that visitors could browse at their own pace. Parallel to the counter, a strip of horizontal LED projectors, also 20 m long, displayed very rapid film sequences.

Visitors wanting more information, or simply wanting to relax, could visit one of the six rooms on the outer part of the stand. These comfortable and slightly more private spaces provided an assessment service, advice and other personalized information.

The upper level took the informal feel of the lower information areas further, while keeping with the overall design and atmosphere of the stand. A bar called the "can smoke Bar" was located in front of a luminous blue screen surrounded by white cubes to sit on and upholstered brown chairs.

The relaxed atmosphere was an important element throughout the stand, encouraging visitors to explore and take their time, so that the stand became a kind of bubble that strongly supported the corporate identity of the O$_2$ brand. This was enhanced by the relaxing effect of the dominant blue coloring, as well as the spacious areas that encouraged conversation.

The most striking element of the stand was the defining "Horizont" bubble-wall, a striking, luminous membrane filled with blue-colored air. On the inside of this membrane, upward scrolling text was used to display information and make special announcements, while the external surface displayed brand names and advertising. Its luminous nature attracted the attention of visitors, creating an association between the company and the stand's glowing blue appearance and leaving a lasting impression.

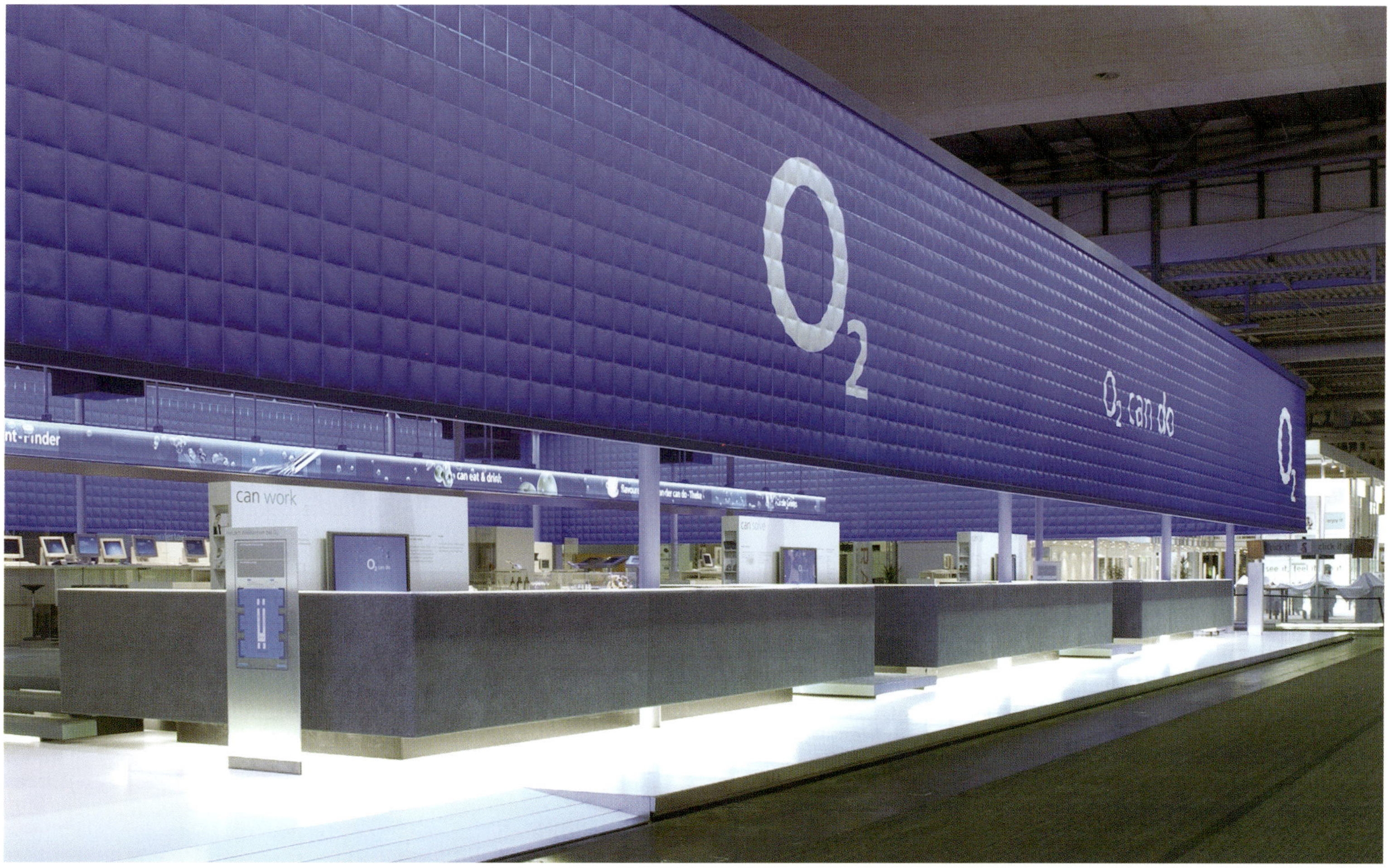
O2
O2 can do
can work
can eat & drink

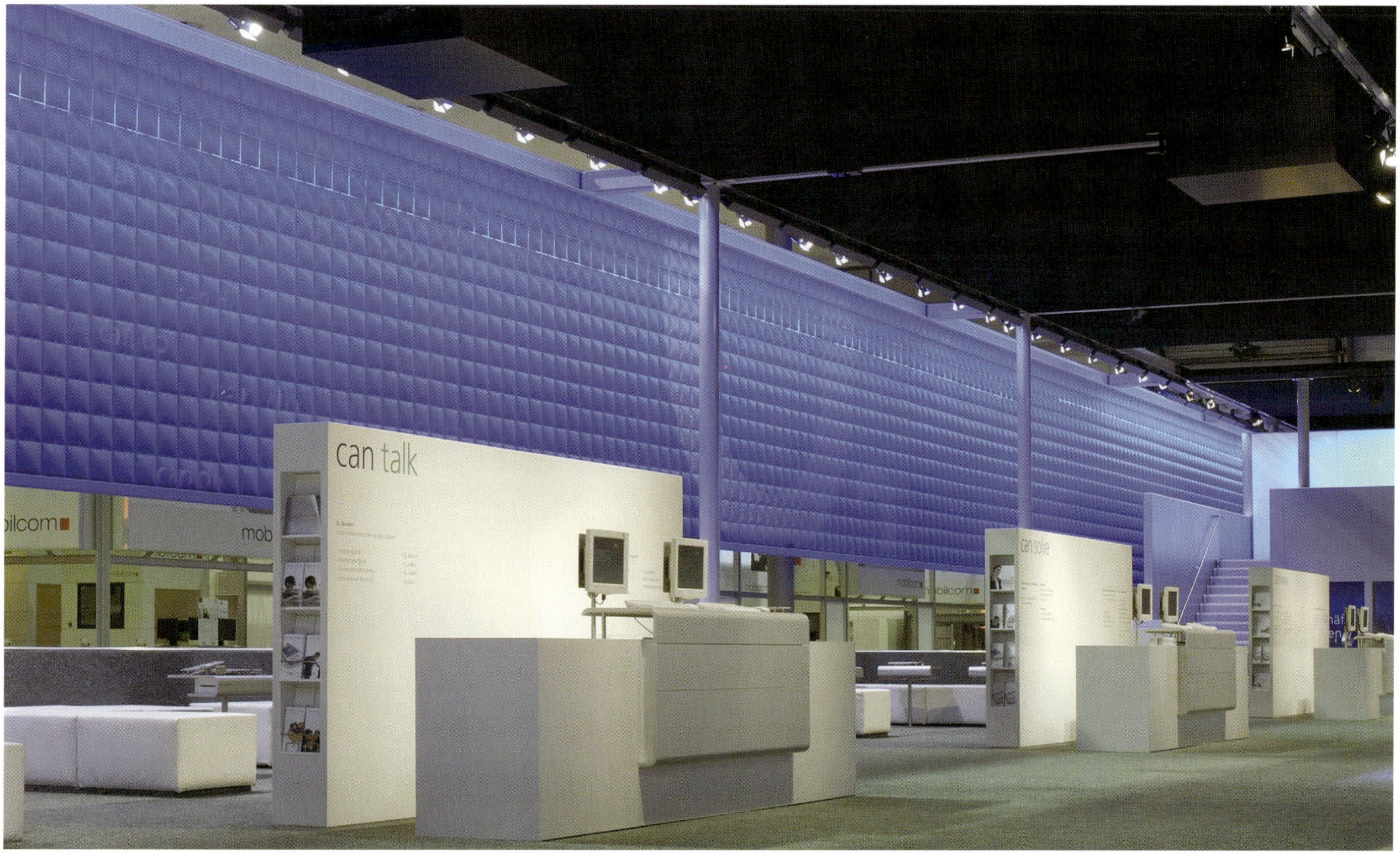
can talk
can solve

The central, street-like corridor allowed visitors to move through the stand and discover information about O2 services, while the meeting areas provided more personalized information. The simple plan and coherent design made it an enjoyable and memorable experience for visitors.

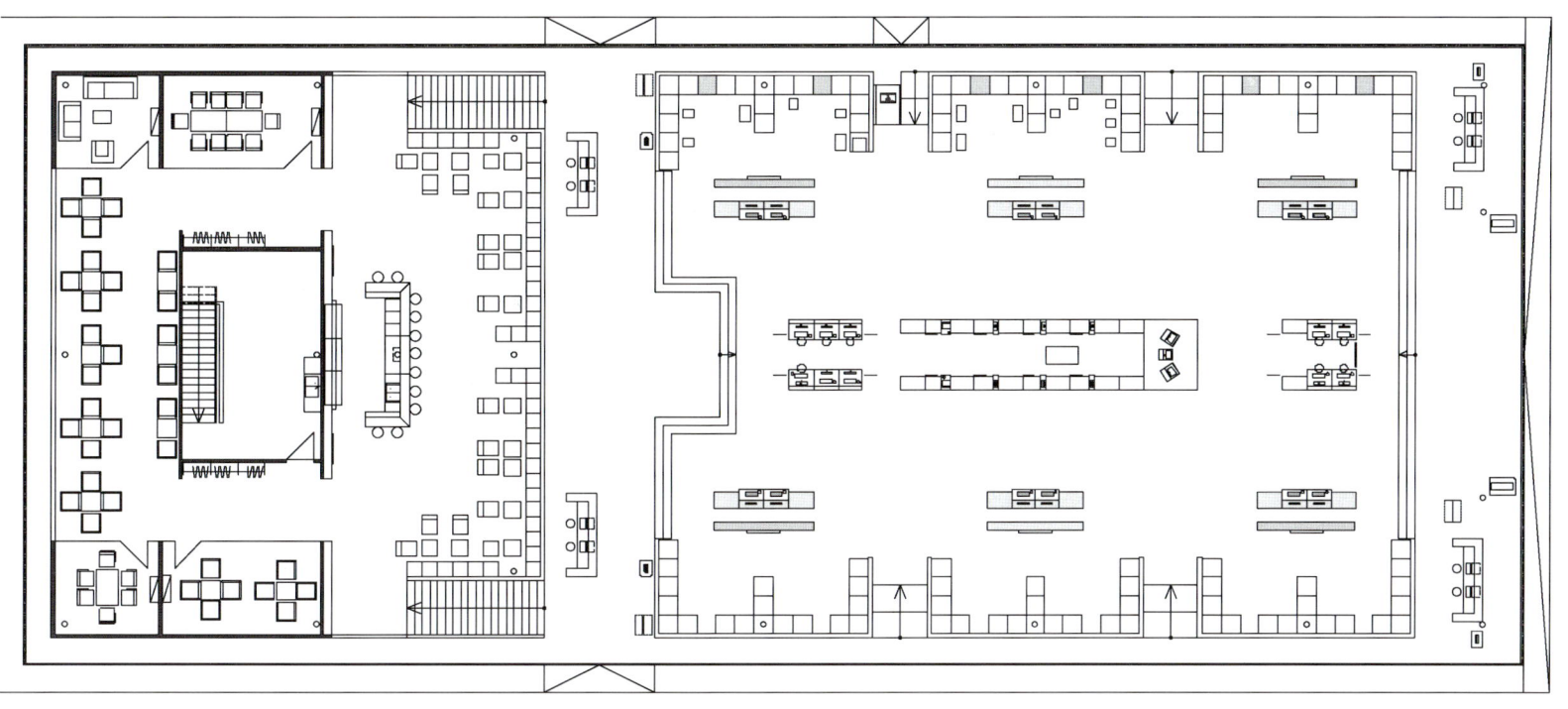

Matali Crasset

casaderme

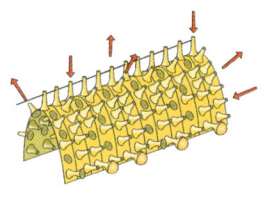

There is nothing more magical than skin, which senses and breathes, constantly changes and regenerates. It is basic to our survival, a sensitive and protective membrane that absorbs sensations and transmits external messages to our innermost self.

Casaderme behaves like skin, filtering and directing its environment. A soft and light shape, made from stretch material. A kind of Sputnik spaceship that could have landed on a strange planet from distant galaxies. Like the body of an alien, with sensitive antennas to perceive the outside world. Like a lung in the act of breathing.

Casaderme represents a new way to think about housing. Soft and flexible, protective and enveloping like a uterus, it is the ideal nexus connecting the interior and exterior of the house through an exchange of stimuli and sensations.

Photographs: Arrigio Coppitz

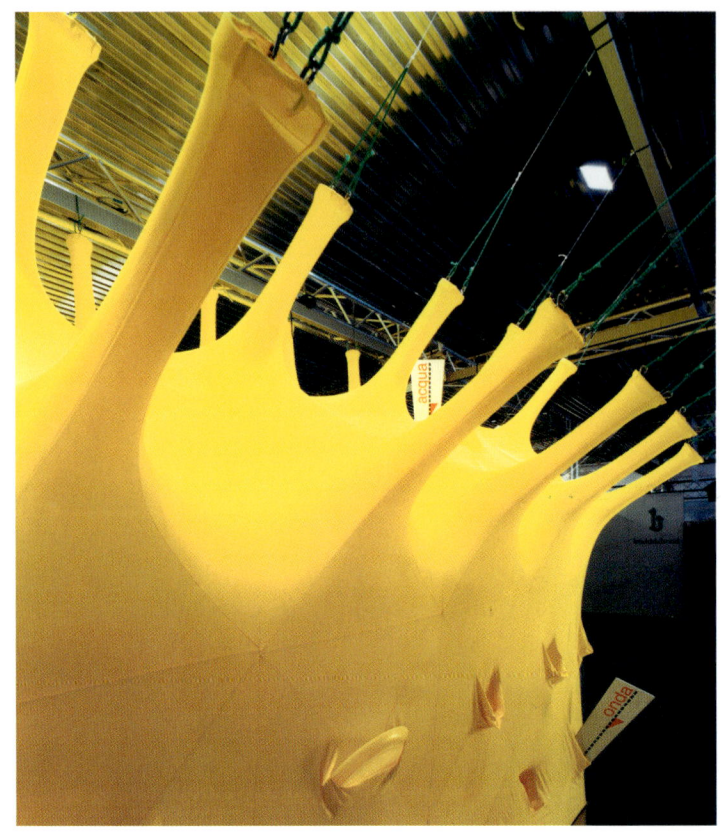

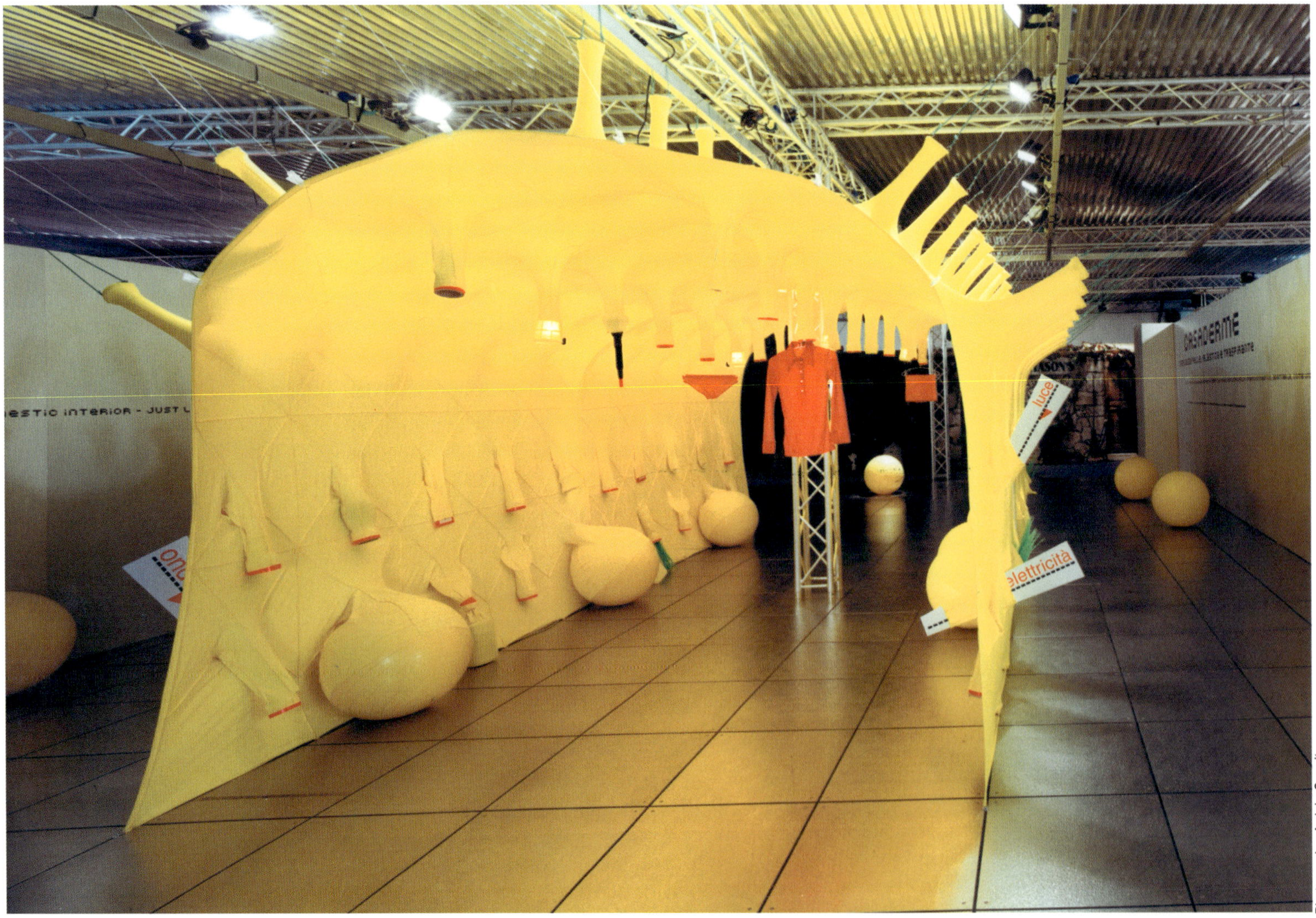

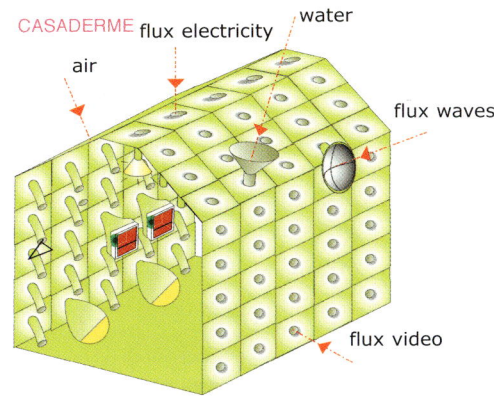

CASADERME flux electricity water

air

flux waves

flux video

Changing and extending, the new house adapts to its environment. It is like a living organism with the capacity to feel, an inhabitable and comfortable space that absorbs the objects and substances necessary for day-to-day living.

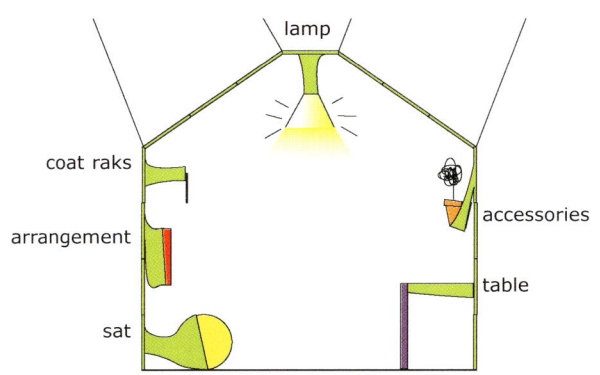

lamp

coat raks

arrangement

accessories

table

sat

Ramón Pico + Javier López
pensar la casa

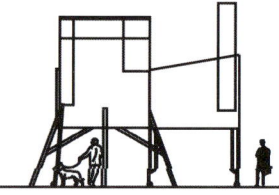

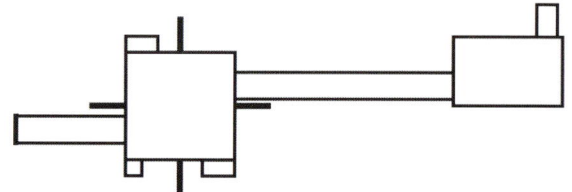

The guiding concept behind this exhibition was to present to the public some examples of the ways that contemporary architects are approaching the idea of the house. The exhibition tried to bring the work of professional designers closer to the level of daily life, to strolls through the squares of childhood, children playing with pigeons in the plazas, and even the agitated ramblings of sleepwalkers. The display was conceived as a touring exhibition, and it is this travelling aspect that gave it meaning. For this reason, it was designed to be housed in a lightweight container that could travel to different public spaces within the province. The structure therefore had to be flexible enough to allow it to adapt to all its potential locations in public spaces. The design concept was to build a movable container, where the volume was a symbol of the modern icon of the home. It consisted of two principal volumes: a central cube with 3m sides, and a prismatic annex. Both volumes rose 1.9 m above ground level, ensuring that visitors could move through the square, and that the exhibition interfered as little as possible on an area's normal day to day life. The exhibition was supposed to visually stimulate pedestrians, but not to force them to enter the enclosure or have to walk around it. The first of the two structures remained fixed throughout the exhibition period, resting on metal supports. Wheels açenabled the second structure and the entrance door into the first to slide out of the way. The container opened up to reveal the exhibition during opening hours.

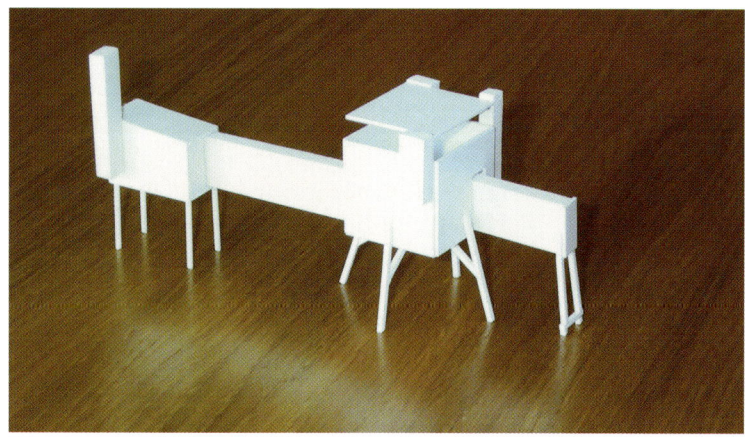

Photographs: Fernando Alda

The panels that were an integral part of the exhibition used advertising language to an extreme degree. Bright colors, huge lettering and very beautifully produced images attracted the attention of passersby and invited them to participate in a very direct and familiar way. The total exhibition area was 18 m, raised off ground level. The display area was divided into four panels, two measuring 3m, and another two measuring 6m. These panels displayed four and eight works each, respectively, in vertical strips. The panels were printed on vinyl support and glued to translucent methacrylate panels. The very modern feel and materials used contrasted strongly with the spaces where it was displayed, inviting the public to think about buildings, concepts and materials in new and unfamiliar ways.

Arno Design
speedo

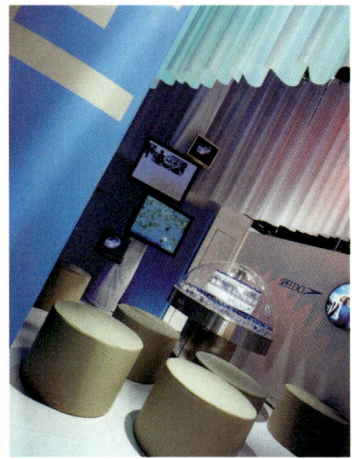

Speedo is one of the leading manufacturers of racing and fashion swimwear and beach clothing worldwide. The brand's success is based on their long experience and the company's philosophy of innovation. For the ISPO Summer 2001 fair, Arno Design GmbH designed a breathtaking ensemble with an emphasis on expressing the brand's unique identity. The colorful, bright and summery range was placed in a glossy white setting, suggesting a museum. Accentuated rounded forms introduced a dynamic element that evoked the high energy and speed of competitive swimming. The trade fair slogan was prominently displayed on curved, luminous orange and deep blue entrance elements in large white letters. An economical design was an important part of the brief for Speedo, so the challenge for the designers was to create an original and dynamic stand through clever use of a limited budget. One of the strategies used was to suspend dramatically folded translucent curtains made of a reflective material from the ceiling. These turned out to be one of the more sensational stylistic elements, and allowed the designers to use the whole permitted height of six meters. Shining like water, and floating above the rounded wall elements, the curtains were visible from a long distance and attracted attention to the stand. Gently pulsating and changing colored lights transformed them into illuminated sculptures symbolizing rhythm and movement. The stand area was structured according to clear principles, particularly Speedo's desire to separate its fashion and competition swimwear ranges.

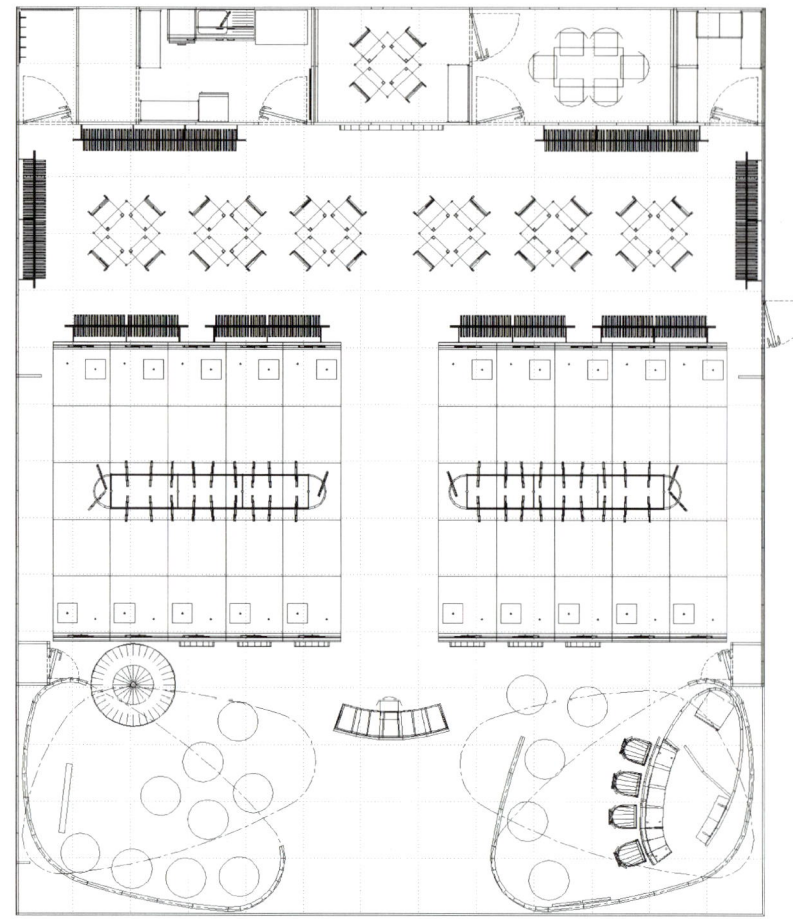

SPEEDO
BEACH
FUN
TIVE
H VOLLE
FABRIC

SPEEDO
TION SWIM
FIT FUN
EACH
ACTIVE
SHELL
BEACH VOLLEY
ERSHORTS
FABRIC
SPEEDO
SPEEDO
ariel

Stefano Colli
husa hoteles

The brief for this corporate stand for a major hotel chain involved designing a central open space that could be used for meetings and information points, a bar, and enclosed office and storage space.

The design centered around a suspended element that functioned as lighting, ceiling and signage support all at once. This idea took the form of a "hat" consisting of an opaque area concealing the power for visible fluorescent lights, with the brand labeling applied to its exterior.

A series of flexible strips made from translucent plastic hung from this external element, acting as a light screen and defining an "intimate" space for meetings. The floor area of the stand was 103 m².

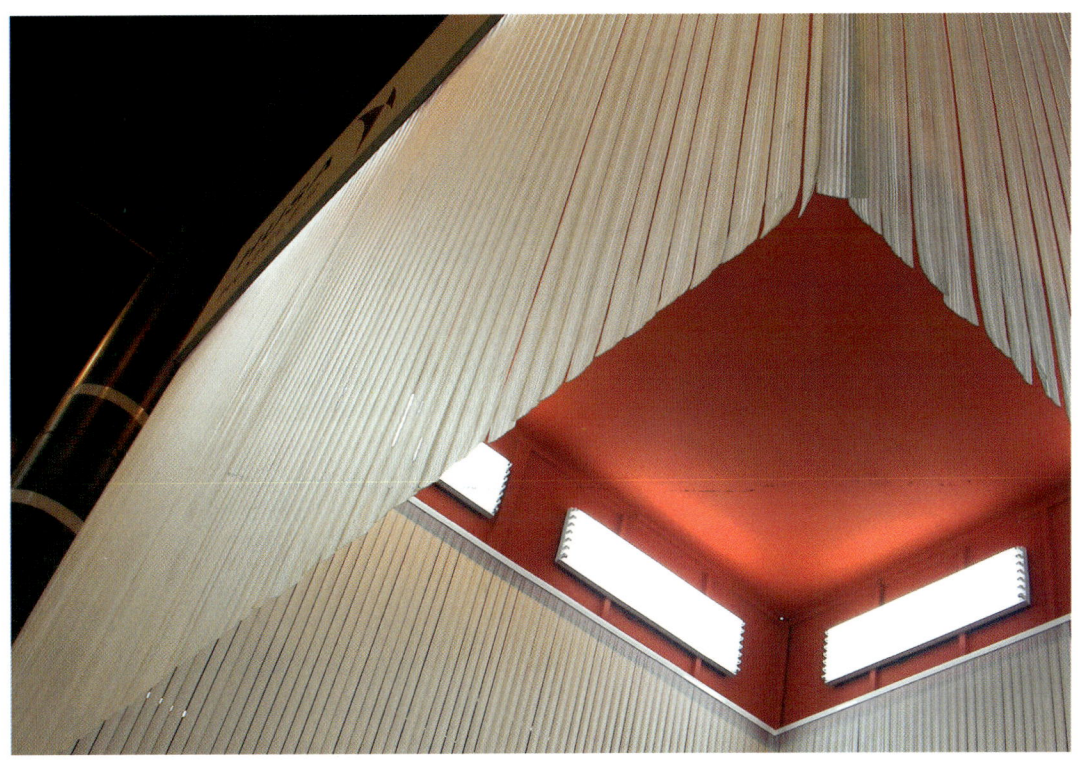

Burkhardt Leitner constructiv

Master of Architecture Rendering - Helmut Jacoby

The exhibiton "Master of Architecture Rendering - Helmut Jacoby" at the German Architecture Museum (Deutsches Architektur Museum/DAM Frankfurt) used constructiv CLIC to create the required partitions and atmosphere. Mario Lorenz and Julia Imhoff from Wiesbaden designed a series of information rooms and divisions with the simple and flexible constructiv CLIC exhibition system. In these rooms, with minimal decoration and furniture, visitors could concentrate on learning about Helmut Jacoby's lifework through videos and text panels. One of the main aims of the exhibition was to entice visitors to spend time in the exhibition room, and to integrate the corporate design of the exhibition in these information rooms.

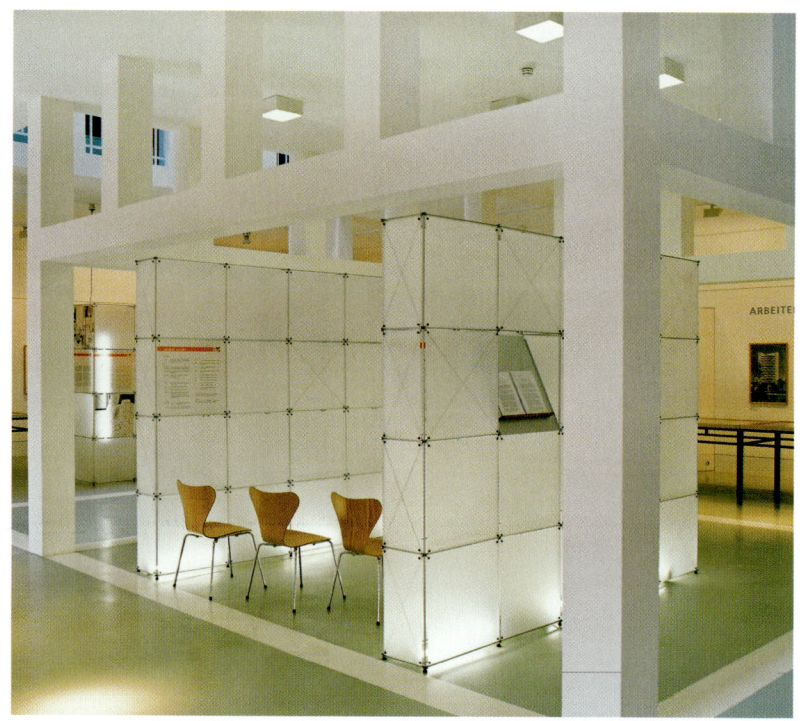

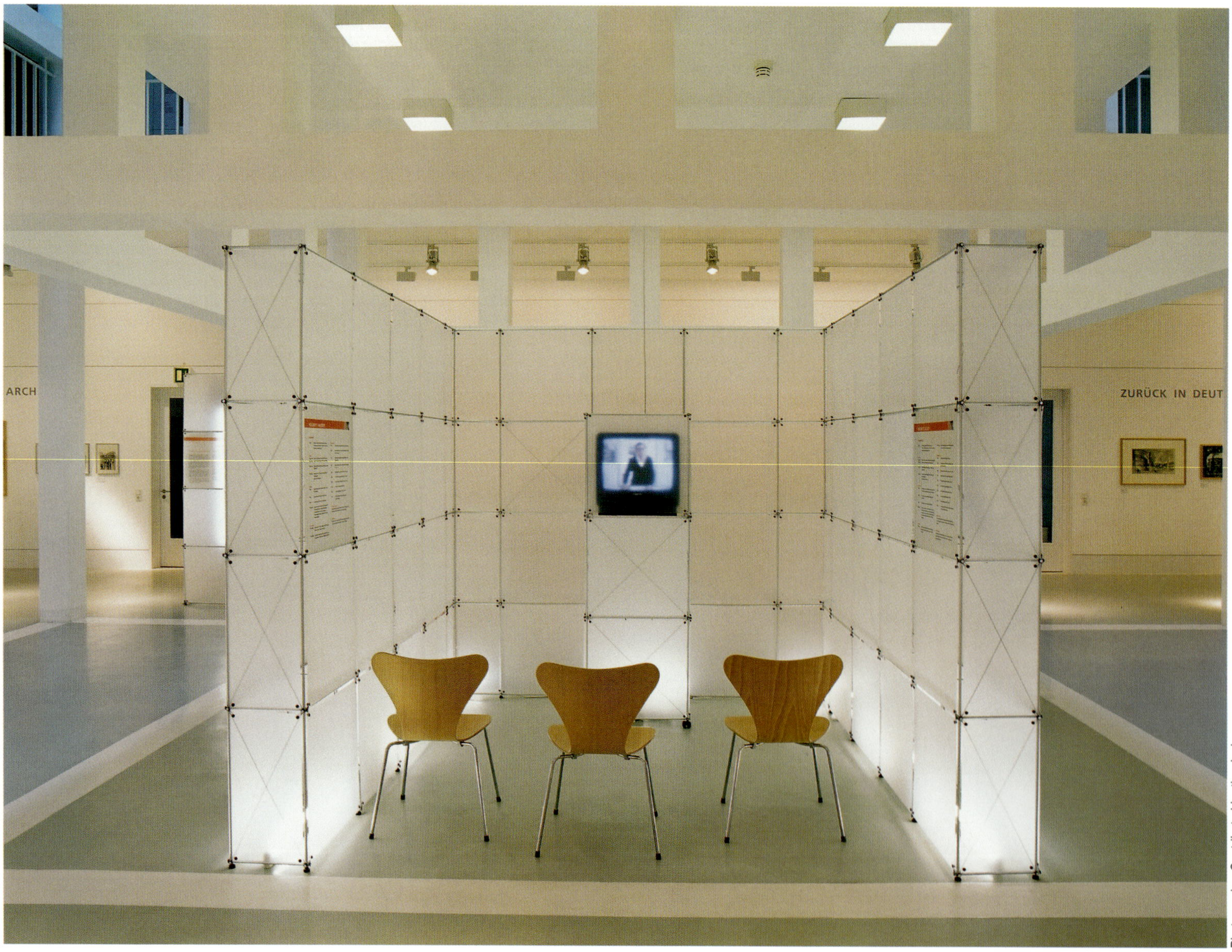

Photographs: Contributed by the designers

Deu i Deu
tafesa

In order to take advantage of a long and narrow site, the designers of this stand created two longitudinal facades, an exterior and an interior wall, on which products were displayed.

The stand was quite simple and purist in terms of forms and colors. The designers decided to use only the color white and straight, perfectly defined lines for the stand structure. Products were displayed in niches, which separated and clearly framed each set of tables and chairs.

The ceiling was covered using black material, making it seem to disappear and creating an illusion of infinite space. Lighting was one of the more spectacular elements, created using light projectors and colored filters for each of the different scenographies. The entire stand was white, but the lighting effects seemed to tinge the spaces with different colors. Using lights rather than paint for color meant that the color was in the air itself, and not just the walls. The lighting design ensured that the color of the products did not change by lighting them with very powerful points of white light.

Photographs: José Luis Hausmann

70

Este año os presentamos a **Carla** y **Andrea**, un duo espectacular y que estamos seguros dará mu

Carla: Es una silla ajustada en medidas y diversa en acabados. Aporta un estilo muy particular;

con la incorporación de médula natural en su respaldo, sin lugar a dudas adquiere un aire

Andrea: No es una silla, es una mesa. En ella hemos aplicado las técnicas de producción más avanzad

su aspecto formal, líneas rectas y limpias, la convierten en una pieza muy especial y que ade

Burkhardt Leitner constructiv

Design: Roland Eberle, Zurich

design prize switzerland

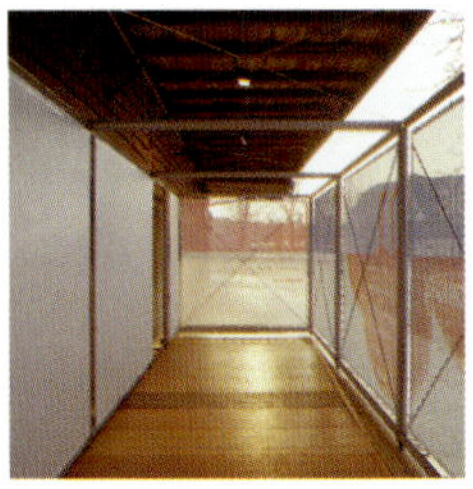

For the sixth time, the Design Center Lagenthal awarded the Design Prize of Switzerland and organised an exhibition of selected works. For the first time, the exhibition of the 80 prize-winning works was created entirely using Burkhardt Leitner constructiv systems.

The exhibition venue was an old farmhouse. Outside, constructiv PILA Petite was used for the cash desk and reception pavillion, while inside it was constructiv CLIC that was used for the 1500 m² exhibition, from the stable level to the double-storey hay loft. The back-lit presentation modules contrasted impressively with the rustic surroundings, and created an attractive interplay of archaic beams and technological systems, of tradition and innovation.

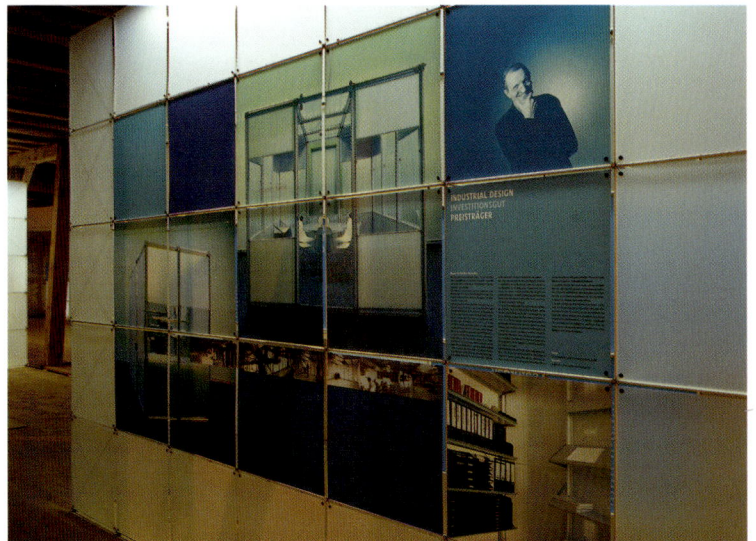

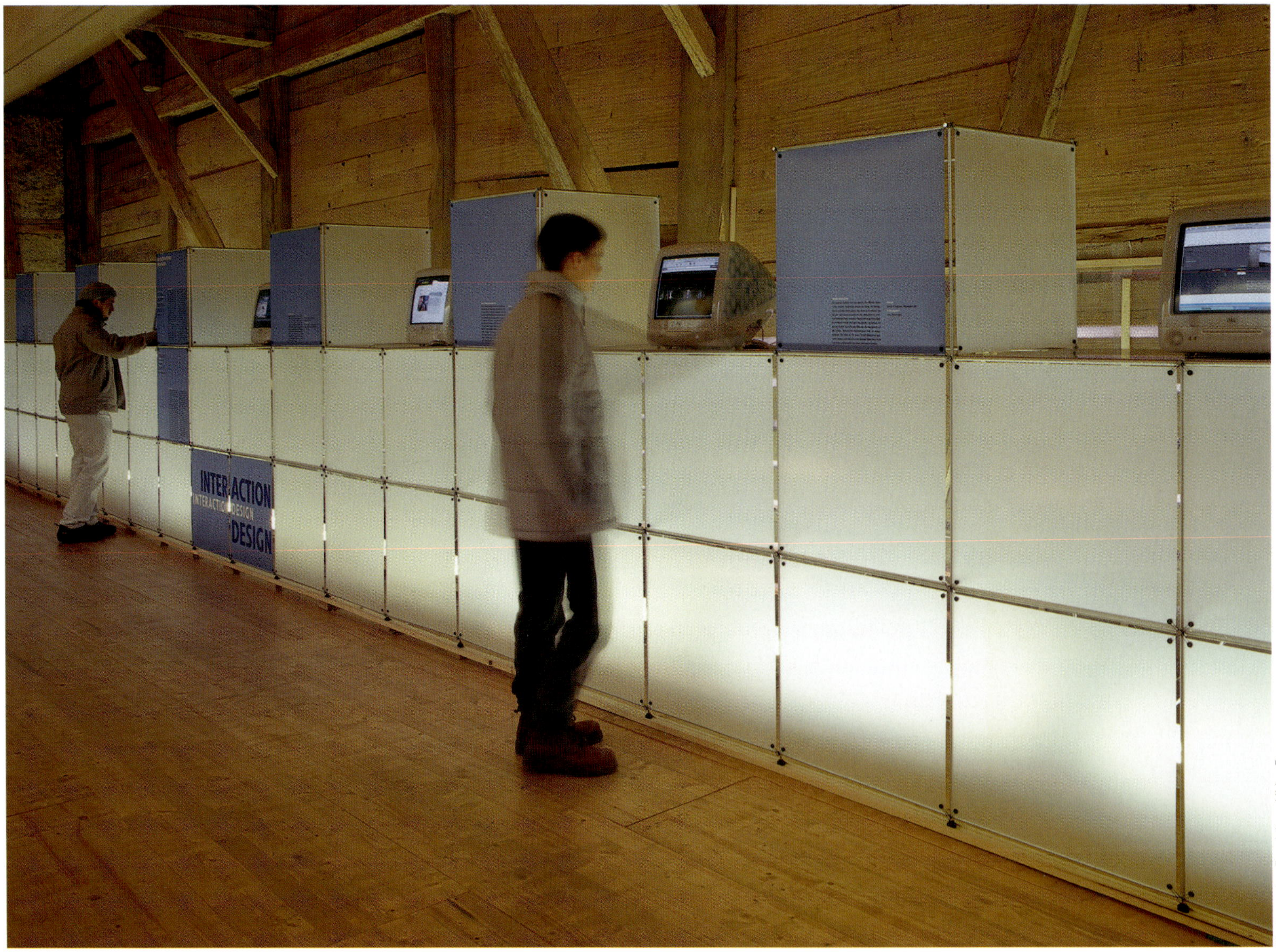

Photographs: Dominique Uldry, Bern

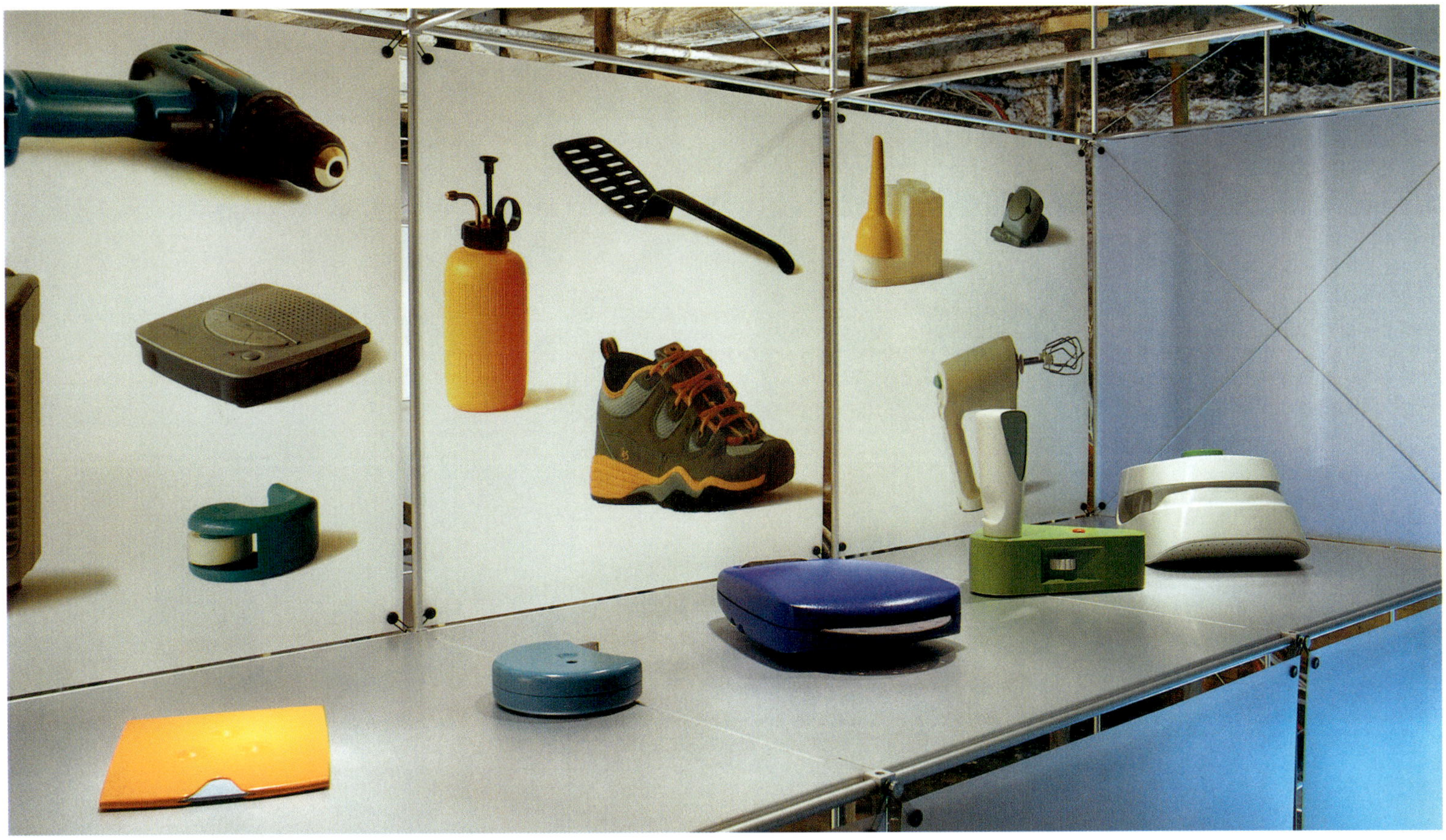

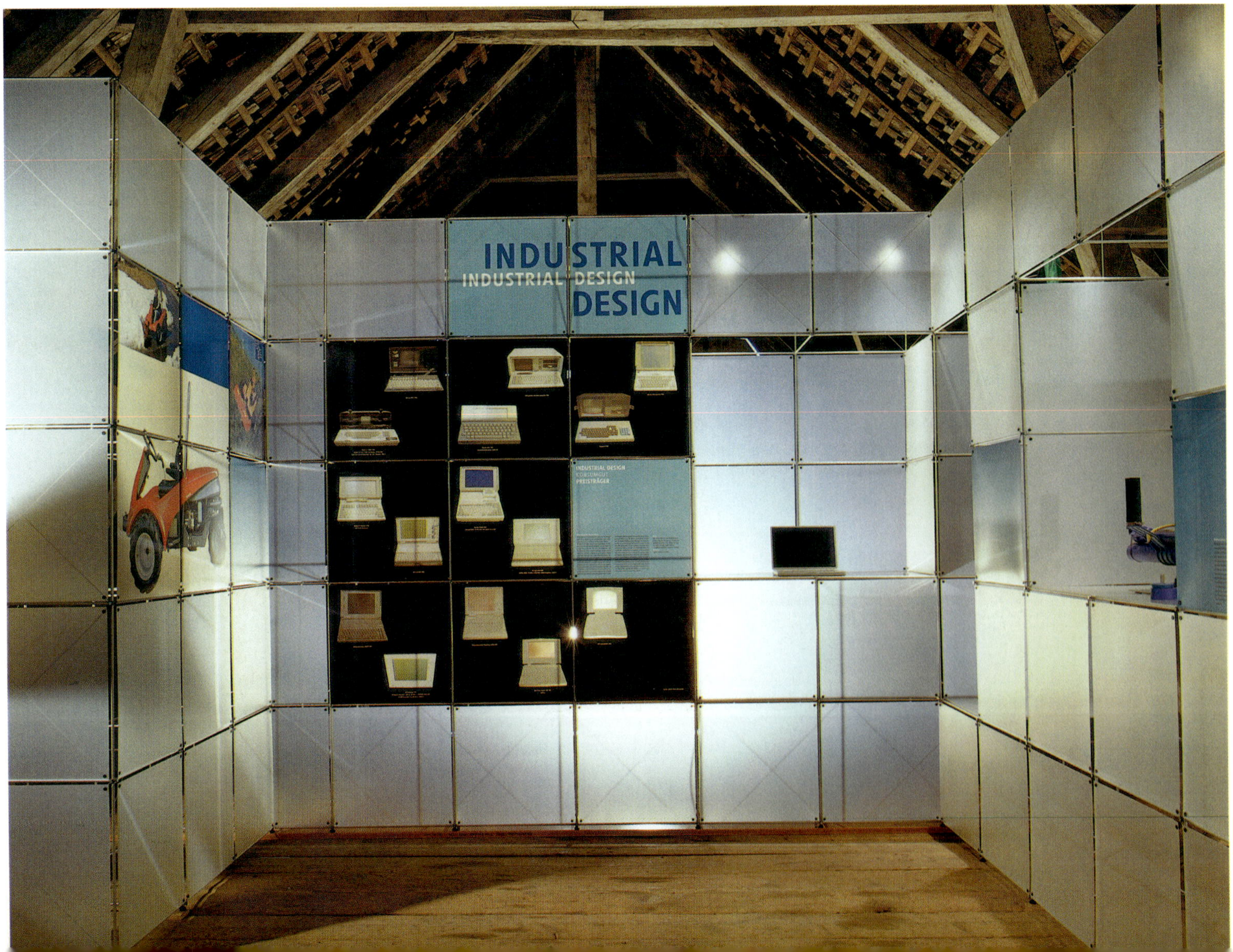
INDUSTRIAL DESIGN
INDUSTRIAL DESIGN

Atelier Markgraph
+ Kauffman Thelig & Partner

eads

As Europe's largest aerospace company and a leading global pla-yer in the aerospace and defence sector, the European Aeronautic Defence and Space Company (EADS) was formed by the merging of DaimlerChrysler Aerospace, the Spanish company CASA and the French company Aerospatiale Matra.

The concept for the new company's trade fair presentation was based on the central design element of the circle, a symbol of unity and identification. The wide reaching roof of the "Space Tower" generously drew together the various business sectors, brands and products of the original companies. Silver colored, aluminum lamellar rings grew from the base of the Space Tower to create a room-defining sculpture.

The finely tuned interaction between the various design elements ensured an easily identifiable corporate image. Architecture, gra-phics, lighting, exhibits and media presentations worked together to create an atmosphere conducive to dialogue and clear commu-nication: EADS is open, inviting and appealing.

The concept allowed for flexible re-implementation at a variety of trade fair venues. Stand elements can be easily adapted to diffe-rent exhibition spaces depending on the conditions of the particu-lar event.

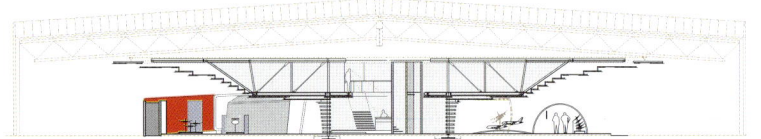

Photographs: A.J. Lipták, A. Keller

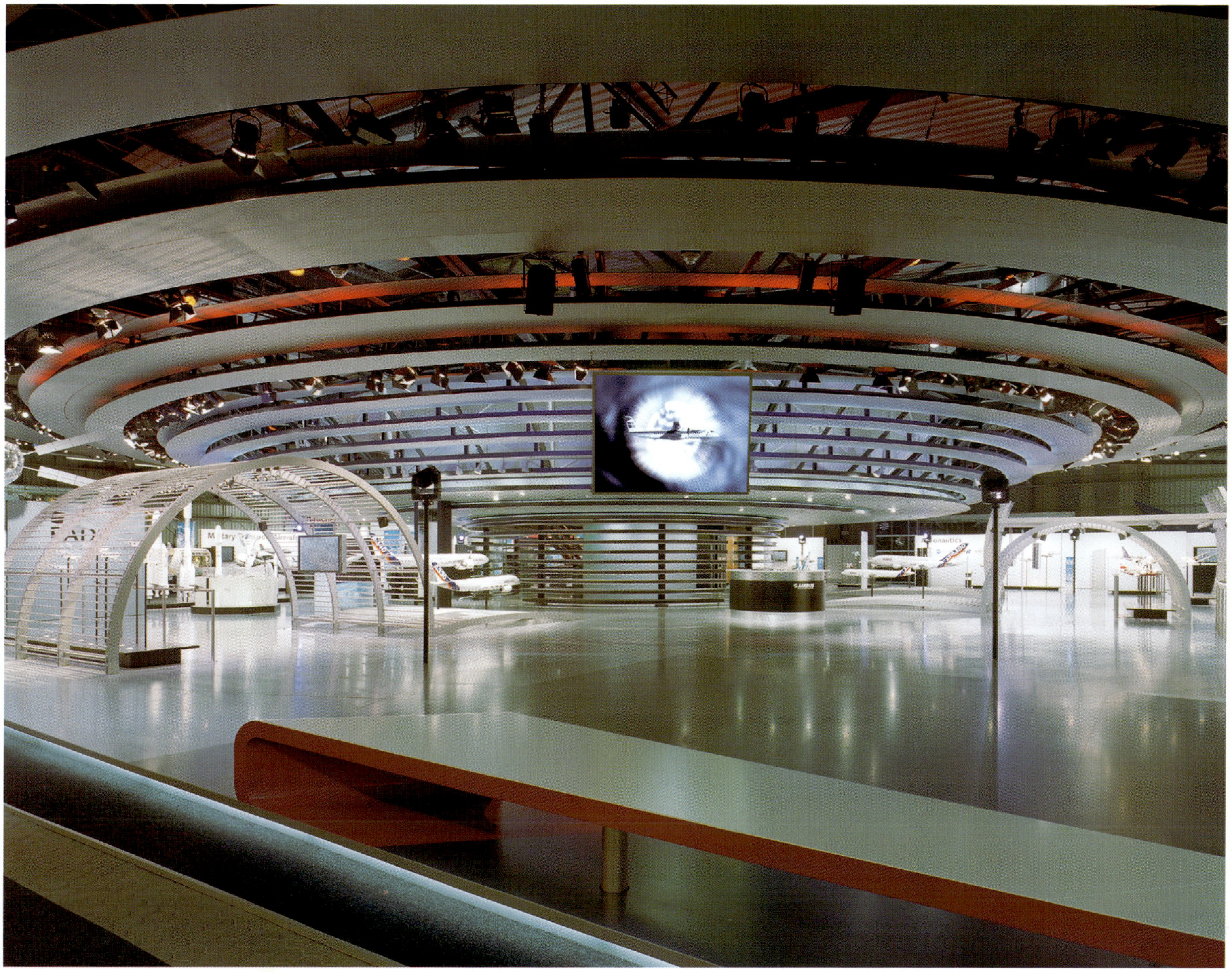

Space
Space
Earth Observation Satellites
Scientific Satellites for Space Exploration

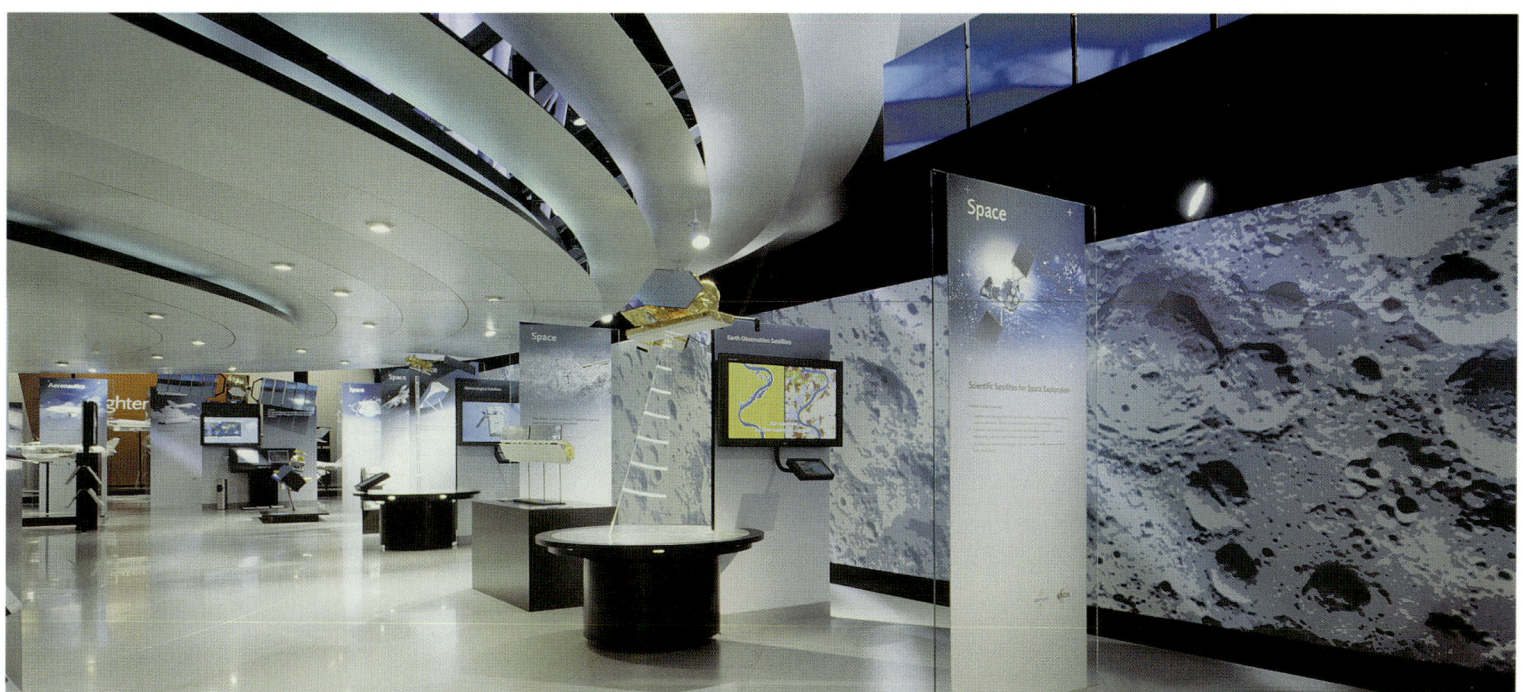

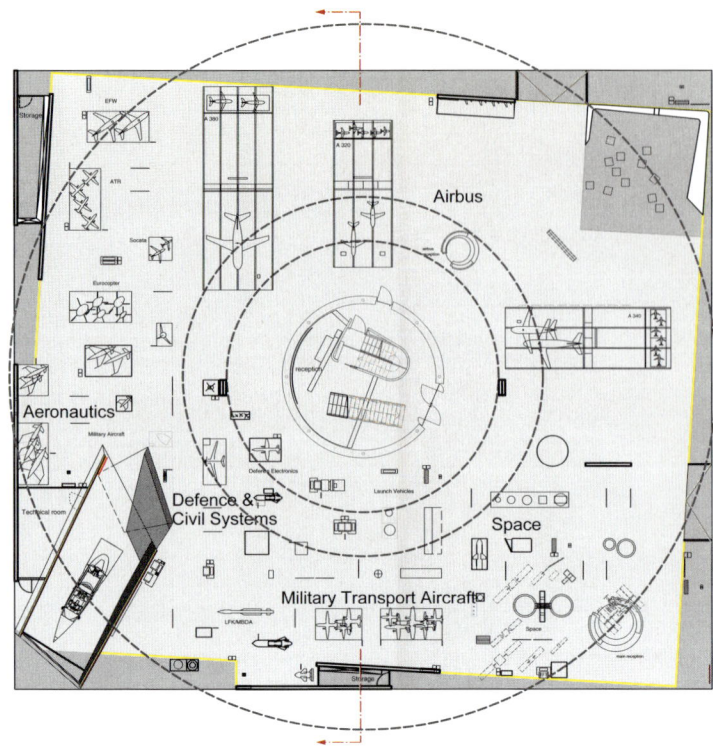

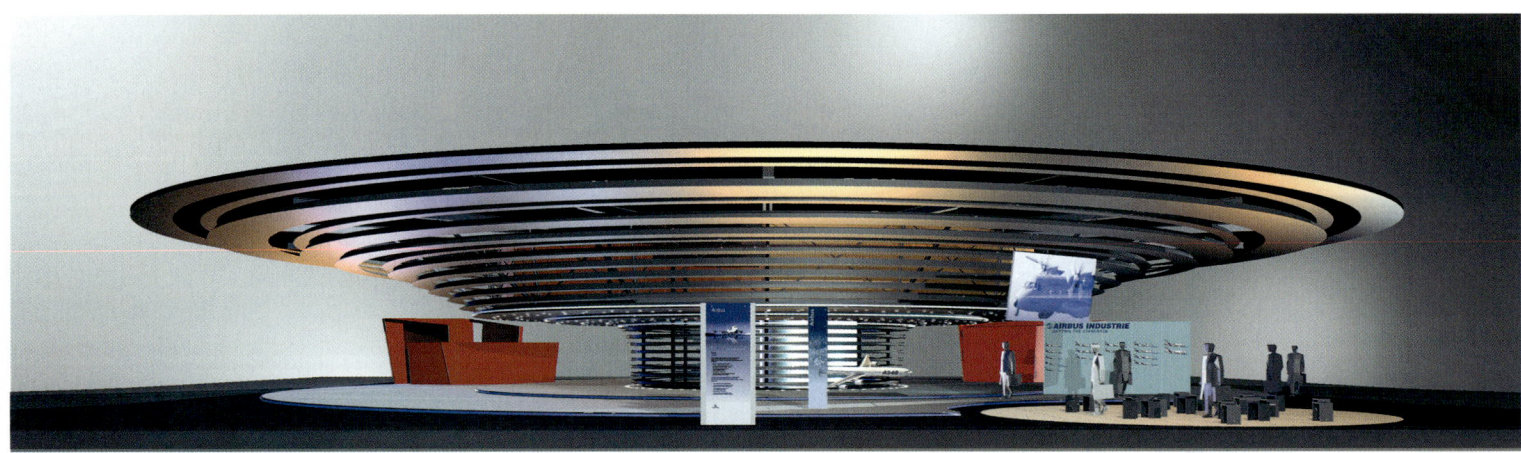

Aeronautics
AIRBUS CORPORATE JETLINER
A320
A320

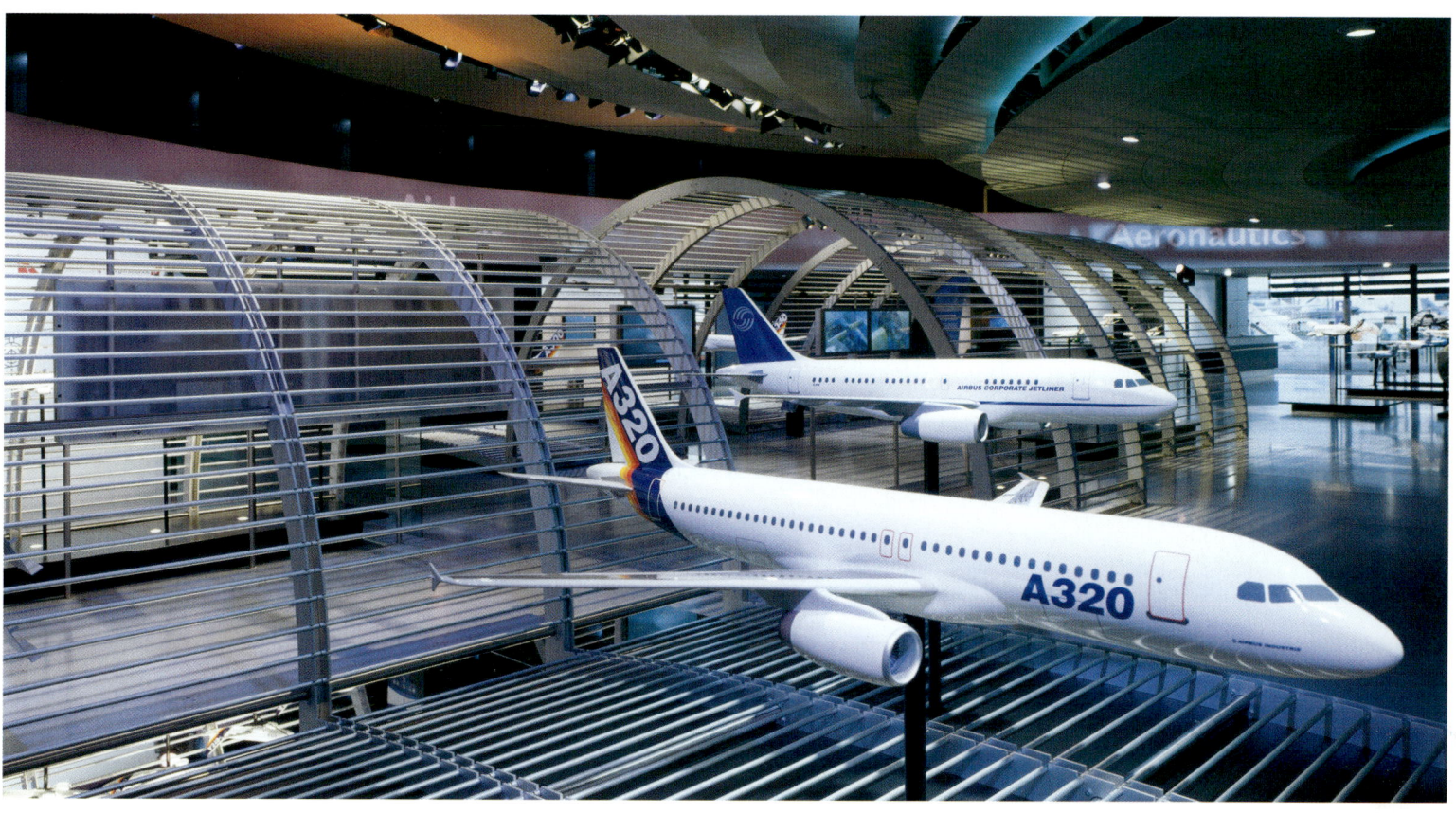

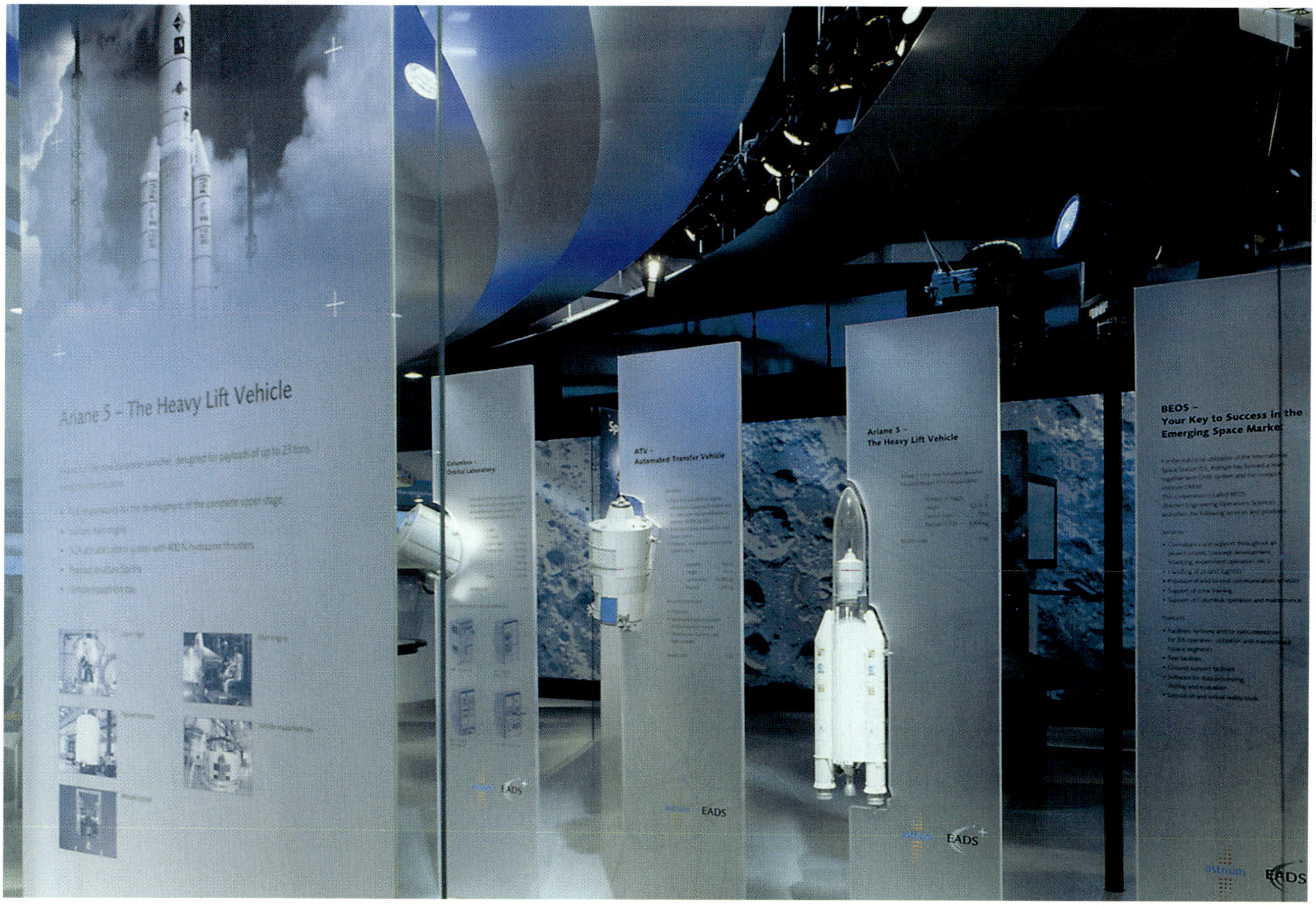
Ariane 5 – The Heavy Lift Vehicle
Columbus – Orbital Laboratory
ATV – Automated Transfer Vehicle
Ariane 5 – The Heavy Lift Vehicle
BEOS – Your Key to Success in the Emerging Space Market
EADS
EADS
EADS
astrium
EADS

The GCGroup AG
orange

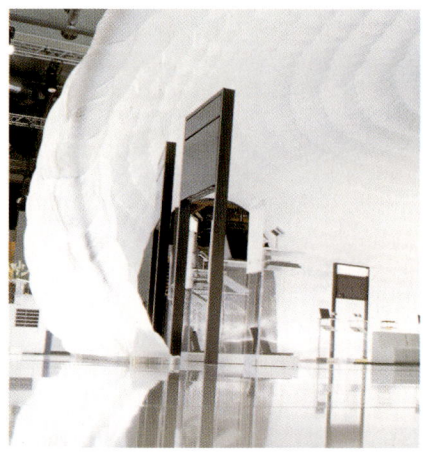

Orange wanted a design that would transmit the message conveyed by its commercials, a tangible expression of their desire to connect people all over the world. The brief was both complex and tempting because it consisted of creating concrete images of the invisible, a challenge that led Patrick Gubser from the GC group, industrial designer Felix Keller and architects Roland Imboden and Stefan Zachleder to develop the concept of an inflatable dome.
This idea embodied the precise feeling of buoyancy that the client wanted, but required a great deal of technical innovation and imagination to arrive at the final structure. The stand's success rested on the way it used the supple and sensuous white roof to add complexity to a simple rectangular site, with lighting, video installations and text all adding to the experience.

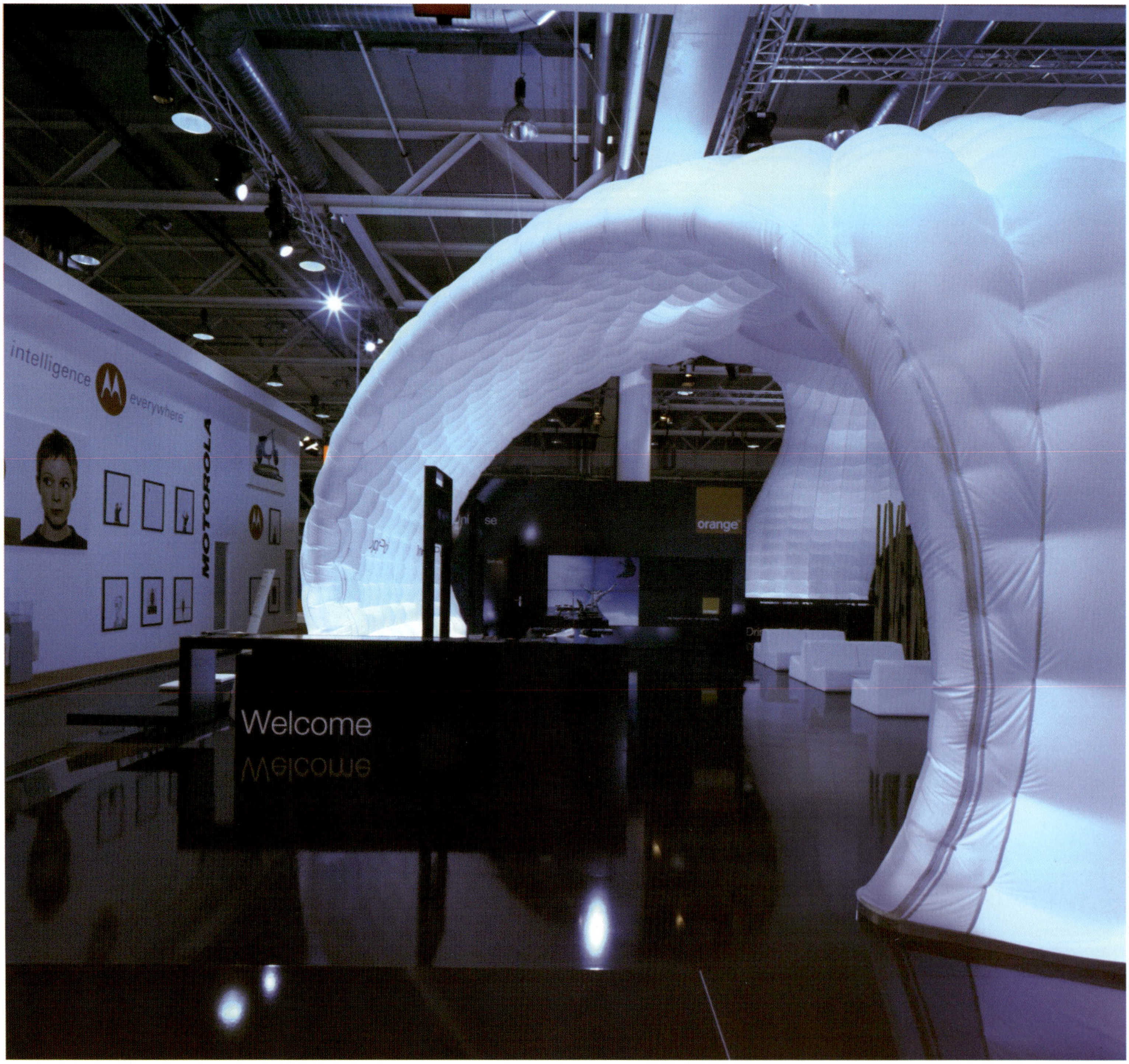

Photographs: Contributed by the architects

Shopping Point   Information Point

The stand defined an area of lightness open on four sides, with arching openings that drew visitors into a calm cool space that housed a two-level central unit. The upper area was reserved for meetings and special guests, but the balloon of fabric enveloping the whole area created a feeling of inclusiveness important to the brand.

Atelier Markgraph

daimler chrysler

The conception and execution of this trade fair presentation defined Daimler Chrysler as a future-oriented global brand, and created a unified space for presenting individual passenger car brands. The Corporate Design was used as the basis for a modular building block system, which allowed for flexible yet consistent implementation of the design elements, including graphics, films and exhibits. The curved roof structure created an architectural bracket supporting the core brand message at the motor show.

With the theme "The Vision of Accident-free Driving" the company further positioned itself as a force shaping the course of things to come and provided its brands with a unifying, visionary theme.

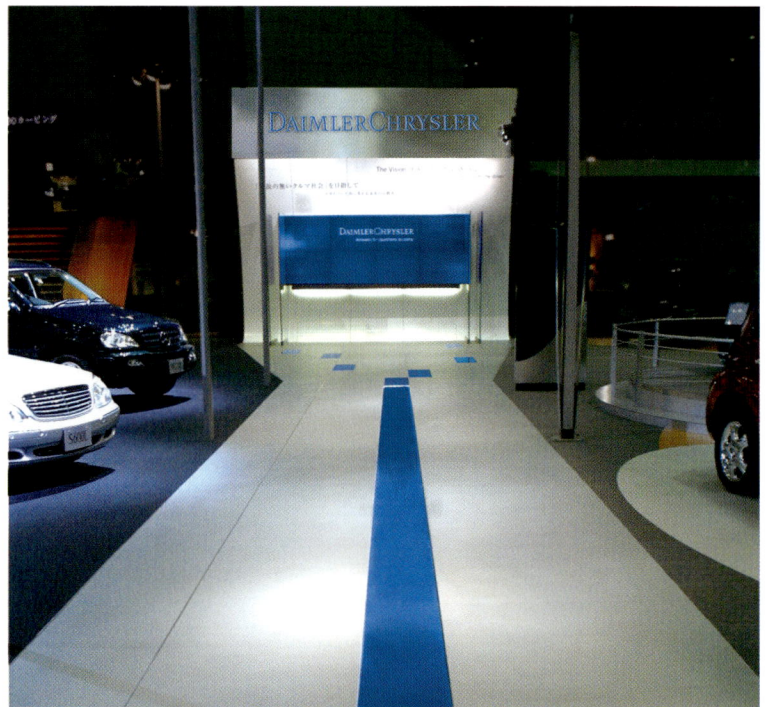

Photographs: Christoph Kraneburg, Andreas Keller

DaimlerChrysler
Welcome
Chrysler
Dodge
Jeep,
Mercedes-Benz

The Vision of 'Accident-free Driving'
Lane Departure Warner • Night Vision
Lane Departure Warner
Electronic Crumple Zone
Night Vision

Artekstands
gas natural

An artist who ignores the difference between natural growth and human construction will produce exactly the opposite of what he was looking for: instead of creating something as natural as a flower, the design will lack exactly that, the condition of being natural.
An object produced by Nature is never unfinished: if it is inorganic, like stone, it is as it should be, and if it is organic, like a flower, then it is just as it should be at any given moment.
This stand is not a butterfly, it is a place to make people working at Gas Natural feel light, natural, and able to soar.

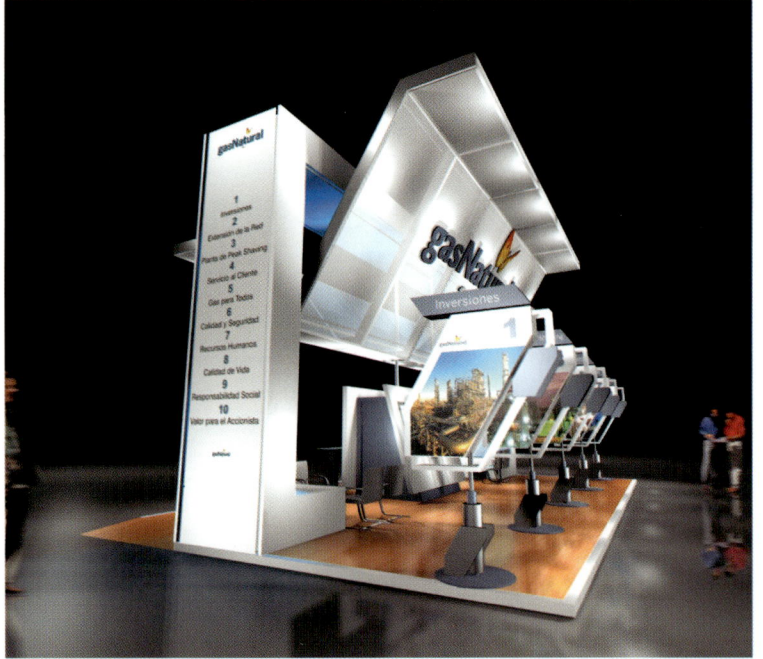

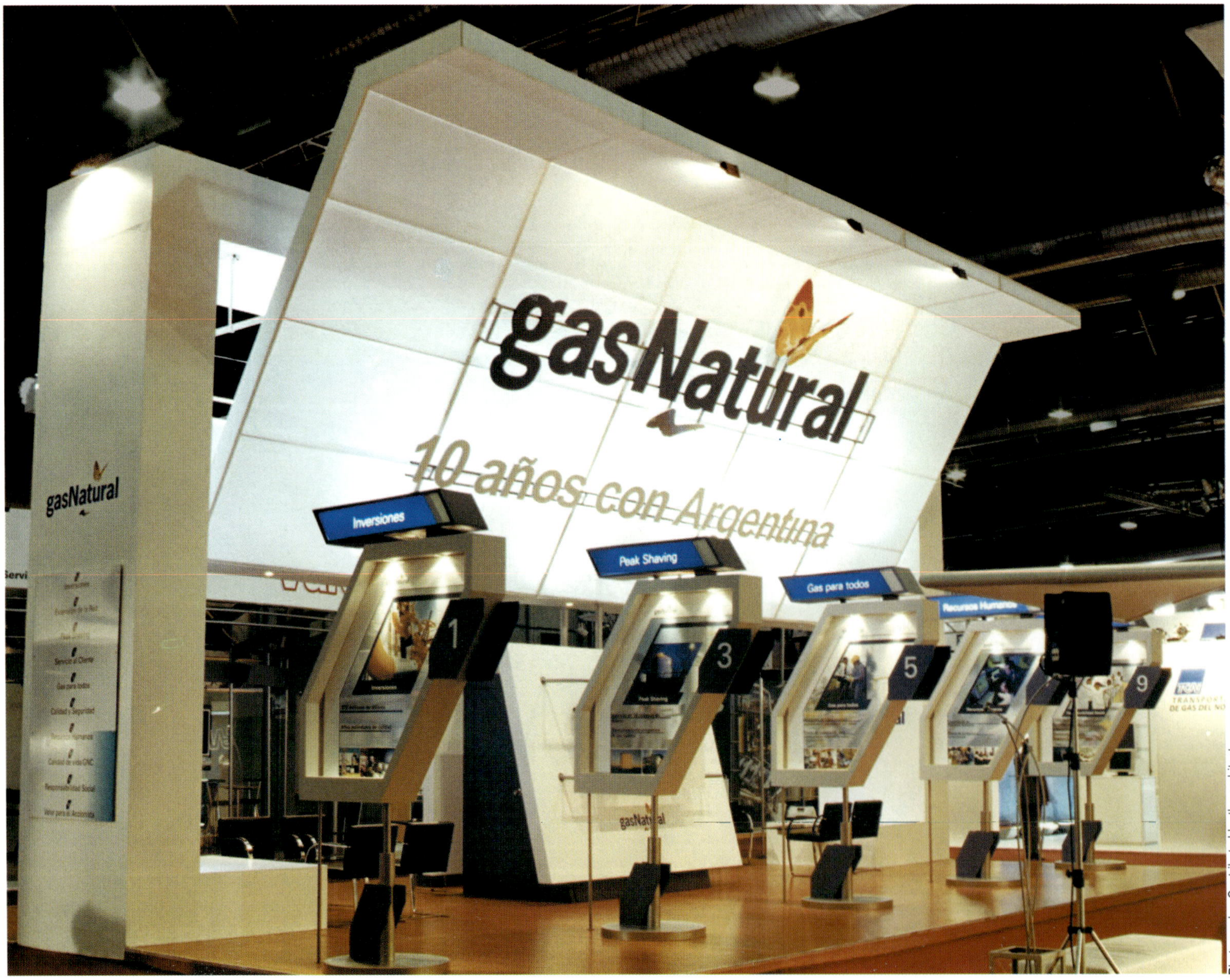

Photographs: Contributed by the architect

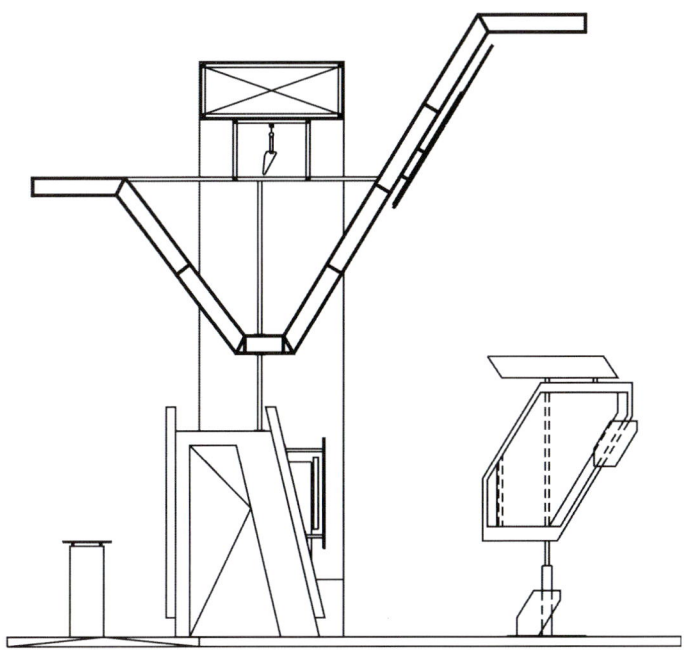

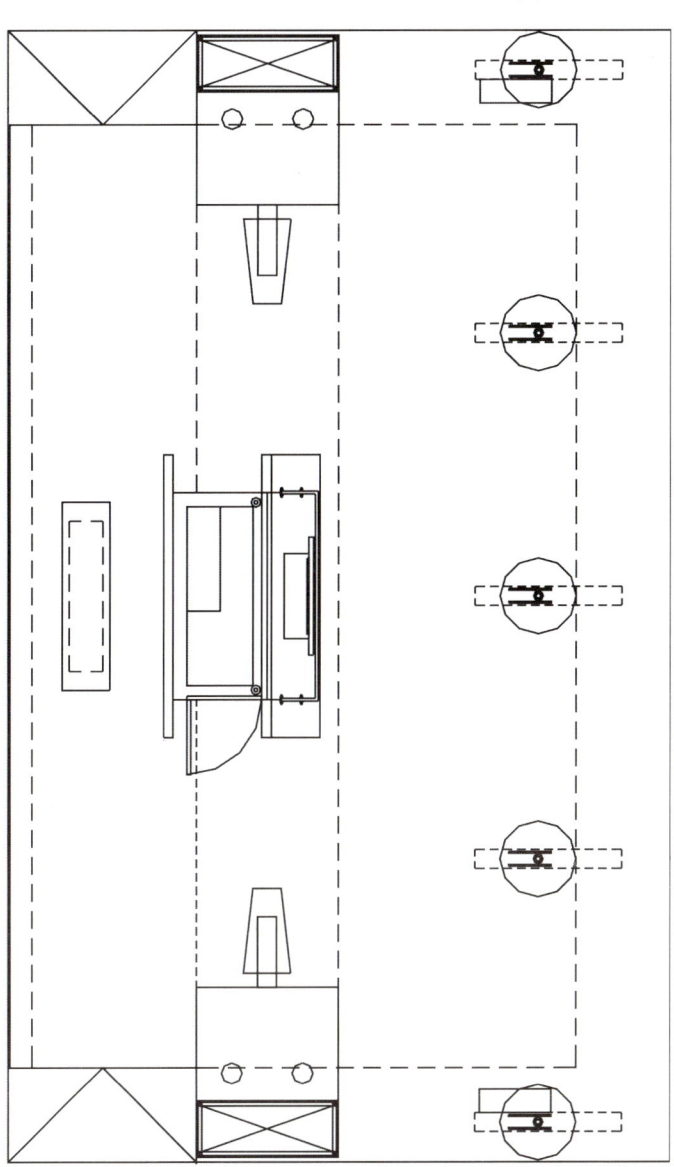

General Graphics Exhibits
monterrey design systems

The idea behind this project was to create a stand that would strengthen Monterrey's image within the electronic design automation (EDA) industry, provide product information in an attractive environment, and lead potential customers into suites for more in-depth information. The obstacle was an existing bulky stand that required extensive, expensive refurbishment, and would still have been in conflict with the company's promise to provide "Advanced Physical Design Software Solutions".

The solution was custom rental that conveyed the brand message, for the cost of refurbishing and remounting the existing stand. The dolphins "playing" on the Monterrey logo suggested an ocean theme, and led the designers to create this sleek design of mesmerizing fluidity. Lights, sound and video were used to evoke an ocean environment, soothing underwater scenes that transformed into a high-energy montage of dolphins playing and jumping in the air. A custom soundtrack of pulsing, ambient sounds of underwater life combined with rippling lights from above alternated with the video presentations.

The stand covered an area of 40 square feet, and consisted of a central box frame tower with a core that supported the state-of-the-art video and lighting equipment. Stretched translucent fabric for projecting the videos, and a semi-transparent black rim canopy for lighting control added to the underwater effect. Opaque wings around the screen were used to display company logos and other information. The product demo areas contained bubble-shaped graphics mounted on clear perplex, and inflatable see-through chairs also suggested bubbles or jellyfish under the theatrical lighting. One of the most important elements was the specially created video and soundtrack featuring underwater scenes, dolphins playing and jellyfish undulating.

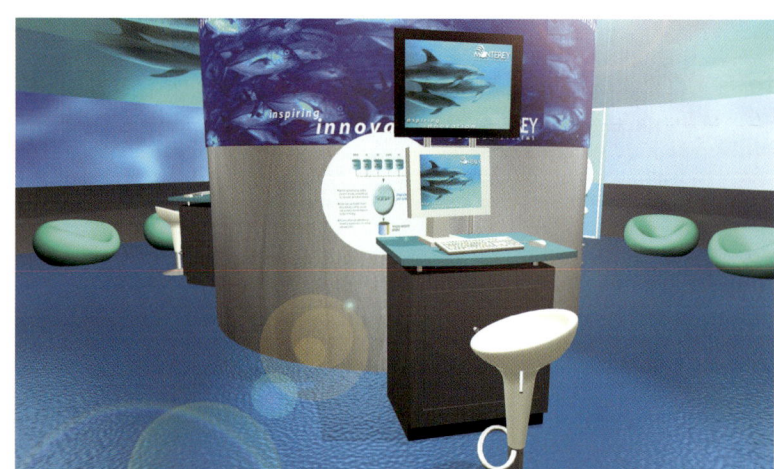

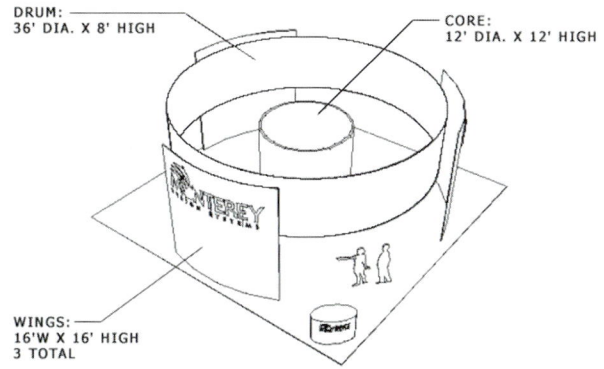

DRUM:
36' DIA. X 8' HIGH

CORE:
12' DIA. X 12' HIGH

WINGS:
16'W X 16' HIGH
3 TOTAL

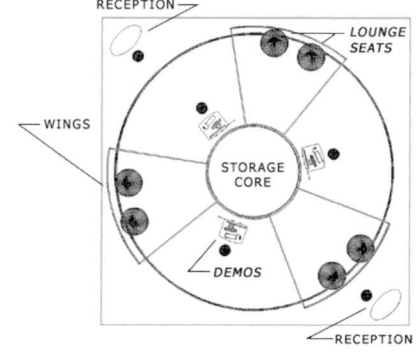

RECEPTION

LOUNGE
SEATS

WINGS

STORAGE
CORE

DEMOS

RECEPTION

MONTEREY DAC 40 X 40

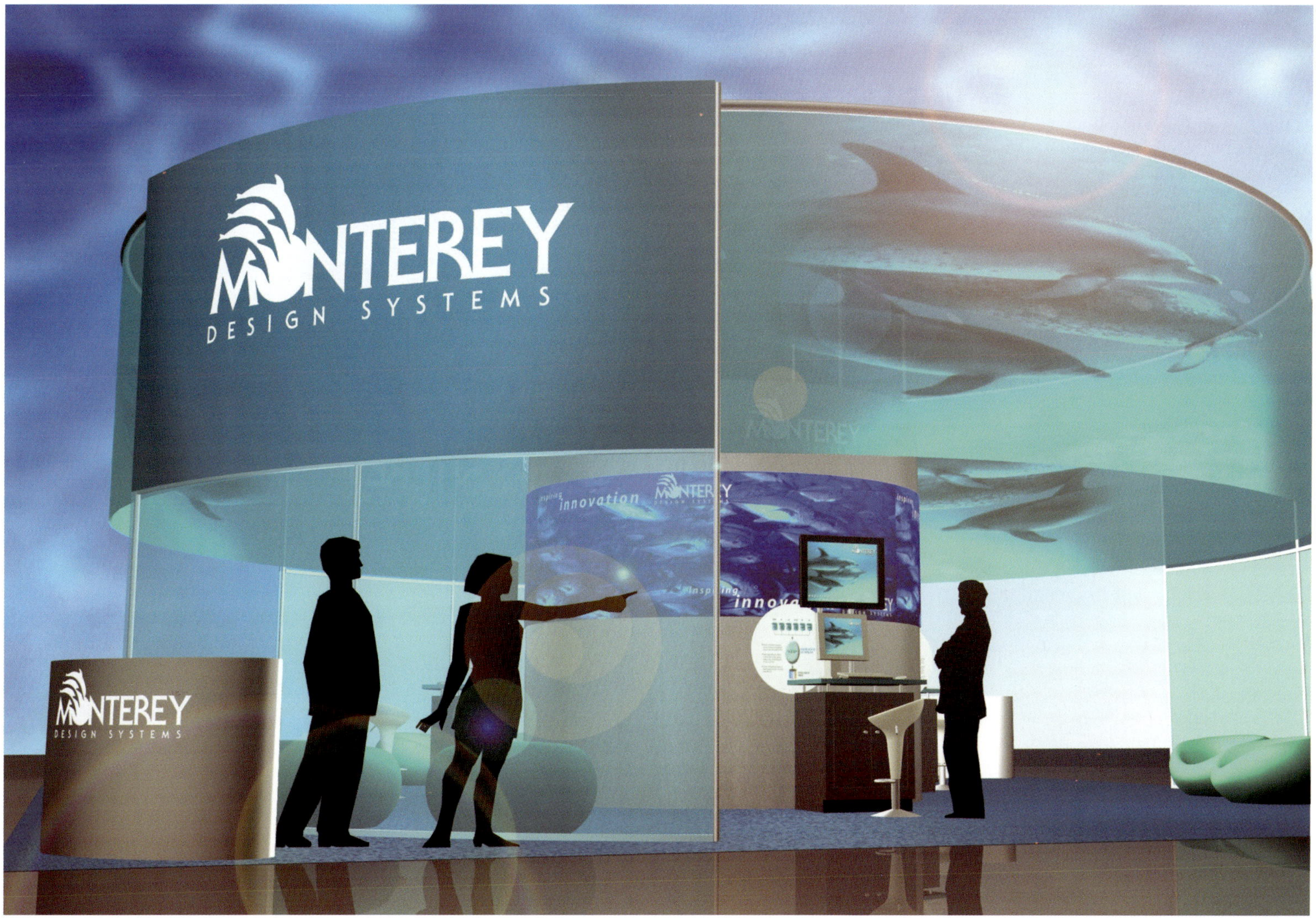

Atelier Brückner
kodak

Stuttgart-based design company Atelier Brückner was asked to develop a design concept for Kodak's exhibition stand at Photokina 2002, held in Cologne. In keeping with its position as a market leader, Kodak occupied a floor space of 8,600 m² at this internationally renowned photo industry trade show. The challenge for the designers was to create a stand with a strong brand identity but enough variety to keep visitors interested in exploring the large area.

Atelier Brückner based the design on two main concepts, creating a sequence of "frames" along a main corridor and different colored showcases on either side of it. Each of these offered its own characteristic world of images and design elements, like scenes in a play. The structure and sequence of the spaces suggested a story told in colors and images that perfectly illustrated the stand's motto - "Share Moments - Share Life".

The stand was designed around a long, winding corridor that varied in width. Wide at some points and narrow at others, this pathway connected the two entrances to the hall. Rectangular shapes, like frames in a photo sequence, divided the corridor into separate "scenes", while brightly colored presentations containing information about Kodak's different business sections were placed along the left and right sides of this central corridor, covering the floor and walls. To make it easier for visitors to orient themselves on the showroom floor, a specific color was assigned to each of the different business sections. A bright yellow-orange unified the stand and gave it an overall coherent look, while the other colors used alluded to the palette of the previous year's Kodak stand.

Photographs: Contributed by the designers

Giant shapes and silhouettes made use of the vast space and drew the visitors' attention to the different cabinets, where they could find information about Kodak's products and services. The simple, striking images and bright colors created a highly attractive environment. By playing with the proportions of these huge, cutout images, the perception of space between the exhibit and the visitors disappeared, allowing them to enter right into this fantastic world of images.

Subdivided into separate, stage-like presentation rooms, the huge stand was transformed into a world of colors and images. This demonstrated the diversity of the Kodak brand, while at the same time a sensitive overall graphic pallet unified the stand and identified it as an integral whole. The intense color scheme of a warm yellow-orange, a strong red, a fresh green and a soft blue turned this stand into a memorable visual experience.

Stefano Colli

tombow

The design concept for this stand was based on the idea of a space that is open on all four sides, and can be experienced as a kind of plaza. A single wall was built using cardboard boxes, with two open windows in the spaces where the meeting tables were placed.
The stand's cedar floor was raised using eight platforms of corrugated cardboard sheets, creating original and attractive display modules for the writing products.
The desktop lamps with flexible stands that were used for lighting matched the design, and focused most of the light on the products displayed.

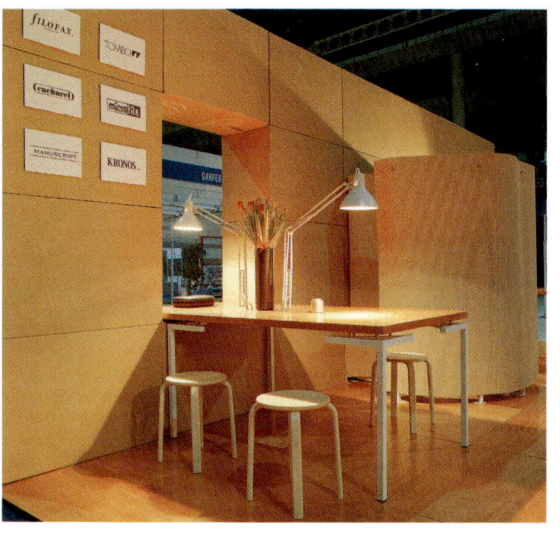

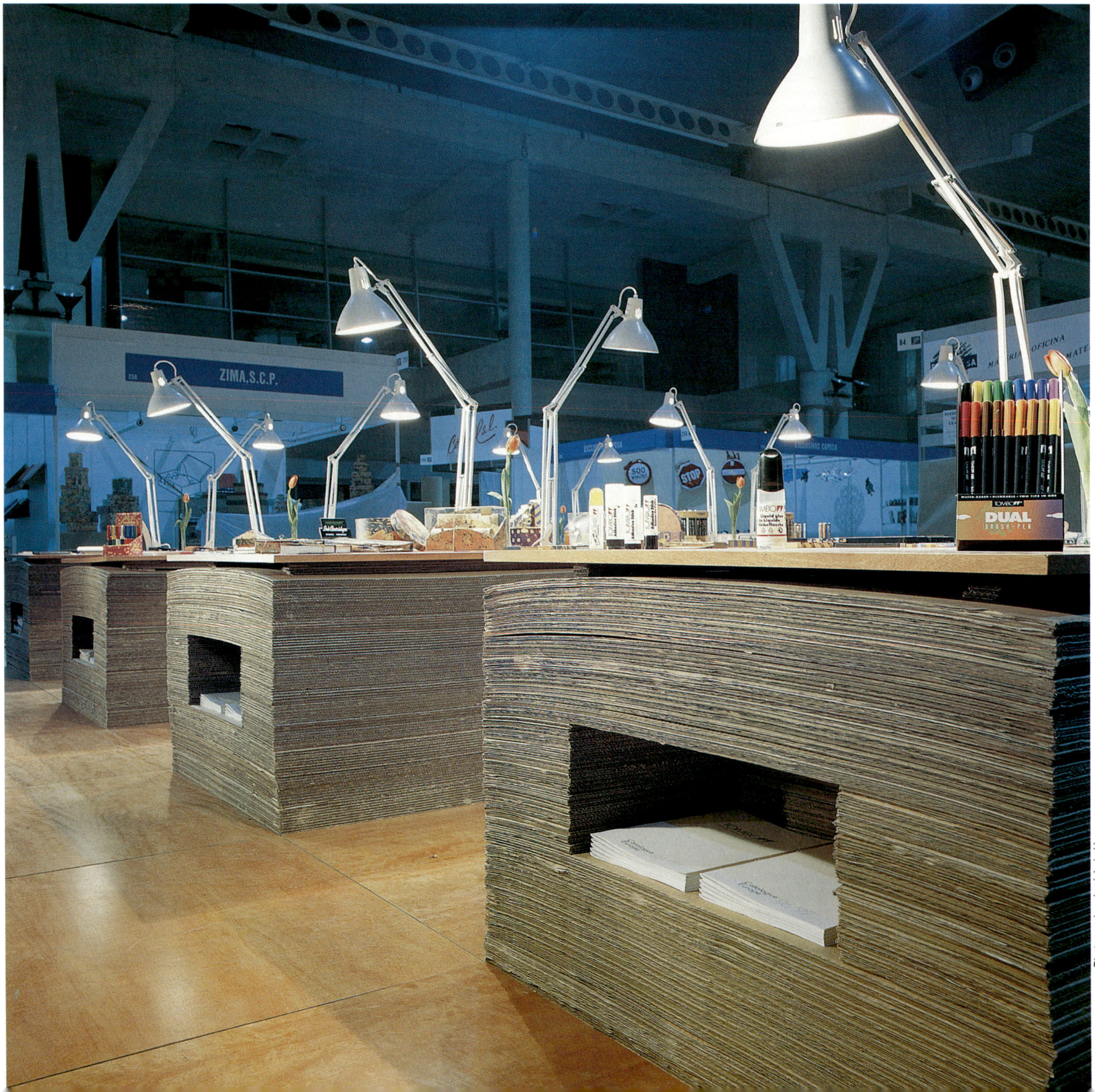

Photographs: José Luis Hausmann

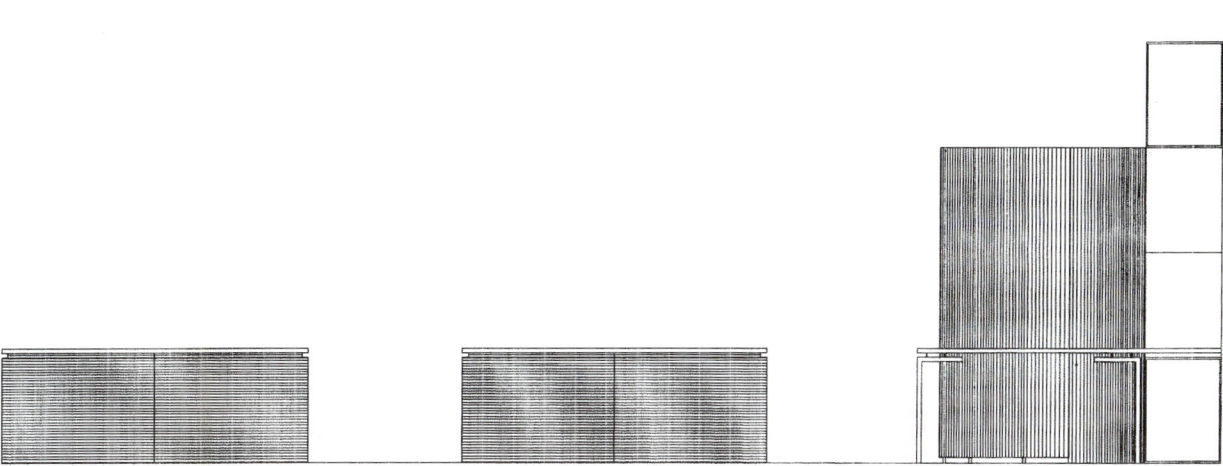

Formpol AG
century

The Century brand was present at the Basilea 2003 Jewelry and Watch fair with a new and totally redesigned stand. A considerably larger floor area allowed the company to expand to three levels and use the external area to stage events and as a bar.

The main purpose of the new stand was to strengthen brand identity and create a space that mirrored the nature and high quality of the products. The design was based around an outer skin made of glass, creating an immediate association between the products and the architecture of the stand. This was further strengthened by the striking use of the design elements and colors of the Century brand. One of the main features was the third floor display area, where the opaque walls contained small openings through which visitors could view the products using binoculars and immerse themselves into the world of sapphire watches.

Another important element was the modular construction that allows the stand to adapt to different exhibition requirements. All components are easy to disassemble, ensuring that the stand will remain useful for several years. At the construction level, the centerpiece is the innovative, mass-produced rubber piece used to join the facade elements. These elements can be joined quickly and easily, allowing the designers to use frameless glass panels that can be arranged in many different ways.

Photographs: Menga von Sprecher

The glass, spaciousness and careful styling allowed visitors to feel at ease while focussing attention on the products. Striking lighting, high-quality materials and bold and simple styling contributed to the atmosphere of quality and simplicity, and created a lasting association between the company and these values in the minds of visitors.

Kaufmann Theilig & Partner
mercedes-benz & maybach

A wooden landscape develops across 1.500 m² in different levels: differentiated spaces and the chance to have an overview of the whole stand are created. Specific views and spatial situations alternating between more open and more spatially defined areas are generated. The office and service rooms go almost unnoticed in the background. The terraced landscape, made of wood, achieves the de-sired warm atmosphere. Partially illuminated Glass arteries playfully cross the ter-races, like quartz veins in a rock. They bind the stand to-gether in its depth and create a technically precise coun-terpart to the atmospher-ically warm wood. A new Brand and a new product are being announced at the Mercedes Stand. The concept of the Mercedes stand interprets the task: a portion of the Mercedes Stand is recogniz-ably separated for the new brand. The new automobile is recognizable in silhouette behind a tinted sheet of glass. The tradition of the Maybach brand is documented with a historical vehicle.

Photographs: Andreas Keller

DAIMLERCHRYSLER
innovations Innovationen
souveraineté Souveränität
High Quality Interior > > > > > AIRMATIC Dual Control > > > > > Siège multicontours dynamique > Fahrdynamischer Multikontursitz

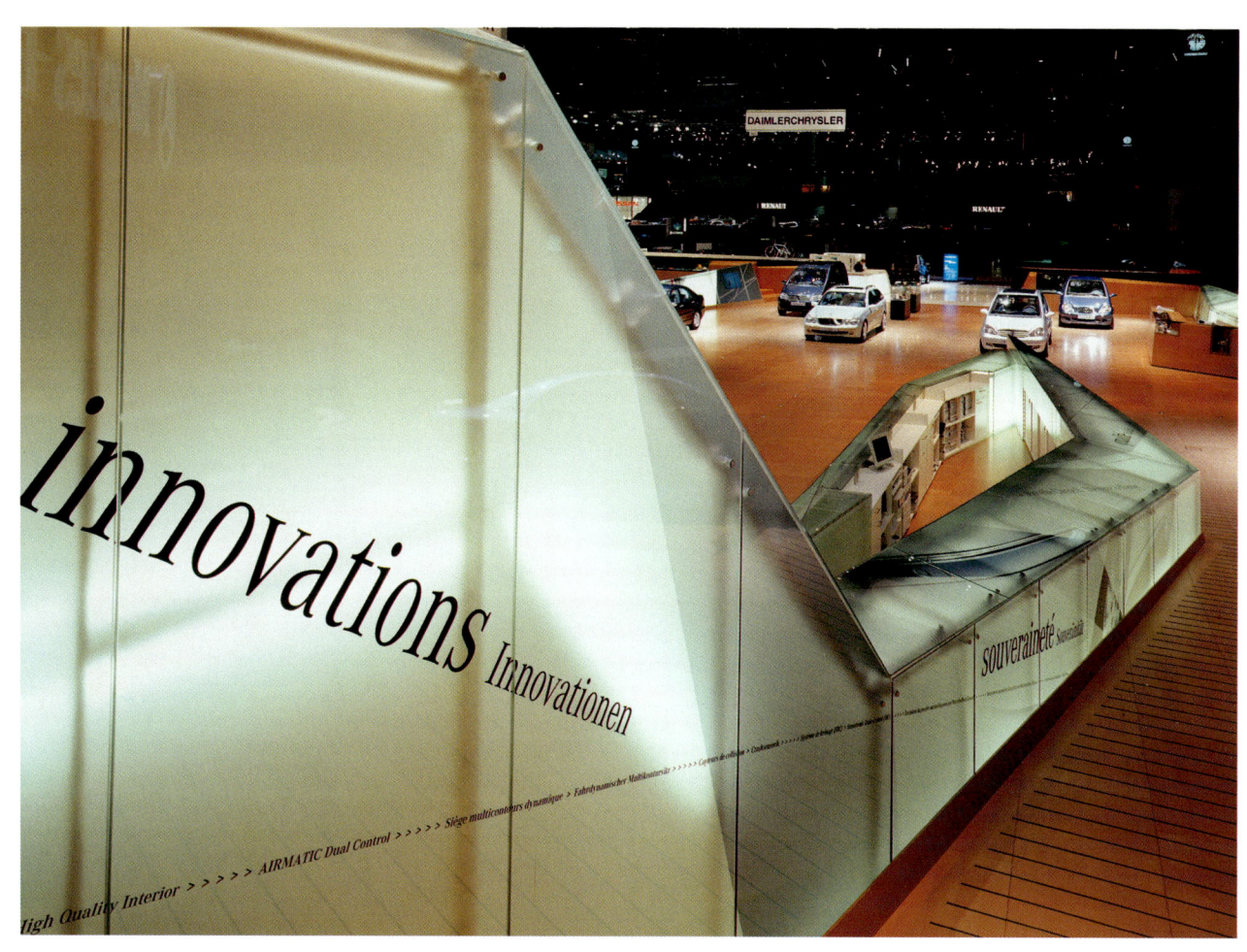

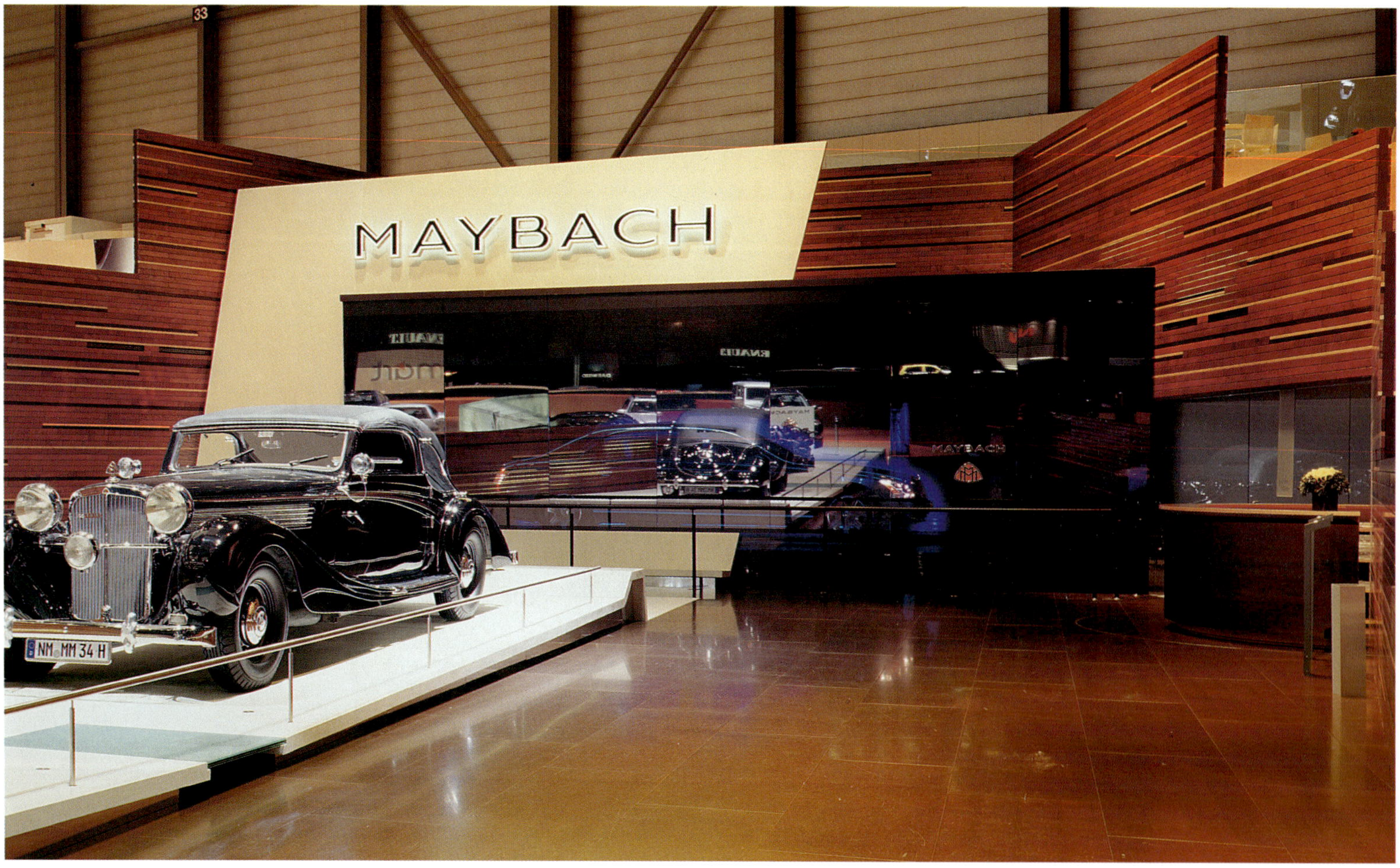
MAYBACH
NM MM 34 H

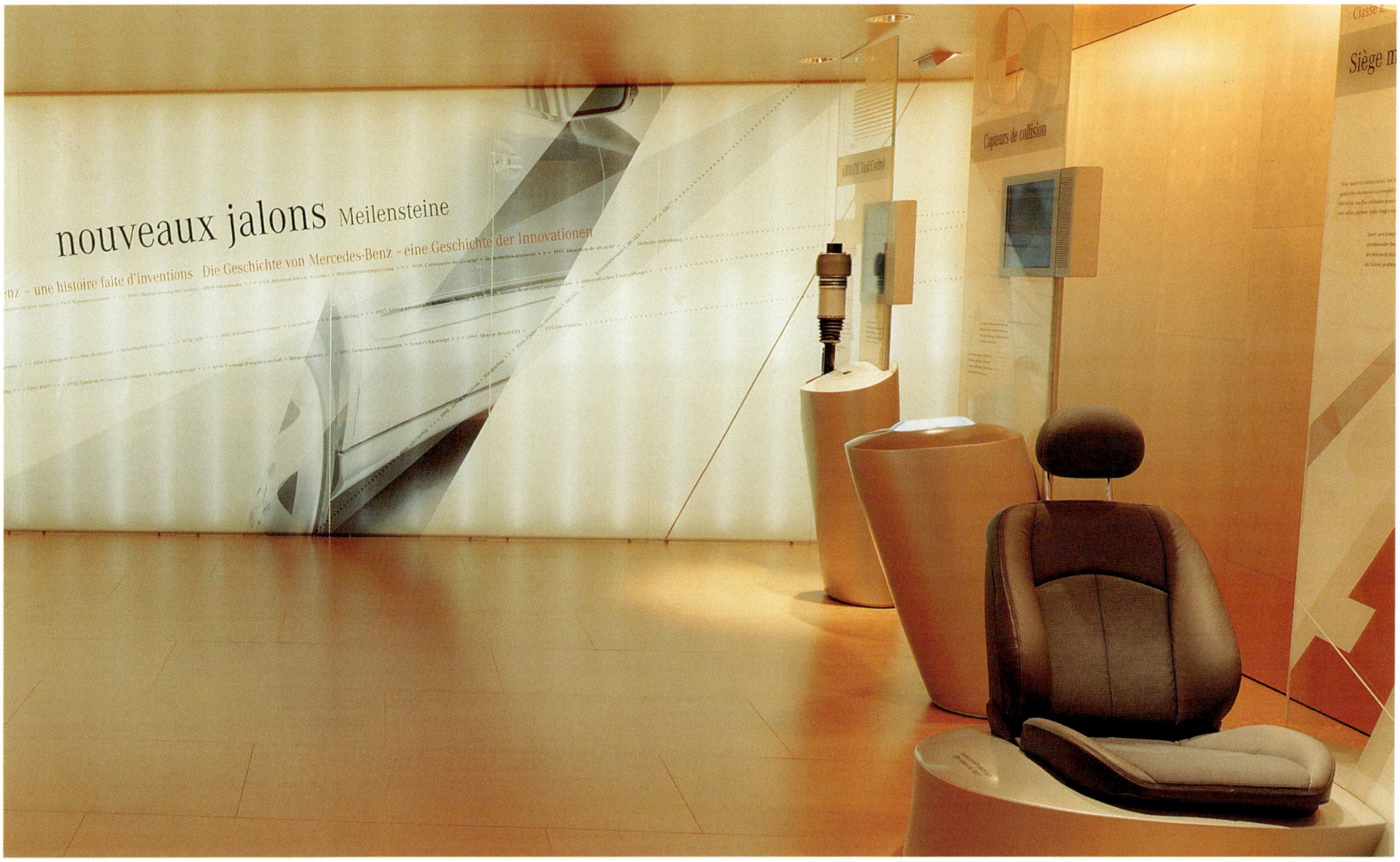
nouveaux jalons Meilensteine
une histoire faite d'inventions Die Geschichte von Mercedes-Benz – eine Geschichte der Innovationen
Capteurs de collision

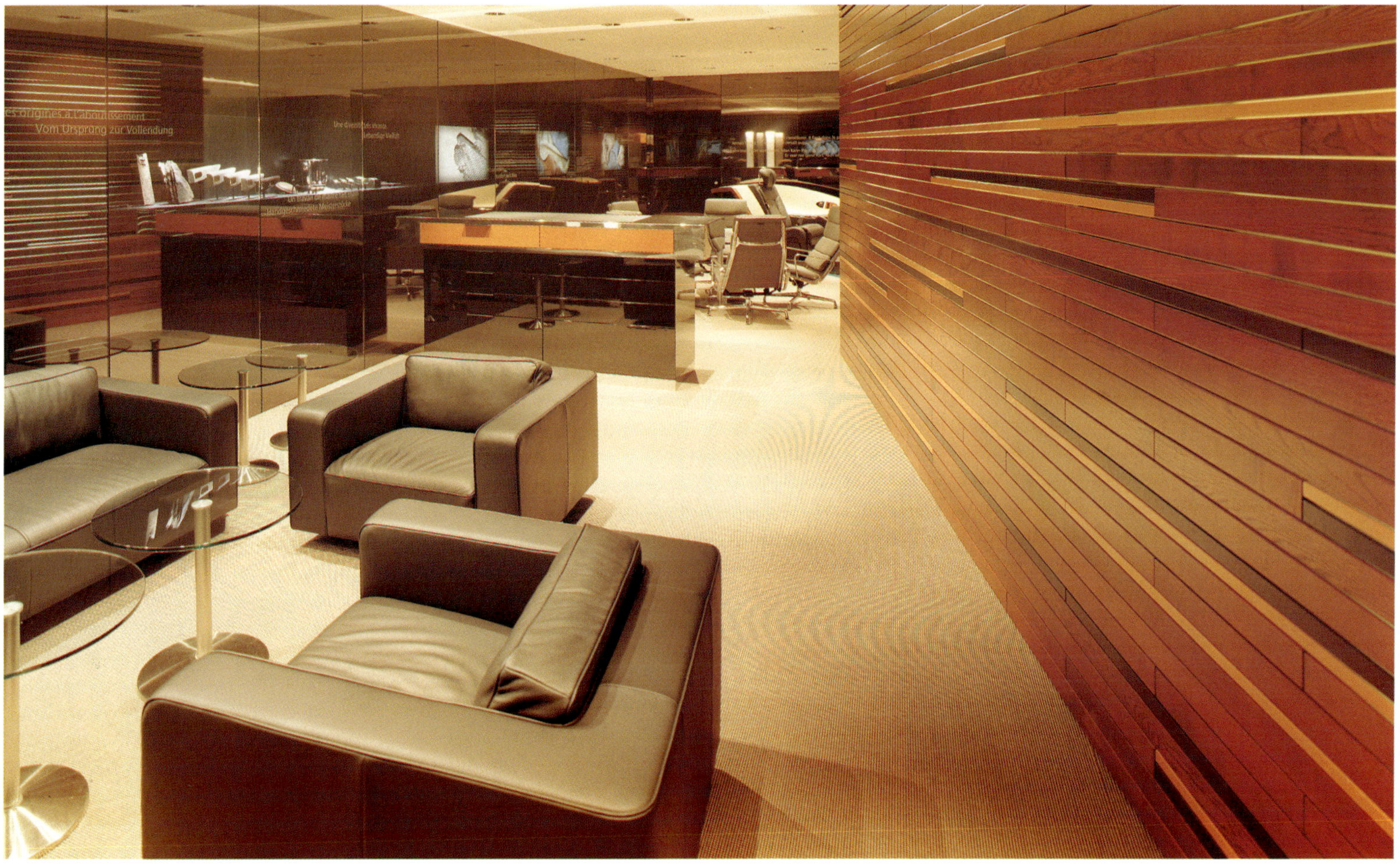
Vom Ursprung zur Vollendung

Stefan Zwicky
legero

The German shoe manufacturer Legero Schuhfabrik specializes in children's shoes, sandals, and waterproof adventure footwear made from the special lightweight materials that inspired the name "Legero". The company hired a team consisting of graphic designers, a copywriter, publicist and the architecture firm Stefan Zwicky to create a new corporate image, including a stand for the biannual GDS trade fair in Dusseldorf.

For the stand, the designers decided to create an atmosphere that would evoke the company's lightweight, all-weather shoes. This was achieved by using scaffolding covered by huge pieces of material printed with the latest models, which would change seasonally as new models are released.

The 12 x 14 m stand was divided into three sections. The first level was the display and exhibition area, with painted walls leading to a courtyard with a table and chairs for semi-private meetings.

The second level was dedicated to personal attention for industry representatives and contained the entire product range, while the back section consisted of a spacious meeting room, kitchen and dressing rooms. The first two areas were made from 5.5 m material-covered scaffolding, and the third level was 2.5 meters in height and built from wood.

Photographs: Contributed by the architect

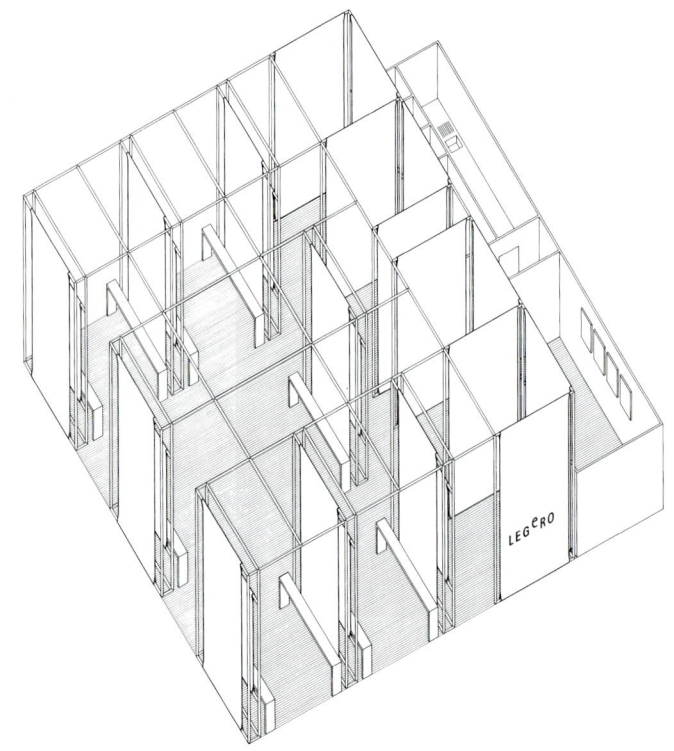

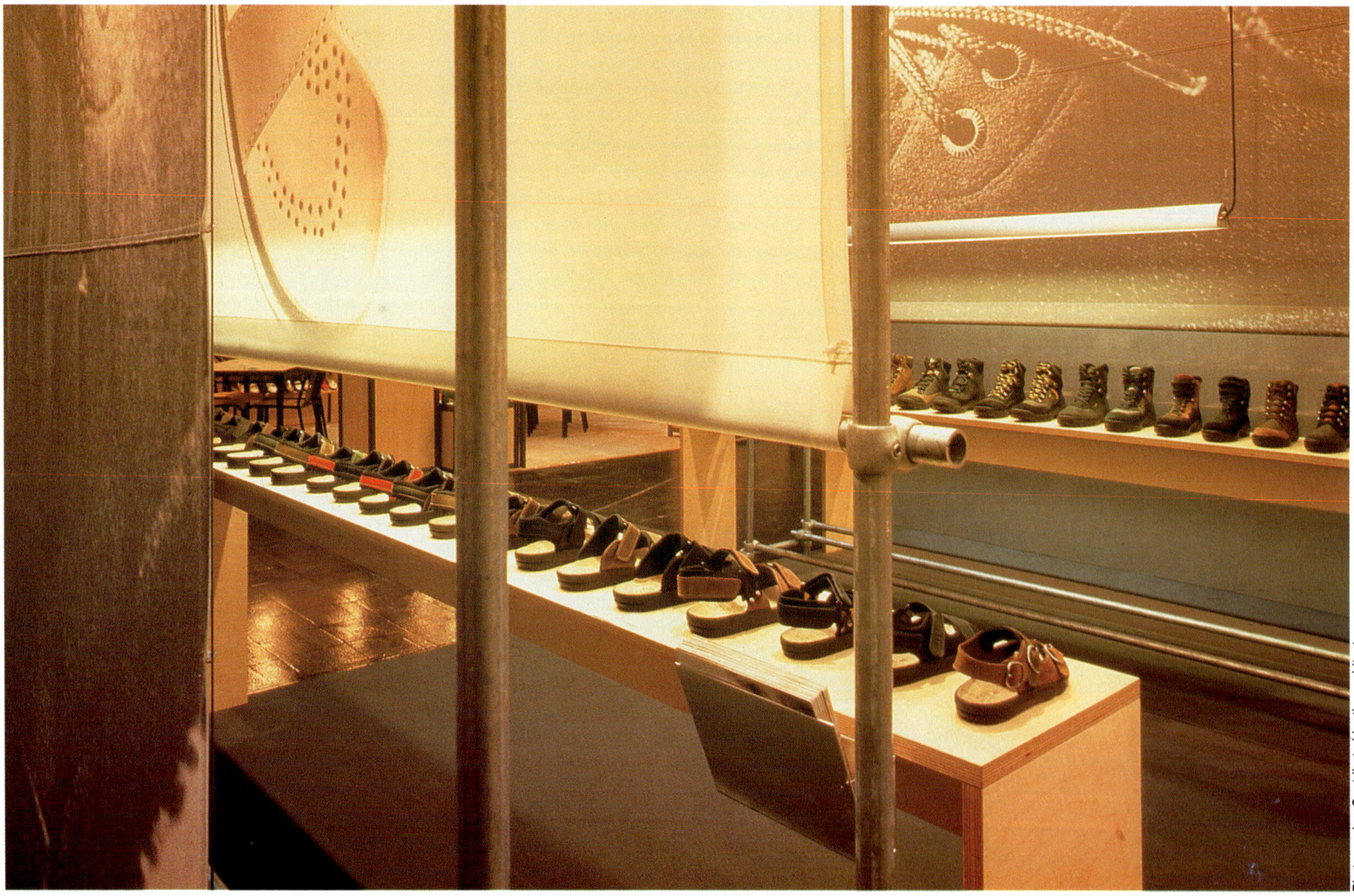

D'Art Design Gruppe
horst

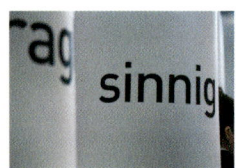

The Horst concept vicariously stands for the Neuss tightrope walk between surface and content. For the designers it is essential to work for and with people, which is why visitors to a trade fair are the element they consider to be most important when designing a stand.

In the same way, this independent group of creators depicts its work as a process-like interaction with wrappers and surfaces. In this display, 154 air balloons suspended from the ceiling described a semi-transparent volume of hints without any real content.

Everything was surface. 154 different words on the balloons formed association chains on the theme of tension "content versus surface". The free mobility of the balloons, their volume and their positioning within the space created landscape architecture references like "park, garden, clearing". The visual effects were underpinned by subtle sound effects (crickets chirping, seagulls screeching, the sounds of insects flying, etc.), which created slowly changing "soundscapes".

Photographs: HG Esch

Traast & Gruson
hidden

This space was designed to present a series of concept products designed by a group of nationally and internationally acclaimed designers and manufactured by Hidden.

Hidden is a Dutch manufacturer with a mandate to produce new furniture designs in the same unadulterated form in which they are conceived. No concessions, nothing hidden. On the contrary, the manufacturer is committed to identifying appropriate technologies and engaging the skill and expertise of the people behind them, in an effort to turn ideas into reality.

Indeed, together they allow us to see the invisible - to discover that which would otherwise remain hidden. This was Traast & Gruson's point of departure for designing the first Hidden show at the International Furniture fair in Cologne, Germany. The company had an area of 100 square meters at the fair and an additional 400 at the Kolnische Kunstverein, a local art gallery. The reason for the two locations is simple: the objects at the fair were furniture, but a gallery setting made them art.

Photographs: Hem Moritz

The Traast & Gruson design for the furniture fair depicted an enormous place setting, with a plate, glass, clutlery. The plate was used as a bar at which visitors could gather, and doubled as a stage. Furniture designs rested in the center of the giant form like petits fours on a plate. The furniture was safely out of reach, visitors could look but not touch. A second plate was shattered. It's contents - another selection of furniture designs - were scattered about but remained upright. This part of the show was hands-on and visitors were encouraged to touch the furniture, to lean on it, open it, experience it.

Sieger design
kaldewei

 This trade fair stand designed for the ISH 2003 not only showcased new products, but also served as a meas of communicating Kaldewei's message: the company stands for more emotionality, but also greater competence in the fields of architecture, design and innovation.

To this end, the designers developed a totally new stand concept within a semitransparent architectural structure, with groups of pavilions arranged arround a central lounge area.

The lounge area was reminiscent of the lobby of luxurious thermal baths, where people meet to chat and exchange views, while a stroll through the pavilions revealed ever-changing worlds with various themes, interior design ideas and screenings.

Photographs: Contributed by the architect

Matteo Thun
zucchetti

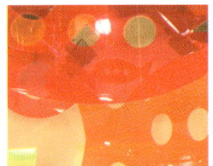

This new formal approach was suggested by the experience of Spain; the inspiration was a landscape of light and colour, where the architecture, graphics and communications have reinvented themselves in a strong and innovative language.
It was in homage to this that the designers decided to construct a story, structured using a new alphabet - an alphabet that can be decoded in terms of color and basic lines.
They designed a story that is all about to Spain!

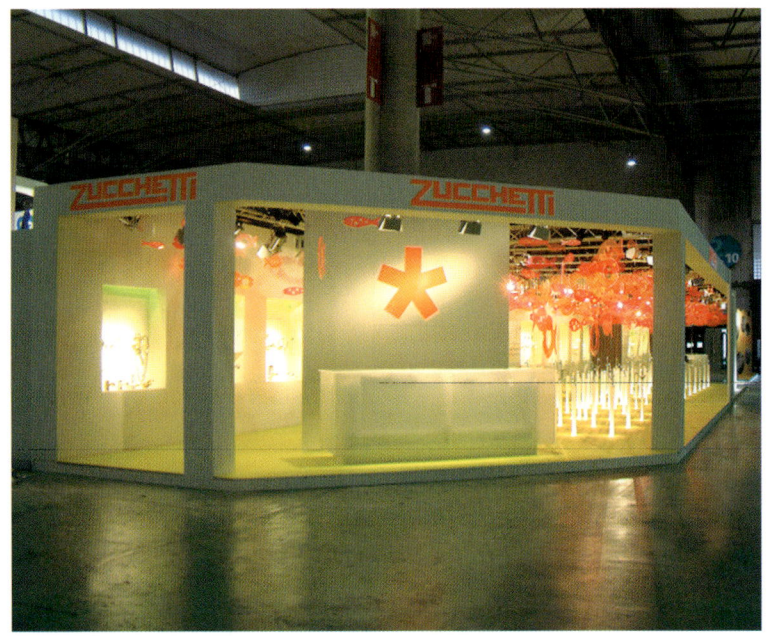

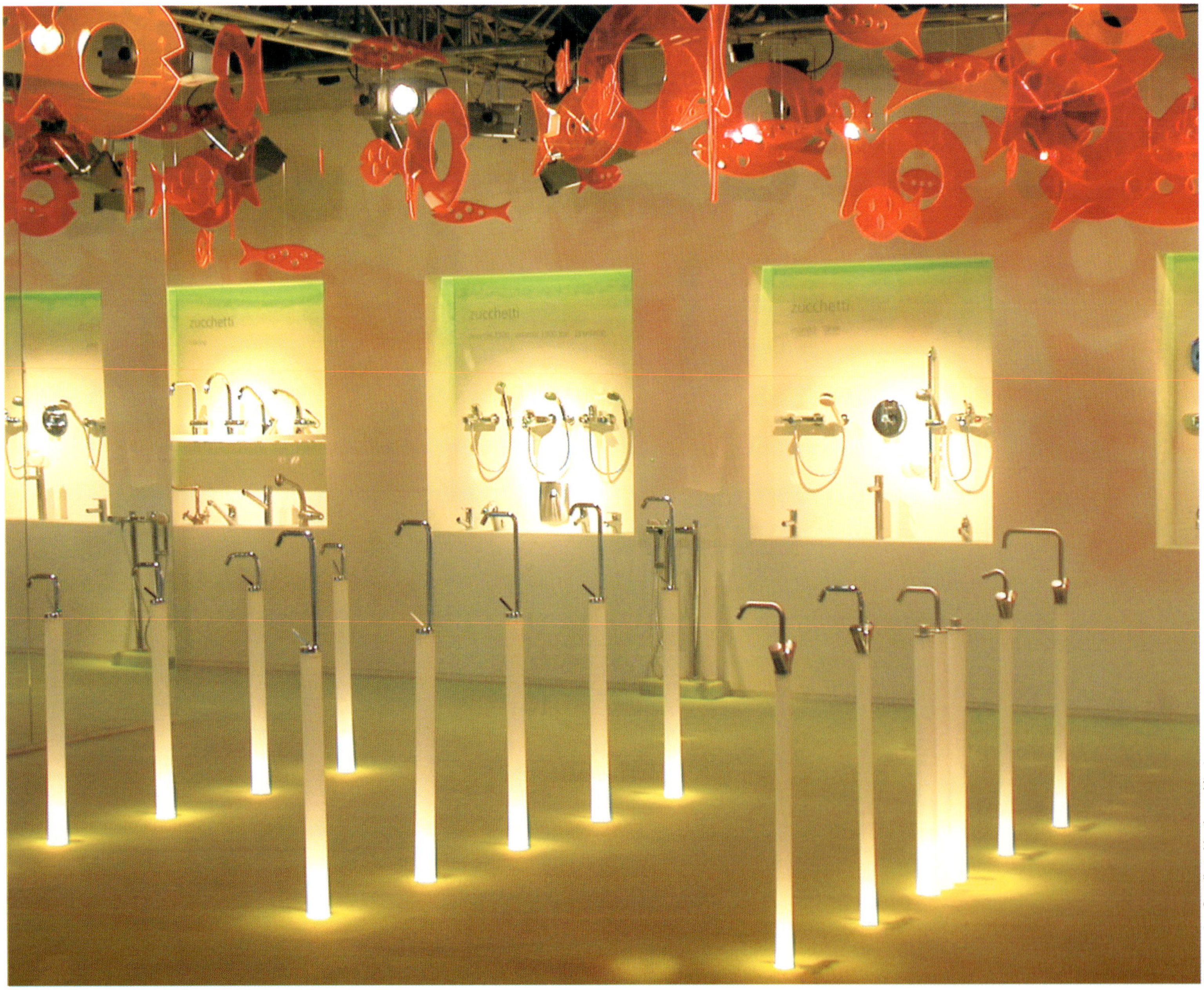

Photographs: Contributed by the architect

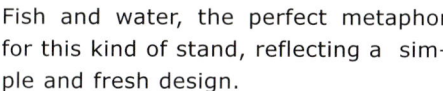

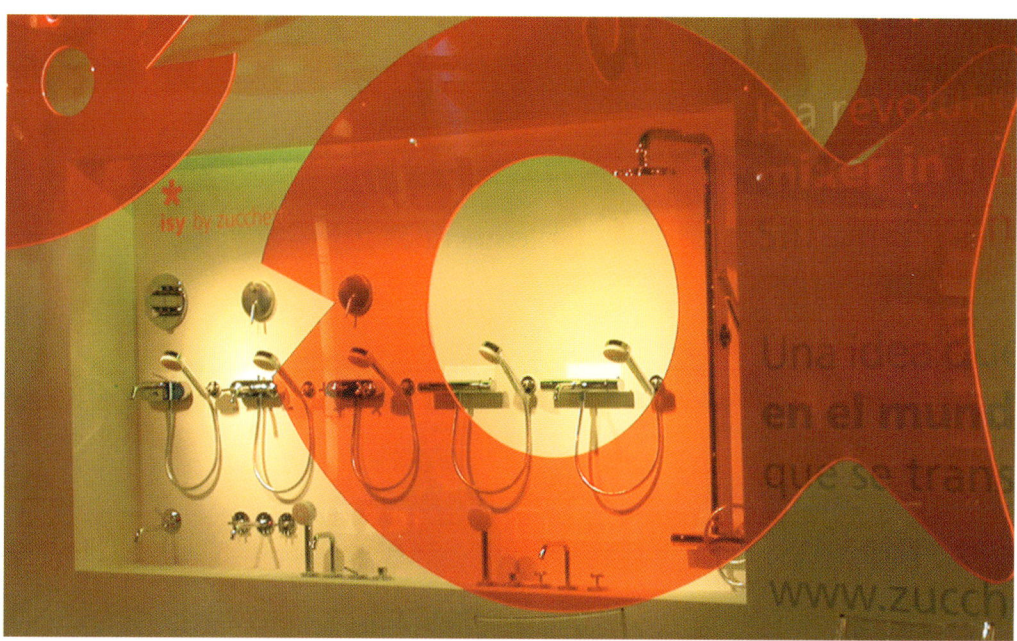

Fish and water, the perfect metaphor for this kind of stand, reflecting a simple and fresh design.

Sevil Peach Gence Associates

visplay & vizona

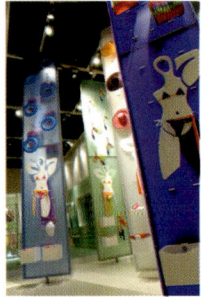

SPGA were asked to design an exhibition stand for Vitrashop - now Visplay and Vizona - for Euroshop 02. The project also included procurement of the fashion and accessories specifically related to the concept, as well as the design of the exhibition brochure.

The aim of the stand was threefold. Firstly, to explain the creation of Vispay and Vizona as two separate identities within the Vitrashop Group and define their basic capabilities. Secondly, to demonstrate the use of Visplay products in a way that was imaginative and visionary, but also real enough to show retail usage. Thirdly, to illustrate Vizona's execution skills. The idea was predominantly based on 'Alice in Wonderland' - larger than life.

The overall 37 x 30.5 m stand was divided into different areas: Reception, Visplay "Invisible Design", Vizona "Visions" and the Cafe, and the whole concept could be grasped from each area. The dimensions, differing height levels and surfaces within the stand were carefully co-ordinated to create a harmonious whole.

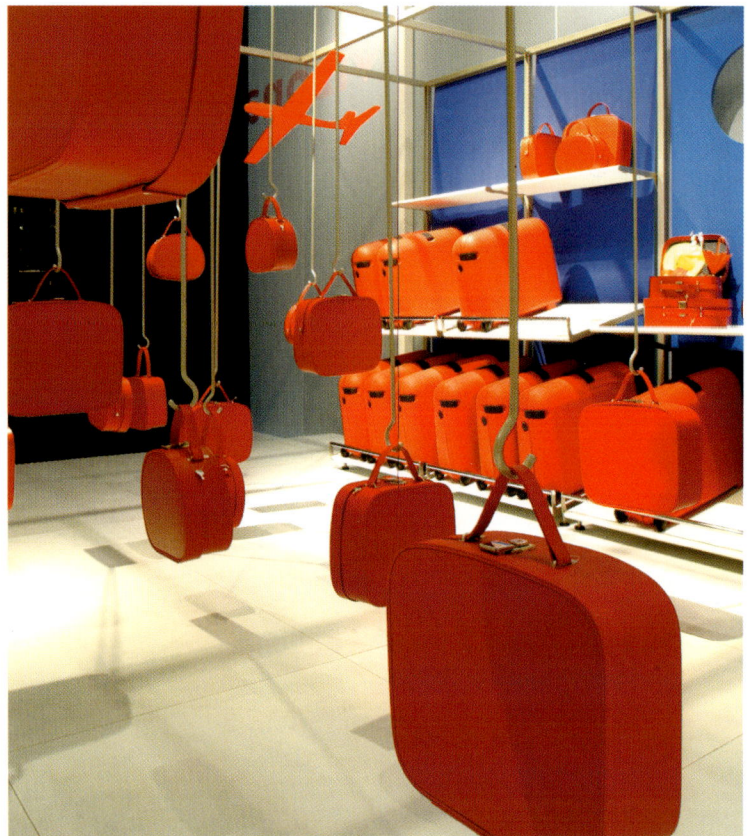

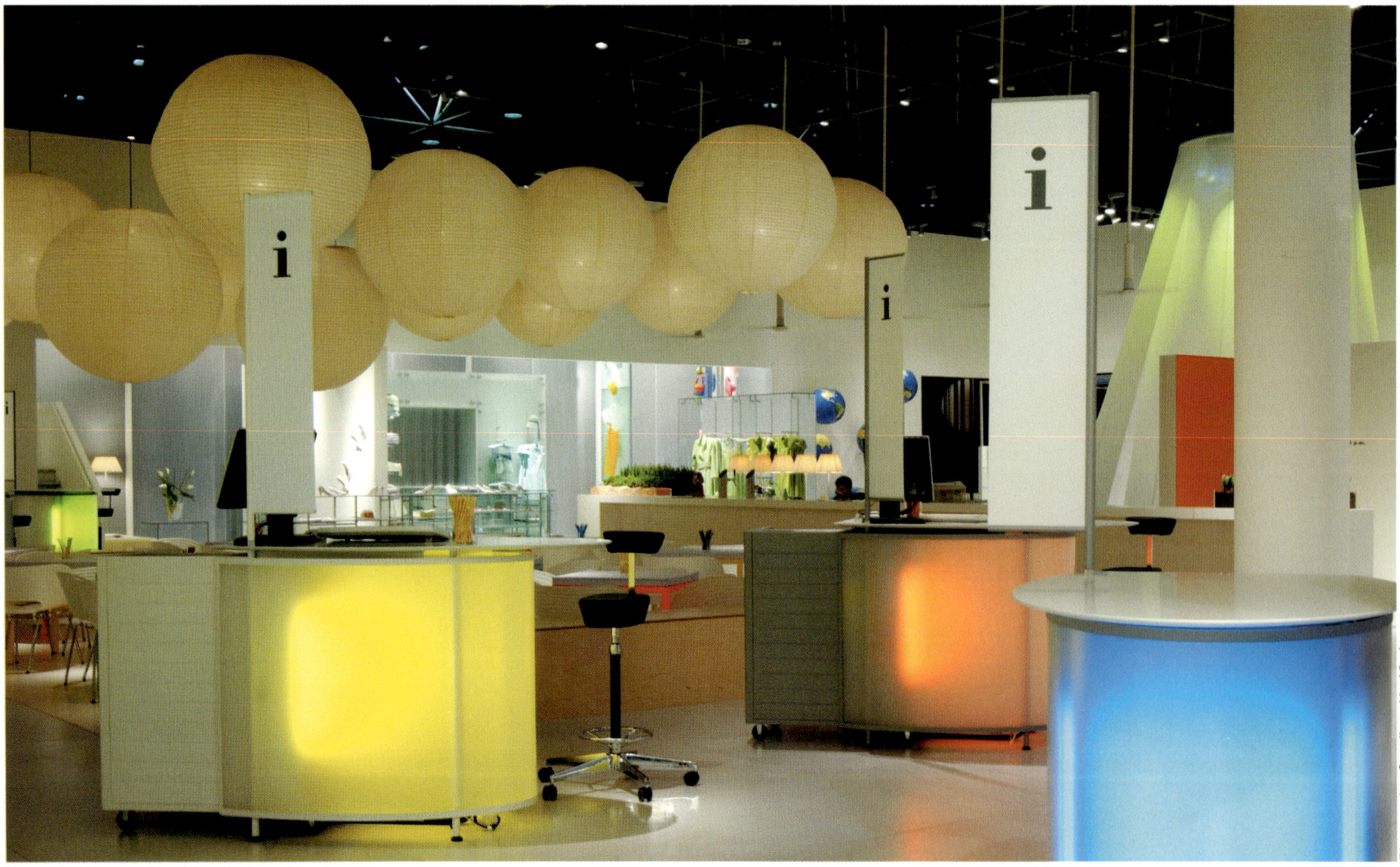

Photographs: Contributed by Visplay

Vitrashop: now **vīzona** and **vísplay**

Opposite the entrance area and the large wall panel, there was a sculptural tent - the "Cone", conference room in the heart of the exhibition space. The Cafe and individual Visions installations were on the lower level. Within the Visplay "Invisible Design" area, Visplay systems were shown as hardware.

The Vizona "Visions" presented retail design concepts that were clearly different from the universal retail language of the previous years. The Visions were based on the use of different design elements and, for visual impact, pushing a particular color scheme to its extreme, in line with the label's attitude: transparent, organised, glowing, floating, horizontal, hanging, playful, curved, mobile. The "Visions" designs were realistic, economic...but at the same time surprising, new, fresh, happy and sexy.

The basic principle was simple: the designers reduced the design to what was crucial in order to create environments with a sense of theatre. and play. Visplay systems were practically "invisible". They became subordinate and adapted themselves discreetly to the design concept while still offering a high level of practicality, loading capacity and flexibility for up-to-date merchandising.

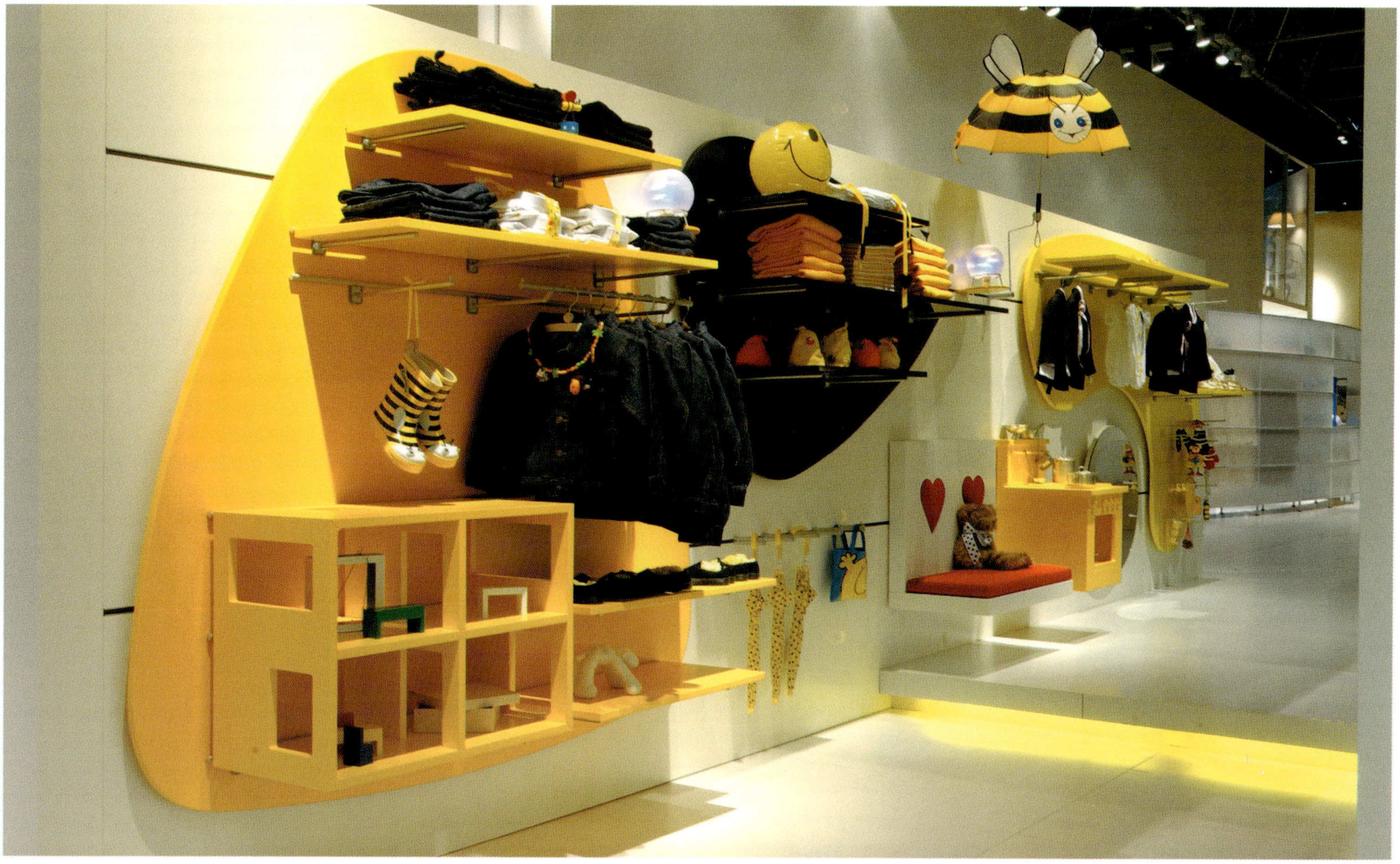

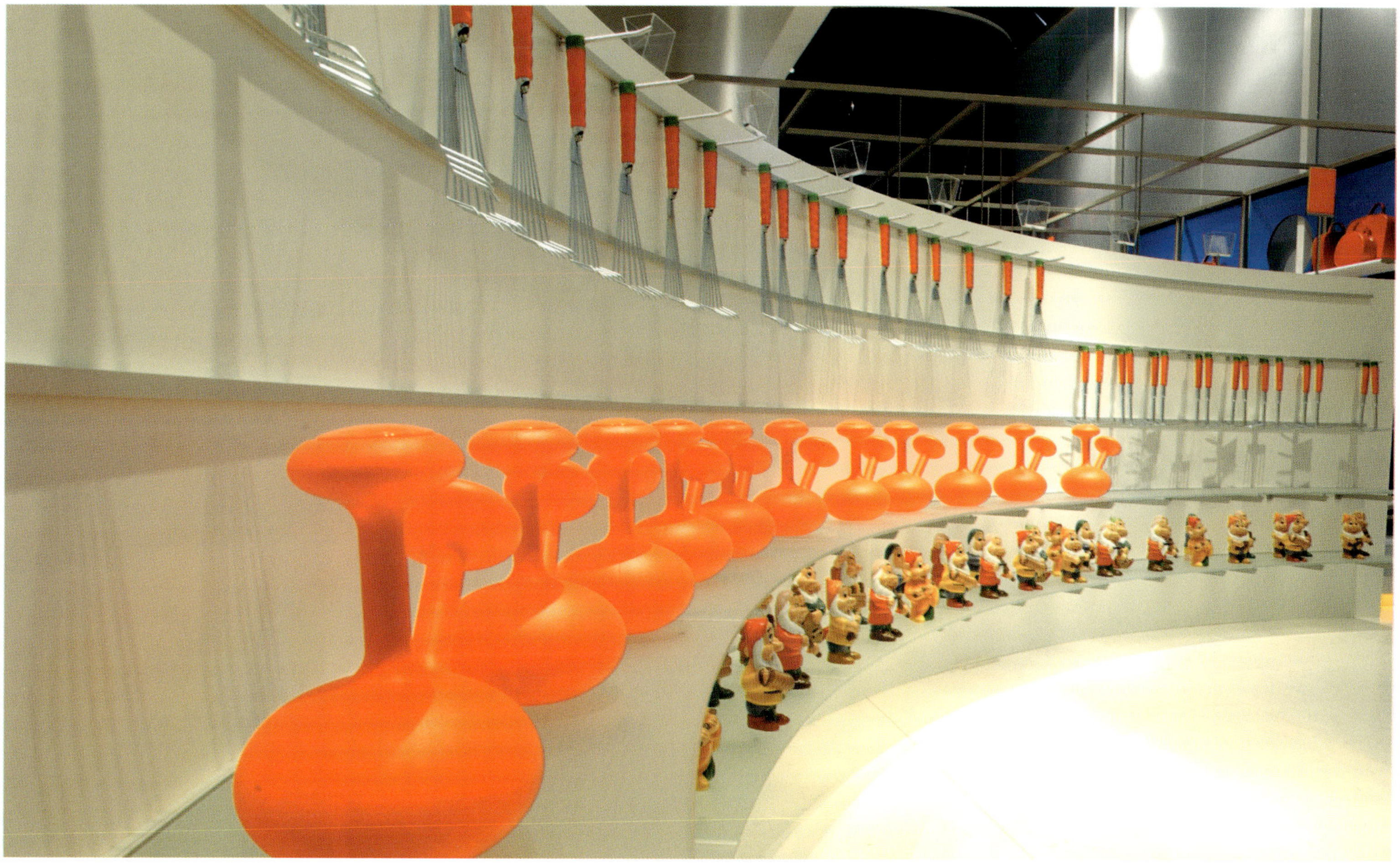

Schmidhuber + Partner
Comunications: Totems
audi

Following the "lane change" at Genf, "acceleration" was the next logical step in the automobile trade fair series - and Audi was off to a great start!
A direct message requires a direct sign, a symbol: an arrow. As a clearly directional element, the arrow embodies the dynamism, speed and acceleration of the Audi brand, and it was the perfect inspiration for this stand, dictating its long straight lines and extensive visual relationships. The floor plan was defined by the shape of the arrow, with the tip, containing the full power of the symbol, representing the strength of the brand. The arrow also provided a clear principle for displaying the vehicles in the large area.

The different groups of Audi vehicles were ordered according to their speed and power. A series of stepped levels following the stand structure divided the space and guided visitors through it. A line of light extended over the surface of the stand, taking on the shape of the arrow and becoming the formal unifying element. Like a comet, it visibly divided the stand and formed the main element of the car displays on the arrow.
The placement and spacing of individual laminated panels in line with the arrow of light created a superimposed effect providing visitors with new and relaxing vantage points. The flexibility of these panels, which can be used with different media and materials, also created a series of visual stages. Orange was the dominant color used on the walls, a memorable and easily identifiable element.
The building was already a regular component in Audi stands, increasing its long-term effectiveness.

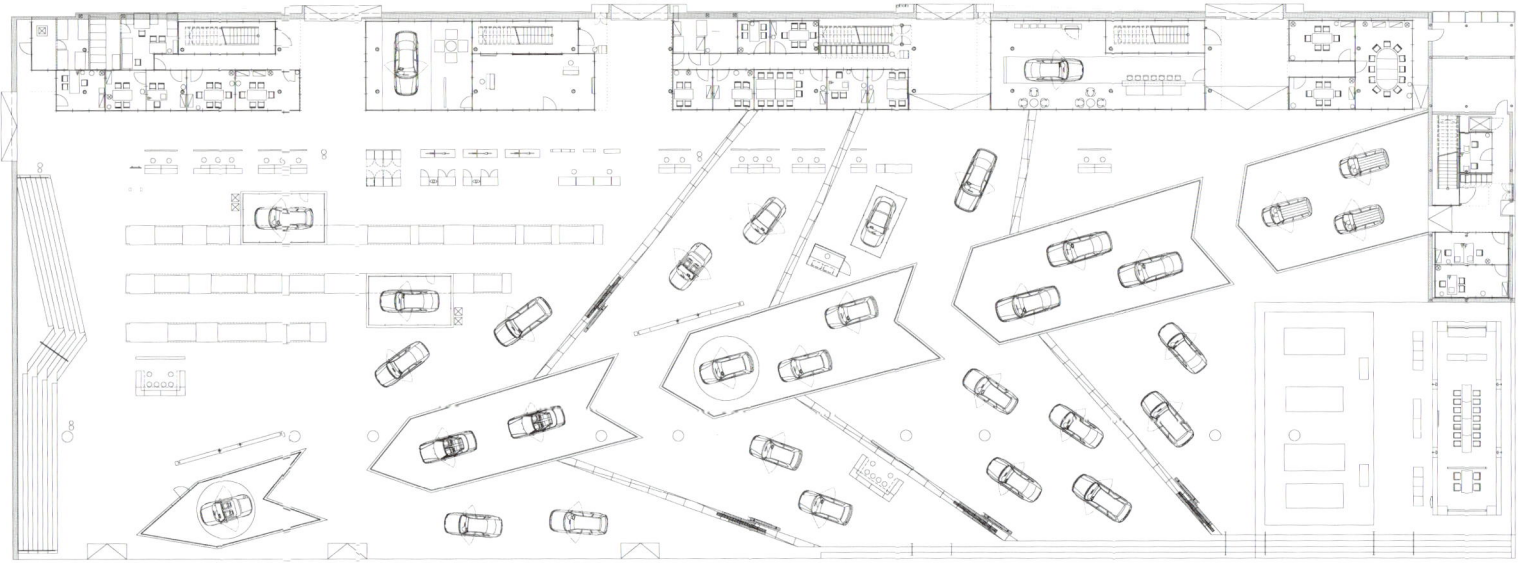

Floor plan

The stand was 115 meters long and 43 meters wide, creating long vistas emphasized by the lighting, which appeared to visually accelerate the stand architecture. Thirty-two cars were displayed along the arrow-shaped floor plan, culminating in a new showcar that was the "spearhead" of the exhibition. This stream-lined and dynamic exhibition was an elaborate construction, requiring many elements, complex wiring and very careful planning.

Each of the 32 vehicles displayed was illuminated by eight spotlights, carefully placed to avoid undesirable reflections. The vehicles were positioned to display their color and contours to optimum effect, within the dynamic, arrow-shaped exhibition area.

Form 3
blend of america

BUBBLES, the key element chosen to represent the brand identity of Blend of America, was designed by the young Danish designer Lene Birgitte Knudsen in 1993, as a part of her graduation project.

The BUBBLES design defines the identity of Blend America, and so it was an important element in the stand. Taking advantage of the clean and modern feel of the BUBBLES, the stand was designed as a futuristic universe with a strong visual identity.

Four of the walls in the stand were covered with white BUBBLES, while the back wall was covered with dark grey BUBBLES in order to create a sense of depth. Mirrors on either side created the feeling of an infinite universe.

Six light towers had built-in sales tables, emphasizing the futuristic universe and "outer space" feel. The furniture also contributed to creating a young, relaxed environment.

Photographs: Contributed by Form 3

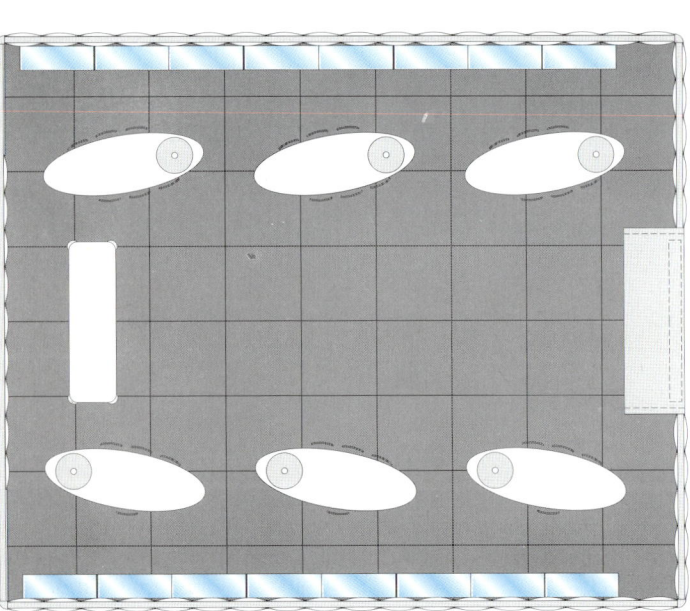

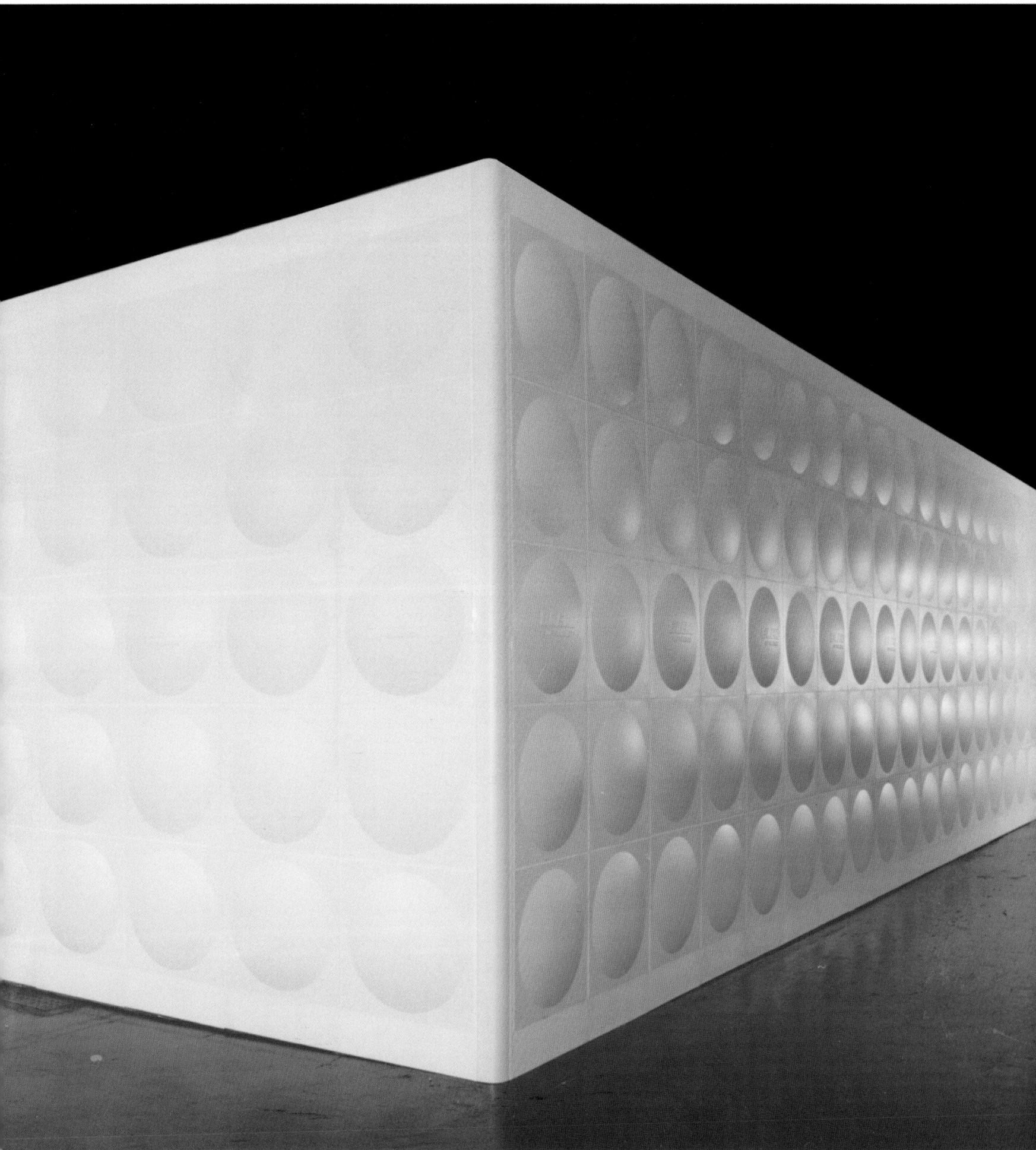

Rotor + Fractal Building Systems

under water vessel

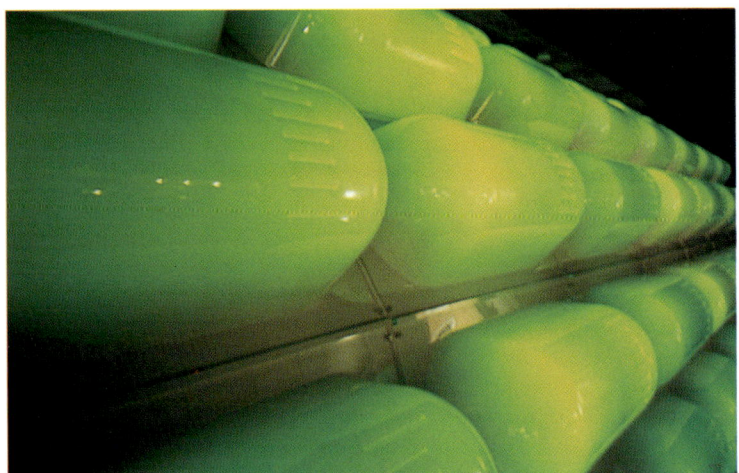

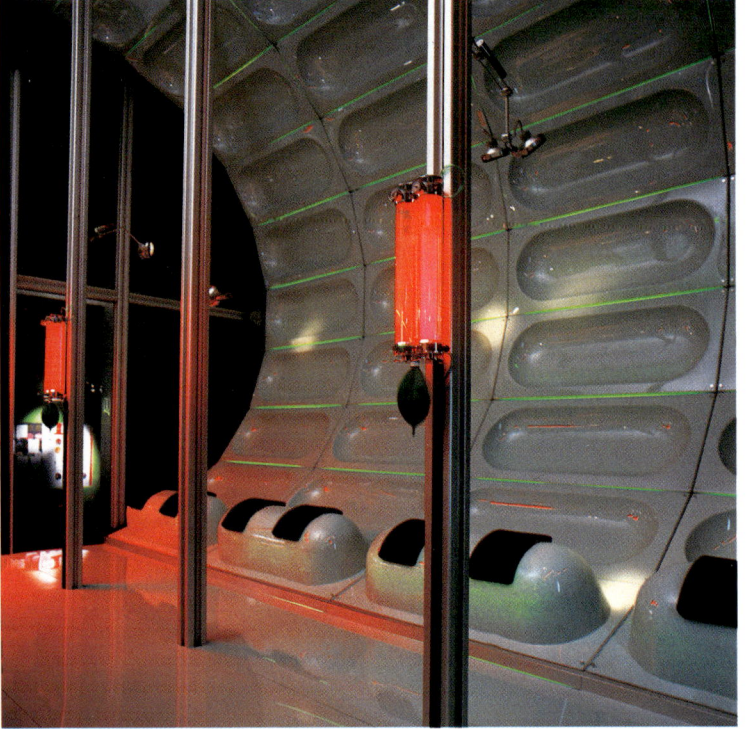

The walls of the vessel were made out of specially formed translucent "bath-tubes", all lit from behind with TL-strips. All other walls and some of the floors were covered with neoprene - diving suit material - to intensify the underwater feel of the stand. Inside, small and large aquariums contributed to the effect, and stand visitors were able to inhale pure oxygen in order to prepare them for the next "dive".

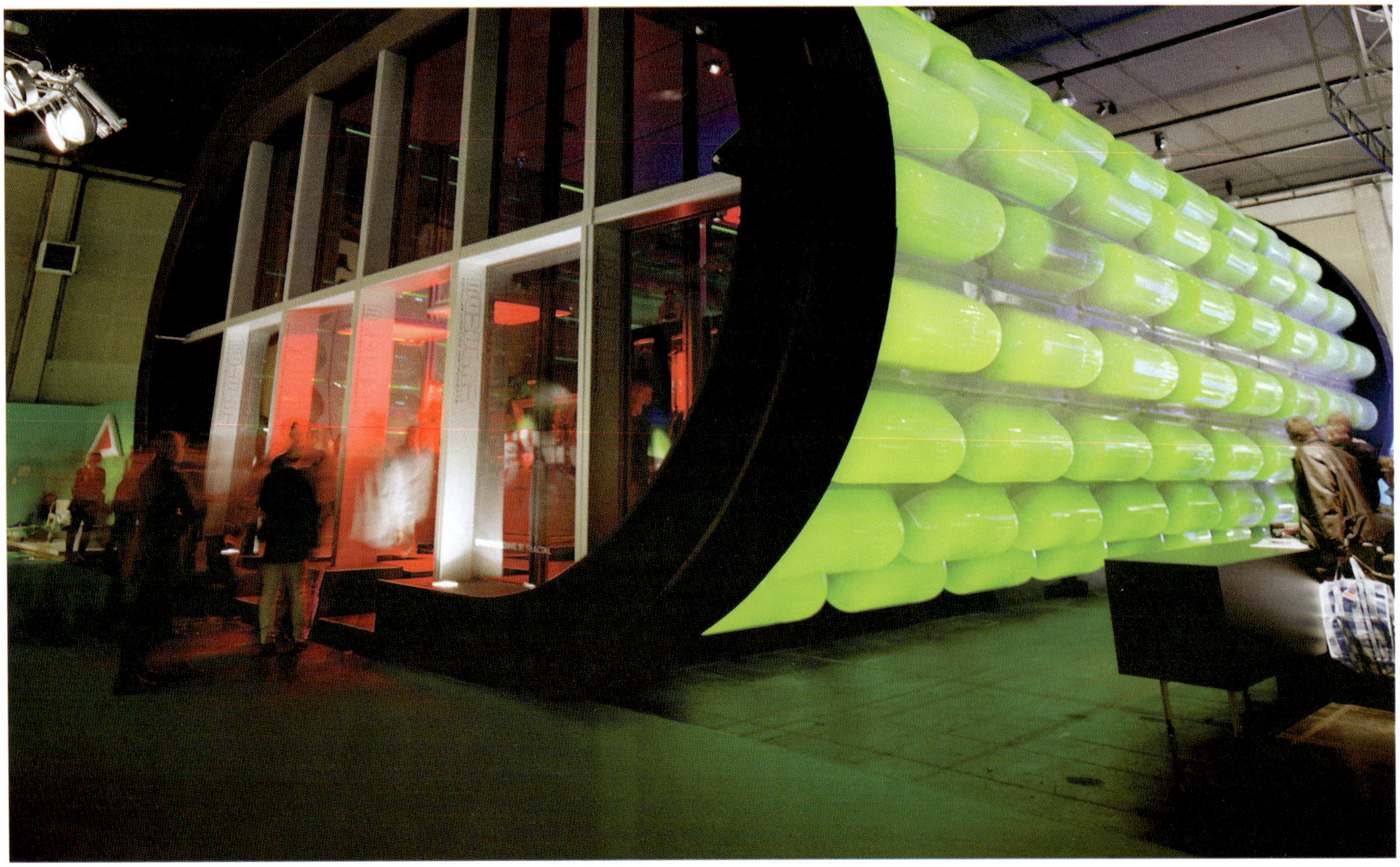

Photographs: Contributed by Fractal

Vicente Sarrablo, Jordi Roviras & Cristina García
dcpal

 The design concept behind brick manufacturer DCPAL's stand at the Construmat 2003 trade fair was based on using the company's own products in an elegant and unexpected way. The designers created a curved surface made from one of DCPAL's principal brick products as the main element of the display. This brick surface area extended like a carpet before curving upwards into a vertical latticed wall.

A storage area was concealed behind this curving latticed surface made of floating coursework elements. This approach created an apparently simple stand that demonstrated the unexpected flexibility and possibilities offered by such a simple product.

Photographs: Contributed by the architects

The organic curve created from bricks was unusual and attracted the attention of visitors, curious to explore further. The curving brick carpet created a gently sloping display area, and specially created box-shaped shelving was used to display other brick styles and colors produced by the company.

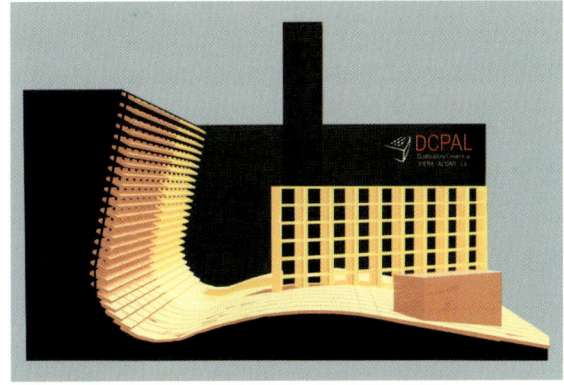

Francesc Rifé
cerámicas diago

In this presentation, a bedroom with a walk-in wardrobe and en-suite bathroom was used as a showroom to demonstrate the creative possibilities of ceramic tiles in interior design, specially in an unusual space such as the bedroom. The interior designer maintained the original interior architectural elements such as ceiling moldings and frames, and chose to simply paint over the wooden flooring that was in a state of disrepair.

The cubic volume with no exterior walls was placed in the center of the space in order to have as little impact as possible on the original elements. This central block divided the rectangular room into two areas, bathroom and bedroom, and different ceramic materials were applied to it in a combination of textures, a mix of smooth and pyramid-shaped tiles. Its function was to conceal and define the bathroom area, and it was closed off by an orange door made of translucent glass.

The bedroom area was resolved by placing a bed over a platform covered with material-textured tiles, as well as extending the wall and creating a background for the relaxation area.

Photographs: Contributed by the designer

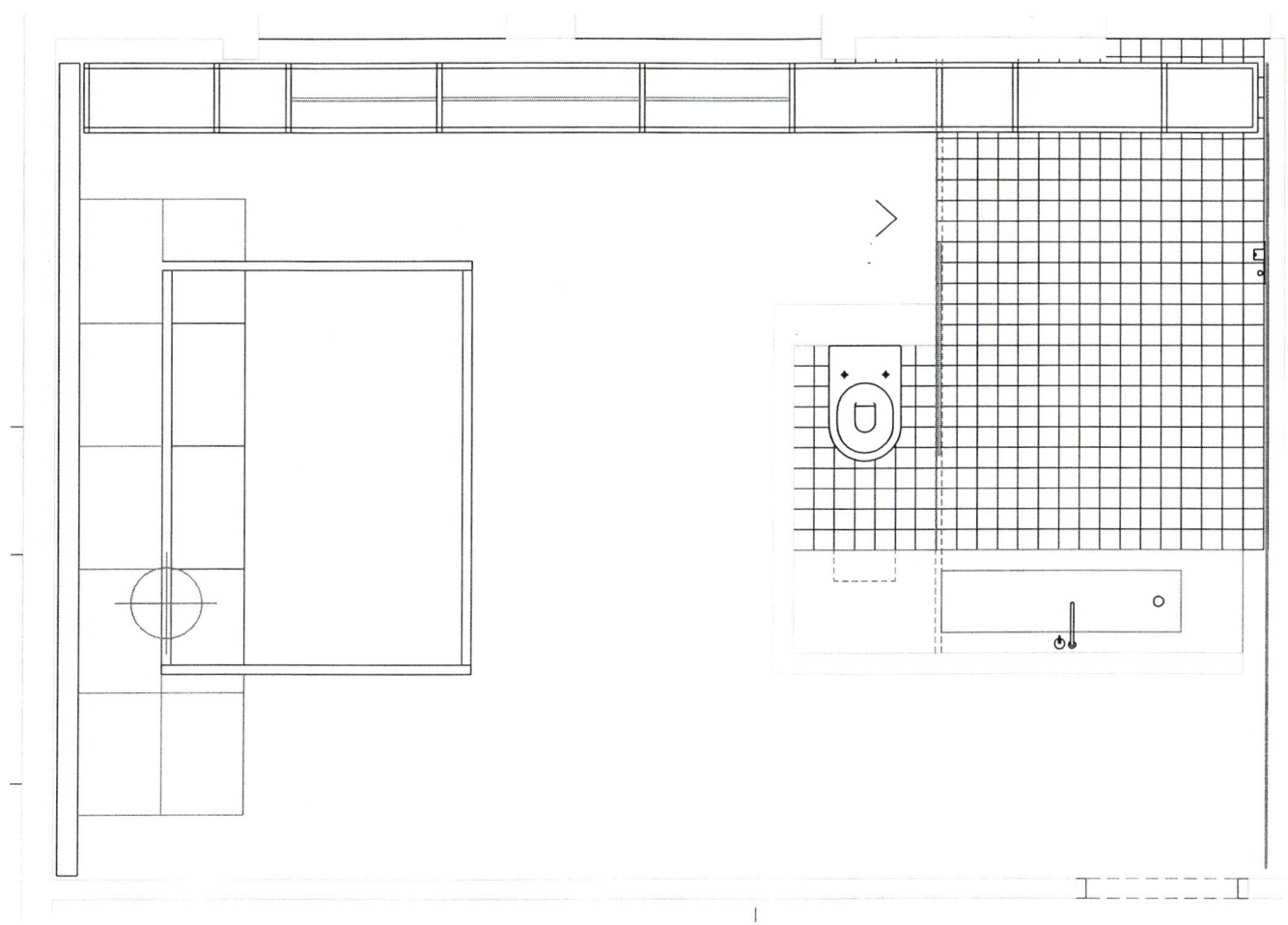

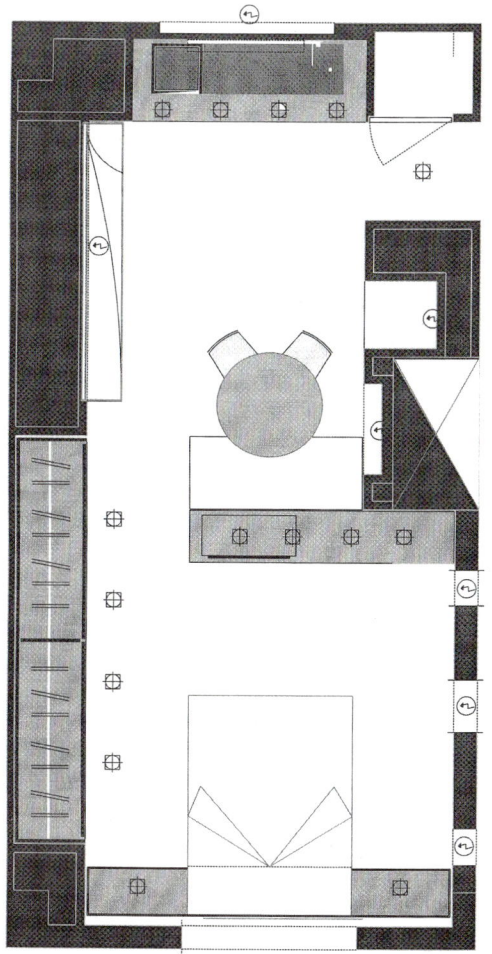

Droog Design +
Traast & Gruson
bang & olufsen

The fluorescent, colored, 3D outline of a house built within a darkened room was the unusual setting for displaying Bang & Olufsen products.

The frame was lighted using black light, and all the furniture displayed consisted of Bang & Olufsen products.

Through "movement" sensors, the public activated different Audio and Video products as they moved through the space. Short movies of children in front of a fire place, children playing in a bathtub or the sound of bottles of wine being opened gave each room it's own identity.

Photographs: Mischa Keijzer

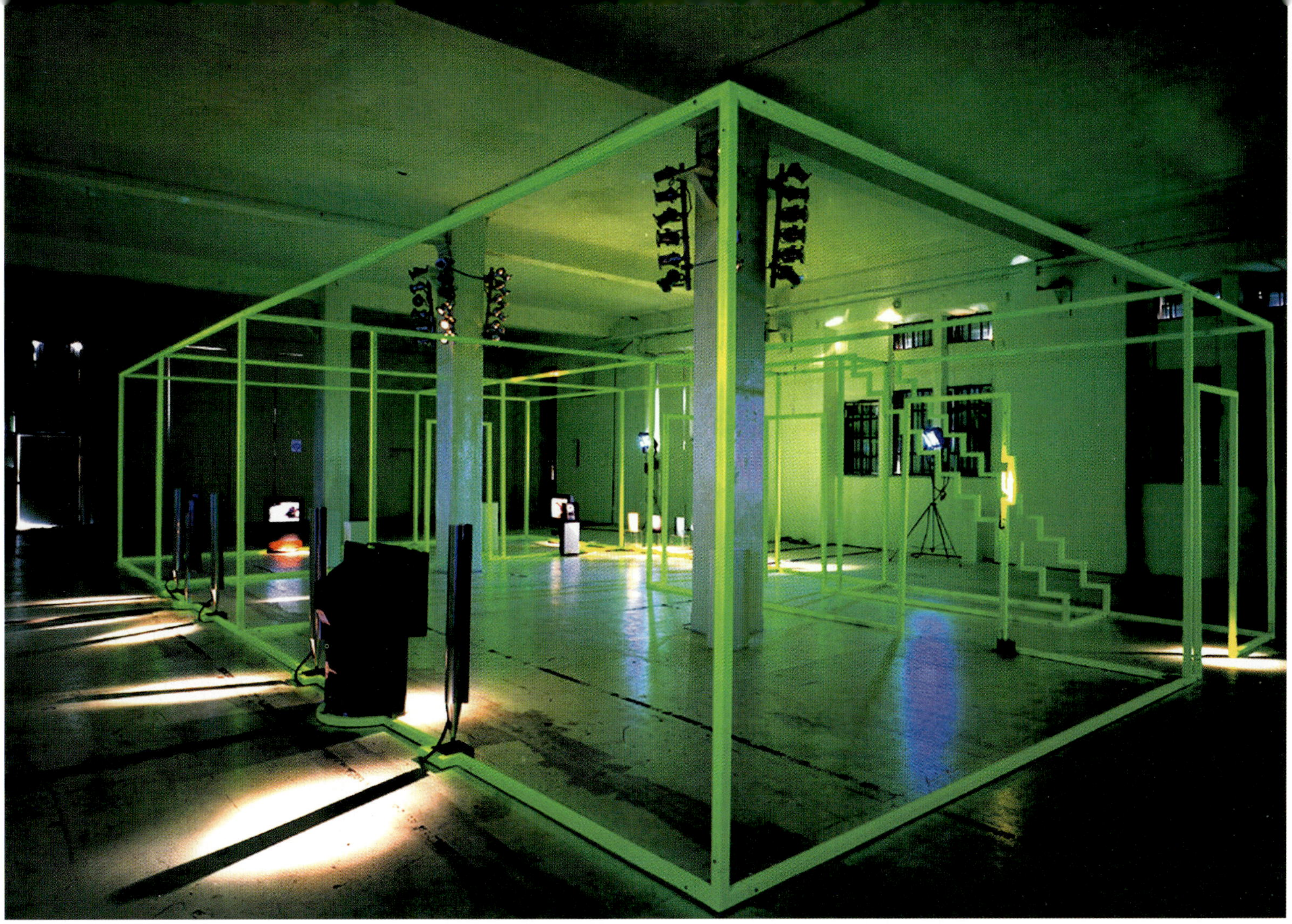

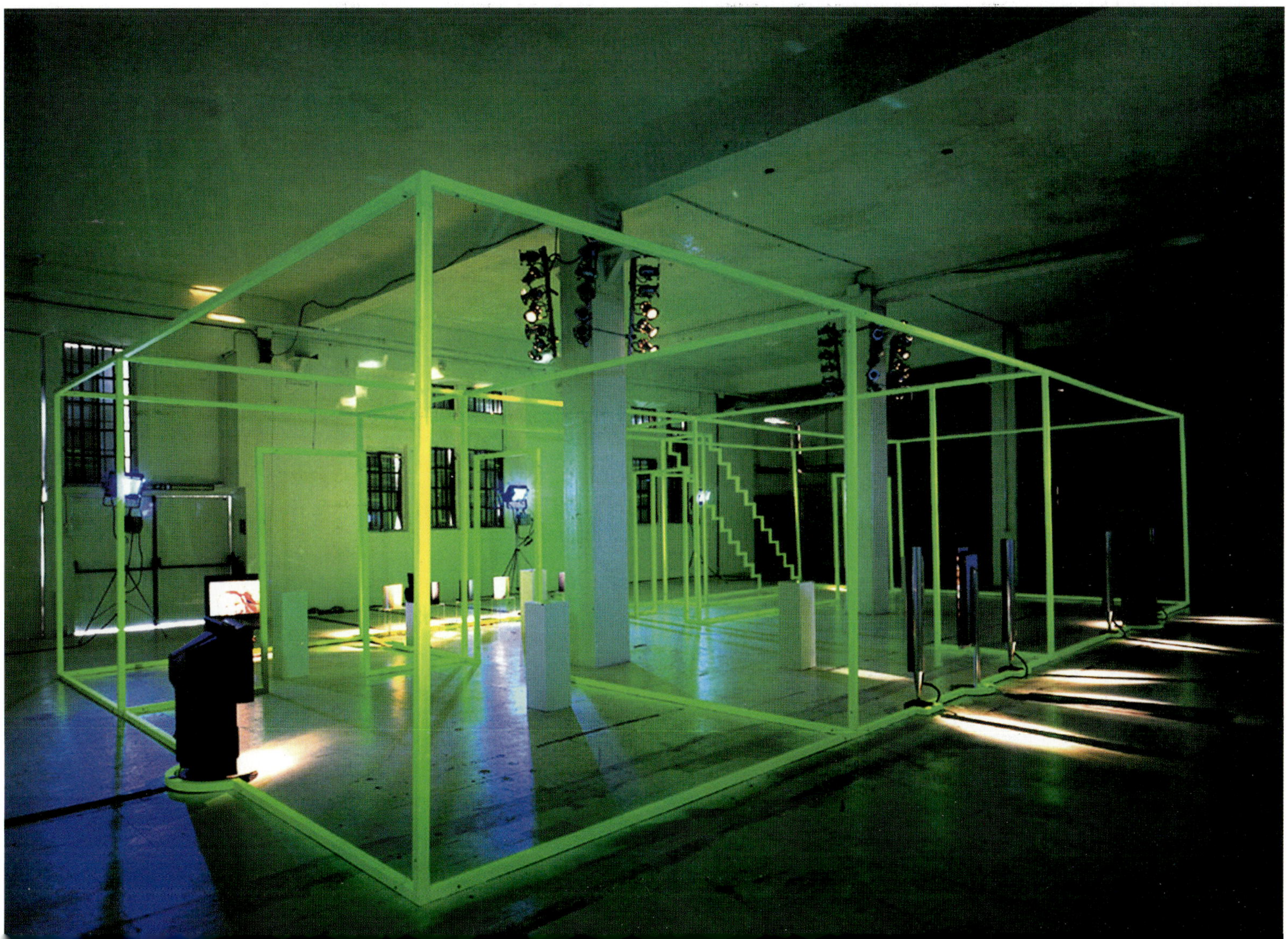

D'Art Design Gruppe
zack

"Follow your Style" was the inspiration behind this design, an expression of style and quality of life. The Zack GmbH stand at the Ambiente 2004 trade fair defined the company as an industry leader dedicated to special design. The stand connected the traditionally ordered nature of trade fairs with the extremely high aesthetic standards of the Zack brand.

The design concept was based on the idea of a stage. It combined a highly structured presentation with an experimental tendency, a surprising and successful approach. The key design aspect was the staging of the "Living/Bathing/News" environments. These were the crucial points for visitors, an expression of the special lifestyle associated with Zack products. The light, colors, and exceptional materials (concrete, glass, wood, textiles,…) were mixed imaginatively in order to emphasize the "atmospheric" nature of the product display. Unusual and attractive objects, such as a luminous glass table or the oscillating wooden tables and sculptures, completed the experience and provided the perfect frame for the company's fine steel accessories.

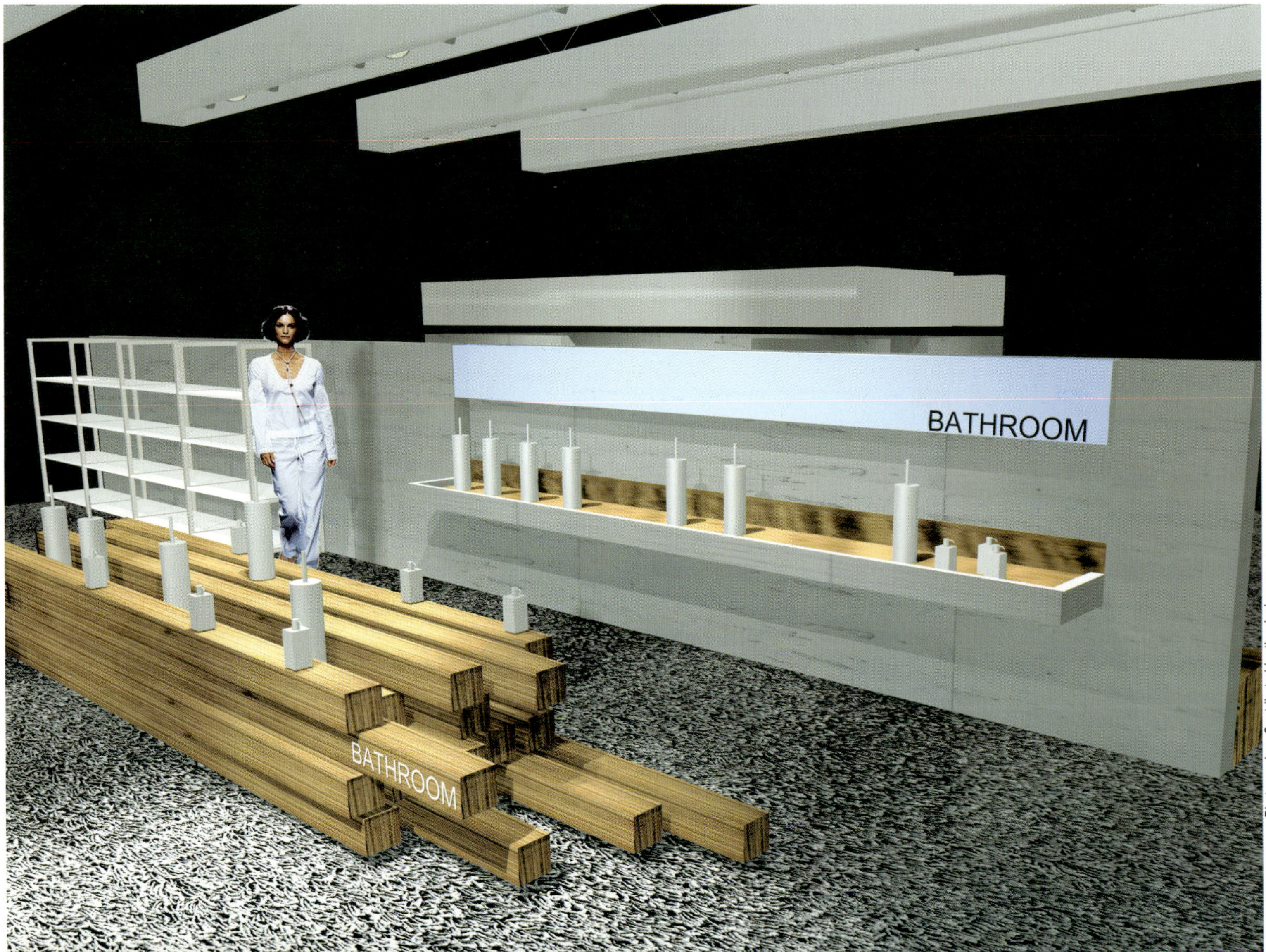

BATHROOM

BATHROOM

Photographs: Contributed by the designers

Rotor + Fractal Building Systems

modular (freep deez)

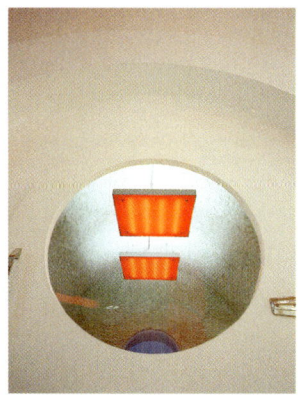

Modular wanted a cold, Antartic environment to display their latest fixtures. In response to this idea, a giant Igloo was conceived by Rotor and constructed by Fractal to meet Modular's needs. To obtain an Igloo shape, a half sphere in a self-supporting insulating material was constructed, then the stand temperarture was brought down to 8ºC, and big ice-walls were mounted. The general structures inside, which followed the same icy theme, were also made by the Fractal crew. Without a doubt, this stand was a "refreshing" experience where visitors could sip on a cup of hot cocoa or a glass of wine whilst enjoying the stand ambience.

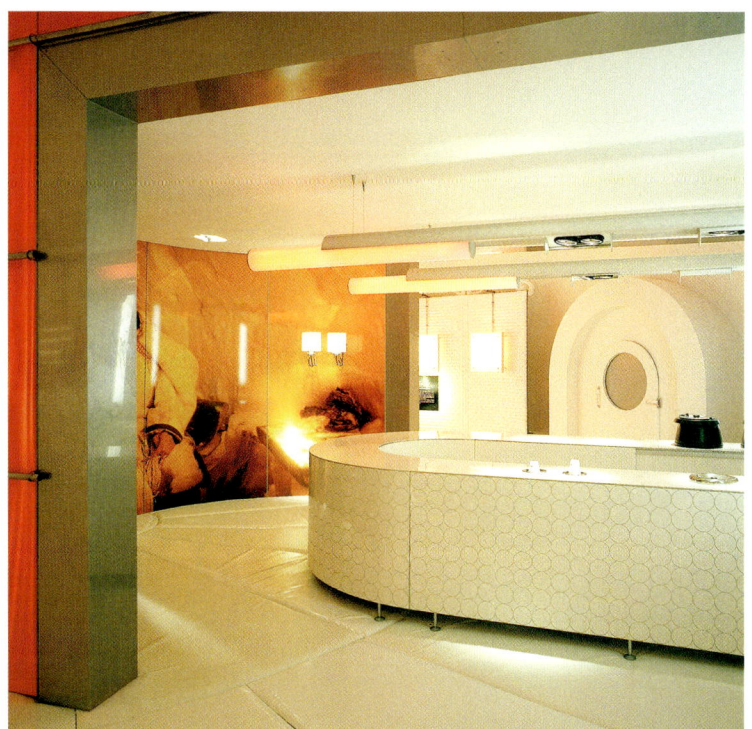

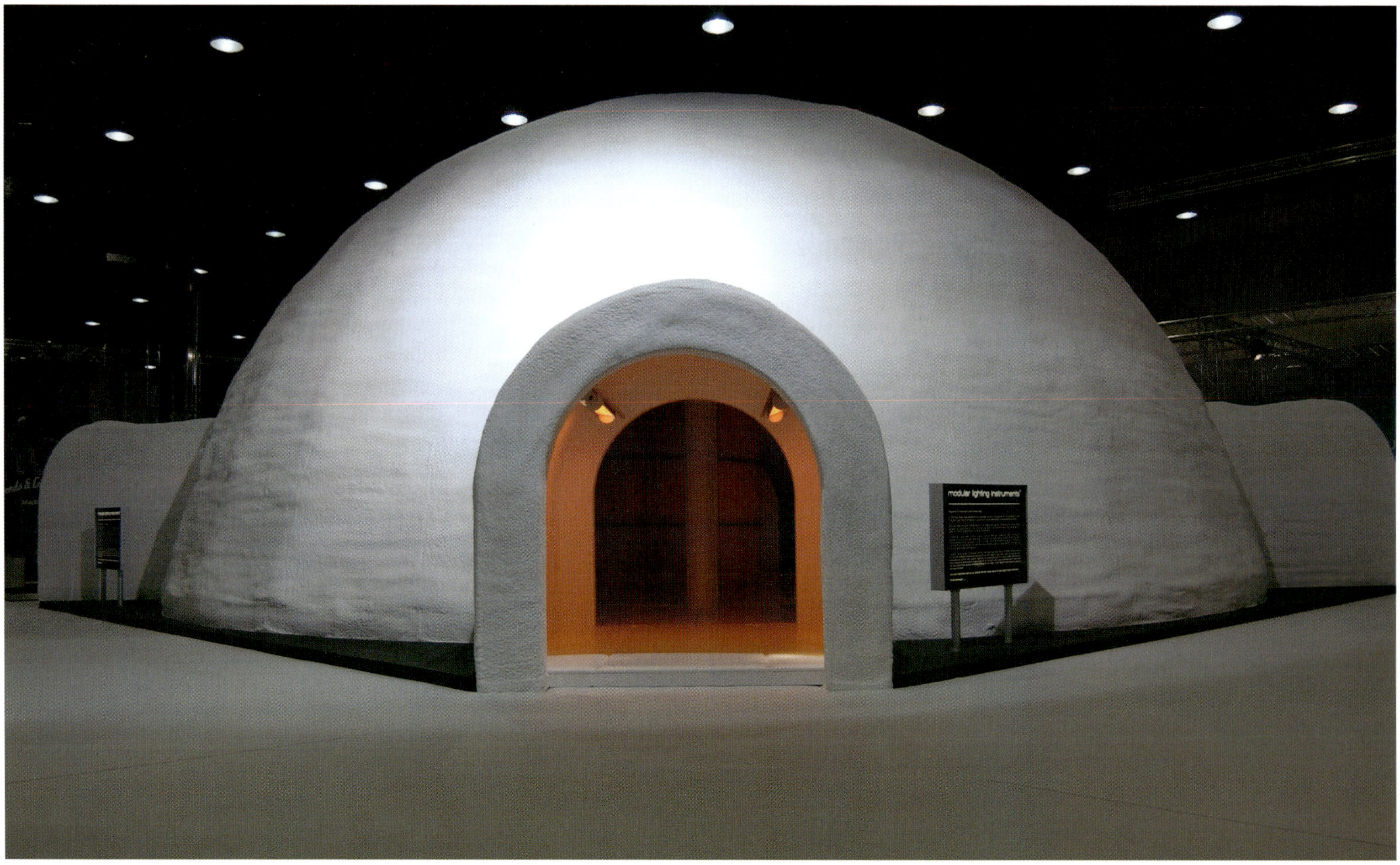

Photographs: Contributed by the designers

Athanasios Megarisiotis & Matthias Siegert

:fepcon

 :fepcon is an innovative company in the metal forming sector. In addition to optimizing metal forming processes, the company also develops 3D software for this area of operations.

The various possibilities offered by these different methods of forming metals inspired the design of this stand. Instead of exhibiting in the traditional way, the designers decided to create a space that would symbolize :fepcon's field of expertise.

The stand was based on a 50x50cm grid: objects were pulled up from a metal plate, with their basic shape and size remaining unchanged.

The individual height of the objects meant that the booth could be used in many different ways. In this way, objects of lesser height became chairs and tables, while higher ones were used as work stations or information points, and a 2.5 m column functioned as a highly visible support for signage.

Nothing but high quality stainless steel and backlit opak blue perspex where used to build the stand.

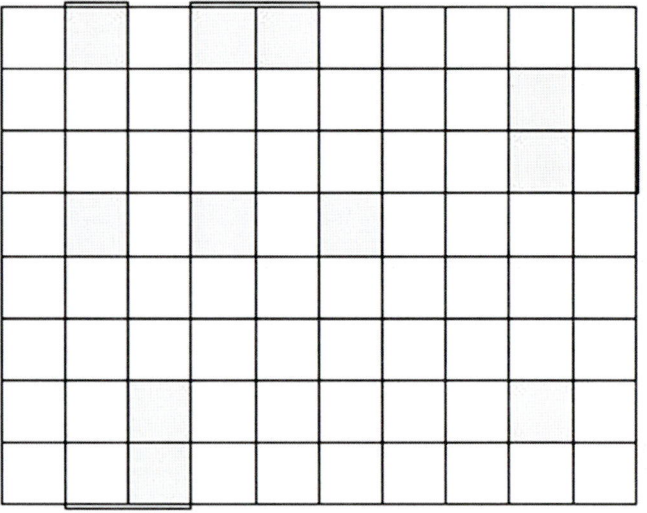

Photographs: Contributed by the architects

5.0.176
:fepcon
MeshView3D

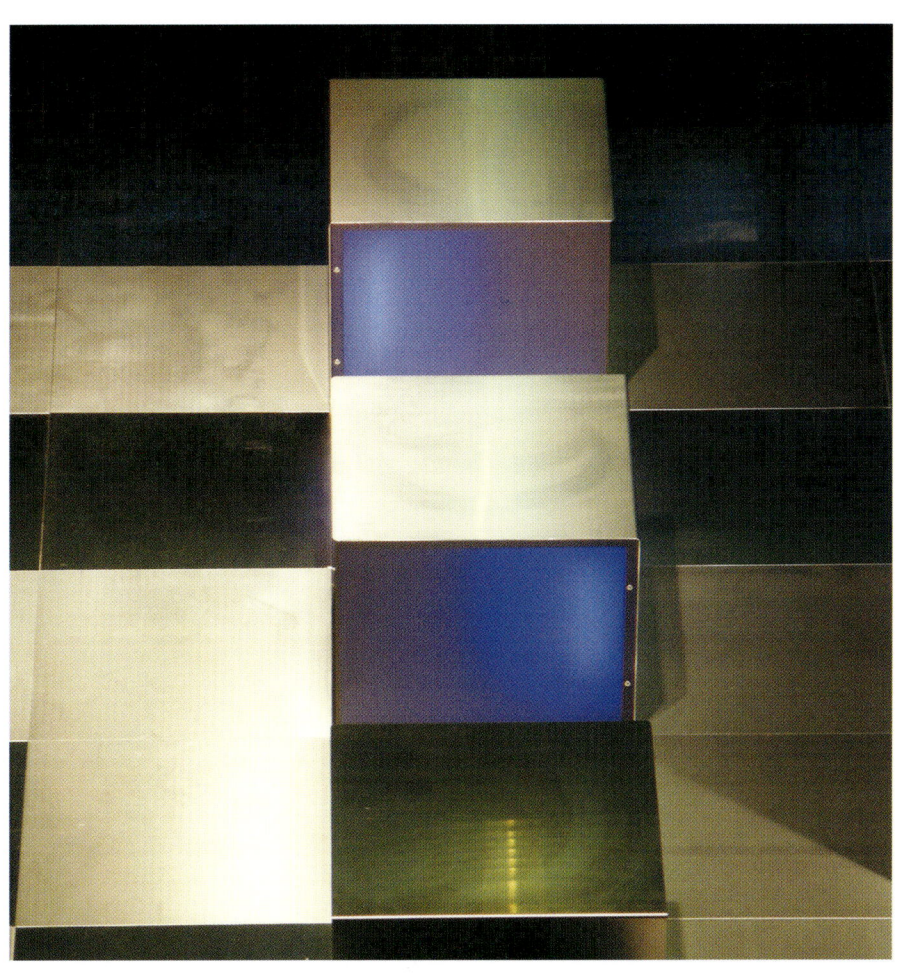

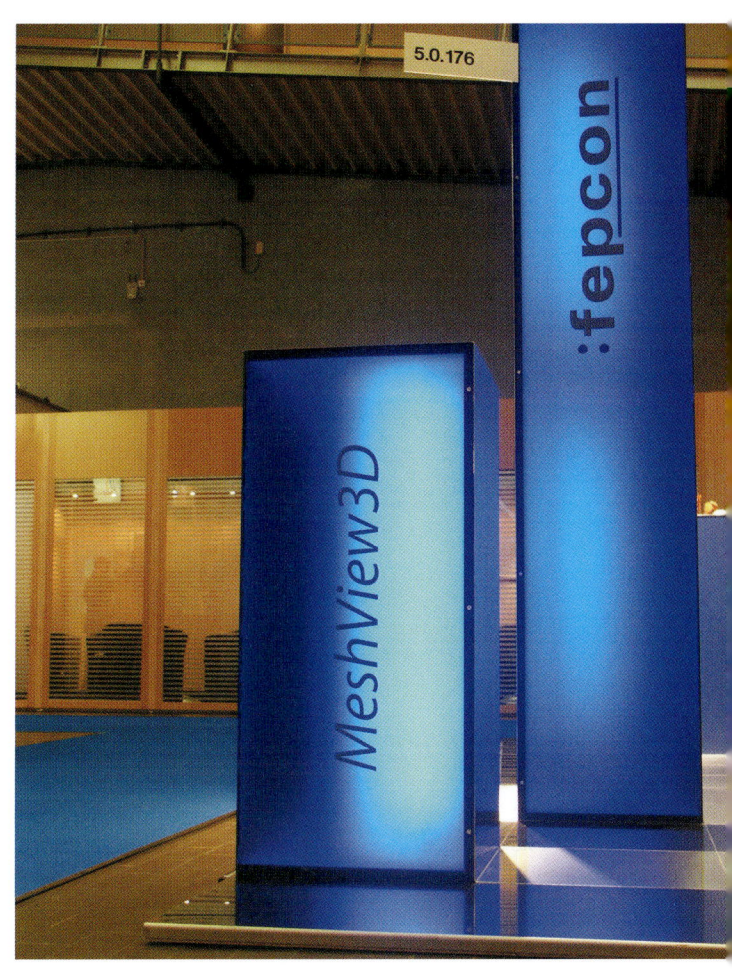

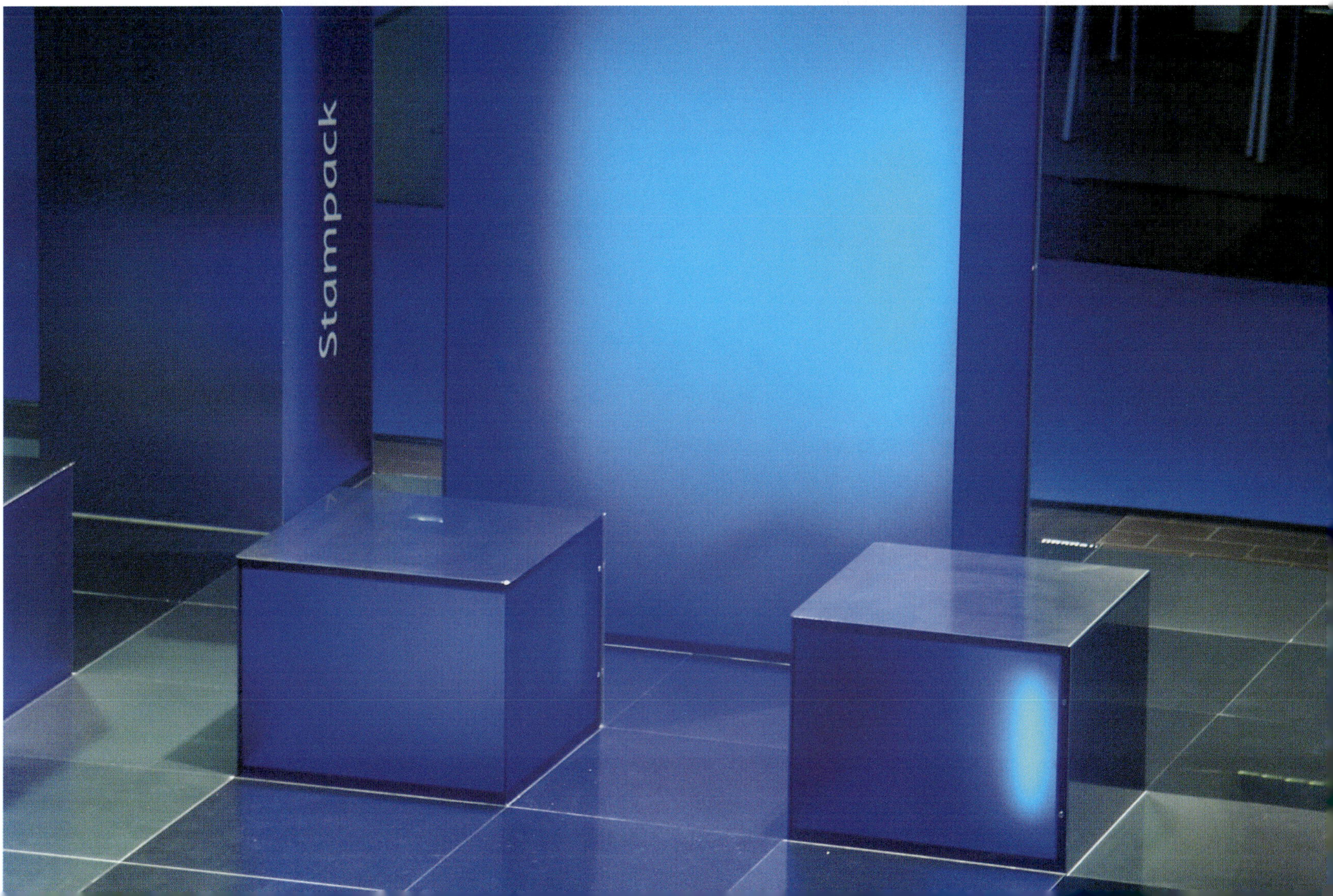
Stampack

Atelier Brückner
panasonic

The new slogan "Panasonic - ideas for life" was the inspiration behind this IFA trade fair design, for which a "Blue Scape", a surreal, abstract world, was created by the Stuttgart-based Atelier Brückner. The space cast a spell over visitors who were immersed into an imaginary universe of architecture, film, light and sound, translating the technological possibilities of Panasonic into a lasting emotional experience.

To create a sense of continuity, the designers developed the concept for the previous year's stand further, adapting the formal language and the color scheme. This time, an open architecture was used to give visitors a sweeping overview as soon as they entered the stand. Dominant blue hues had a unifying effect, strikingly contrasted with red and yellow elements. The space was structured by a network of lines covering 1,700 m² of floor space and 960 m² of wall space, which created an abstract, wire frame landscape. This was the heart of the "Blue Scape" concept, which consisted of "presentation islands" and "product fields" as well as an "artificial cloud".

A labyrinth of fabric ribbons that covered the ceiling over the three main attractions, the substage, and the mass DVD and SD displays, formed the colorful cloud with moving lights. These elements were aligned with the wire framework, and surrounded by a "changing horizon", a 360 degree panorama of 22 LCD projectors, screening films that were created in collaboration with Marc Tamschick.

Along the side of the booth, bright yellow hues infiltrated the blue world through small openings in the changing horizon. Behind these openings, furnished home cinemas, just like ordinary living rooms, displayed different Panasonic products. The overall effect was to showcase Panasonic products as well as creating an experience that appealed to all the senses and the imagination, and would not be quickly forgotten.

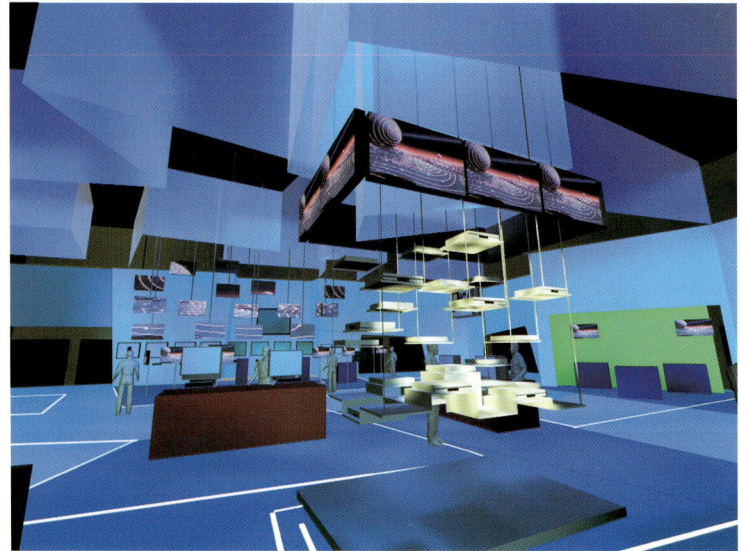

Photographs: Markus Mahle

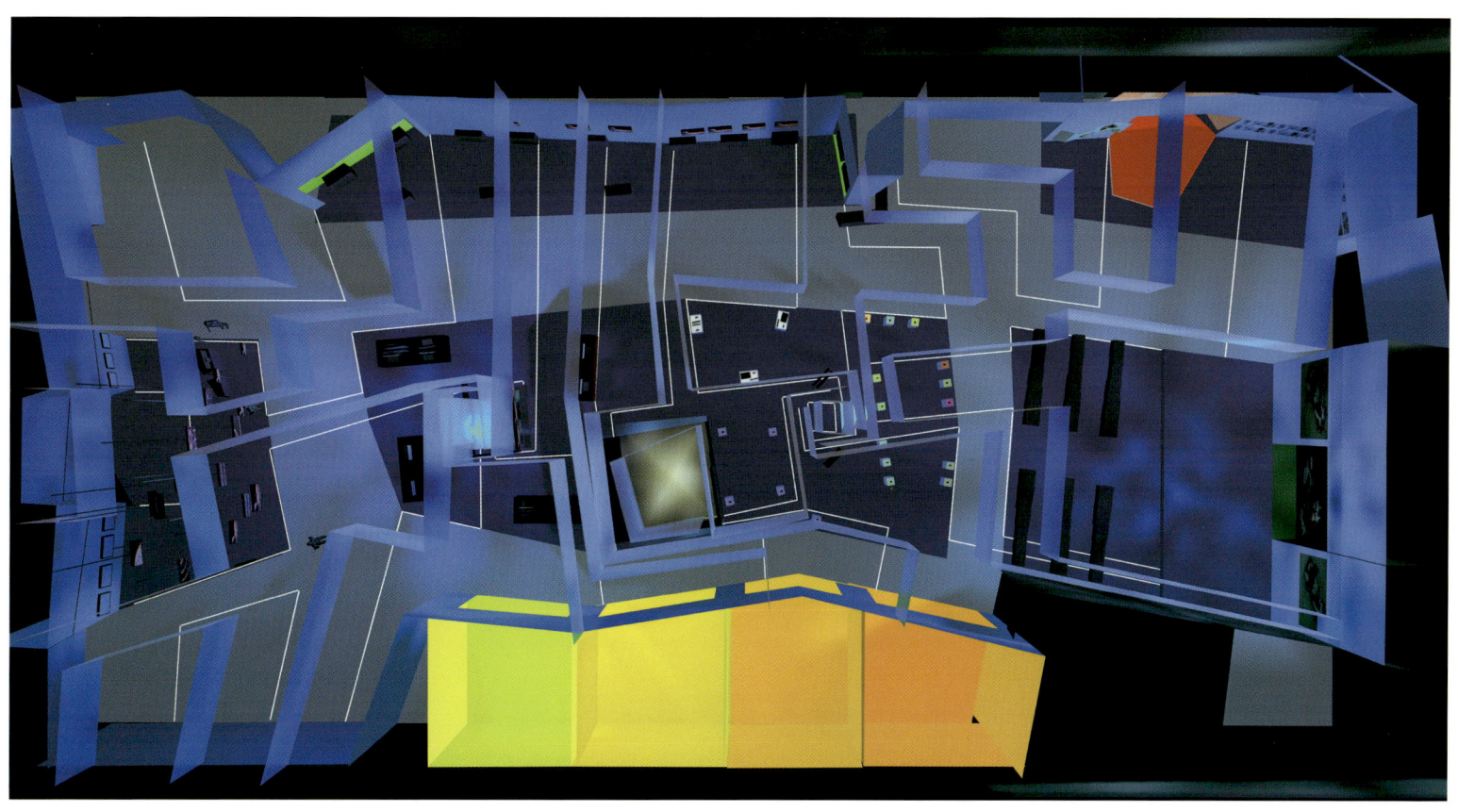

The open architecture and dominant use of blue created a strong first impression, while the network of lines captured the attention of visitors and invited them to explore the stand. The wire frame on the floor and walls continued visually into the screens and became an inorganic moving grid, which integrated three-dimensional objects and small, self-contained spaces.

A woman in a red dress, a protagonist at the previous year's booth, was part of this wire frame world, and through her interactions the lines occasionally transformed into three-dimensional product worlds and fantasy landscapes.

On one side, a multitude of hanging plasma screens called the "plasma stage" showed sequences from a 360 degree projection, on which the same plasma screens appeared again as objects. The main stage was located opposite, and the whole multimedia installation was designed to draw the attention of visitors to the ongoing shows on this stage every hour.

The heart of the "Blue Scape" concept were the "presentation islands" and "product fields" on which products seem to grow.

Panasonic
Panasonic ideas for life
future vision ideas

D-snap

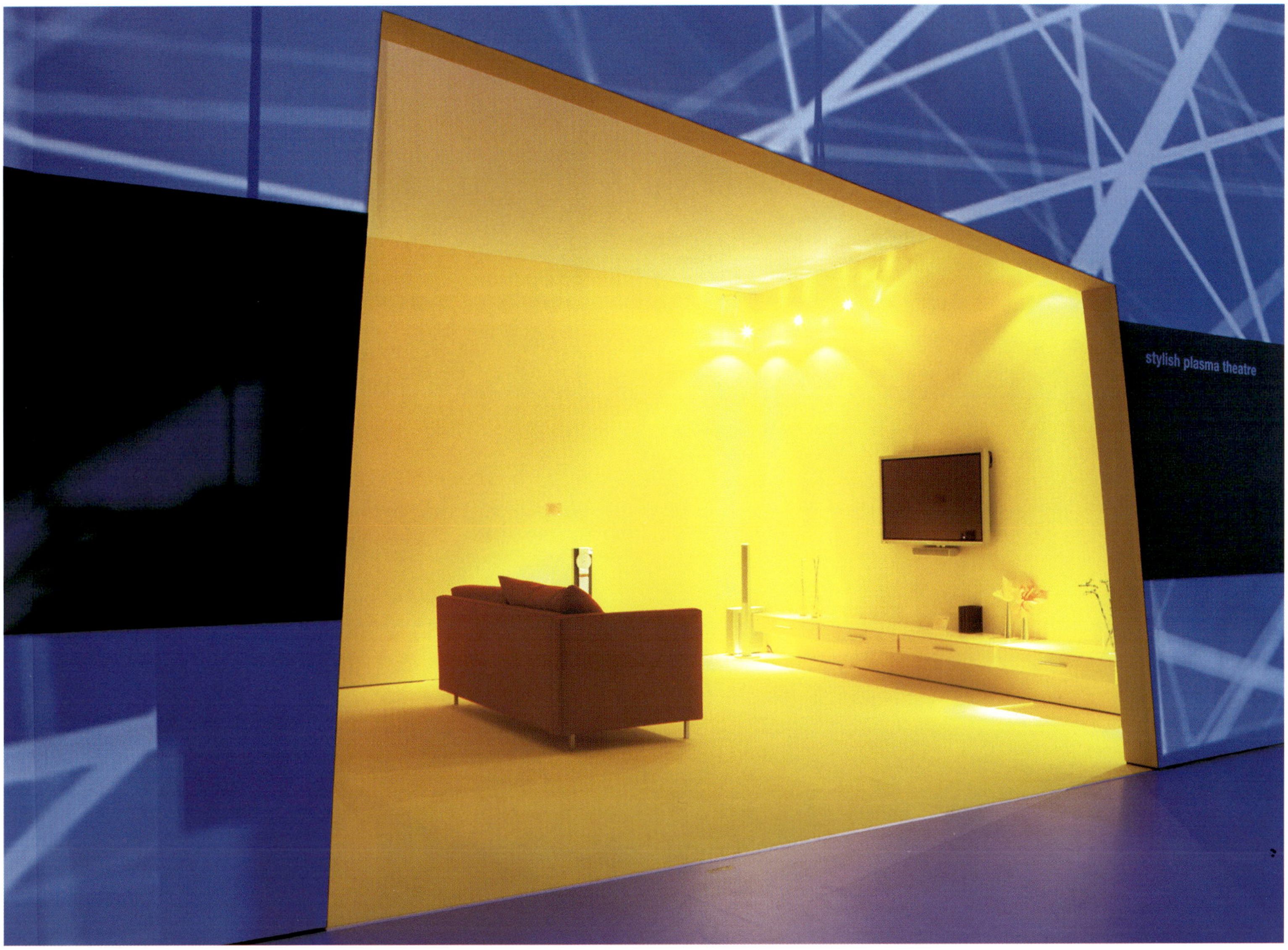
stylish plasma theatre

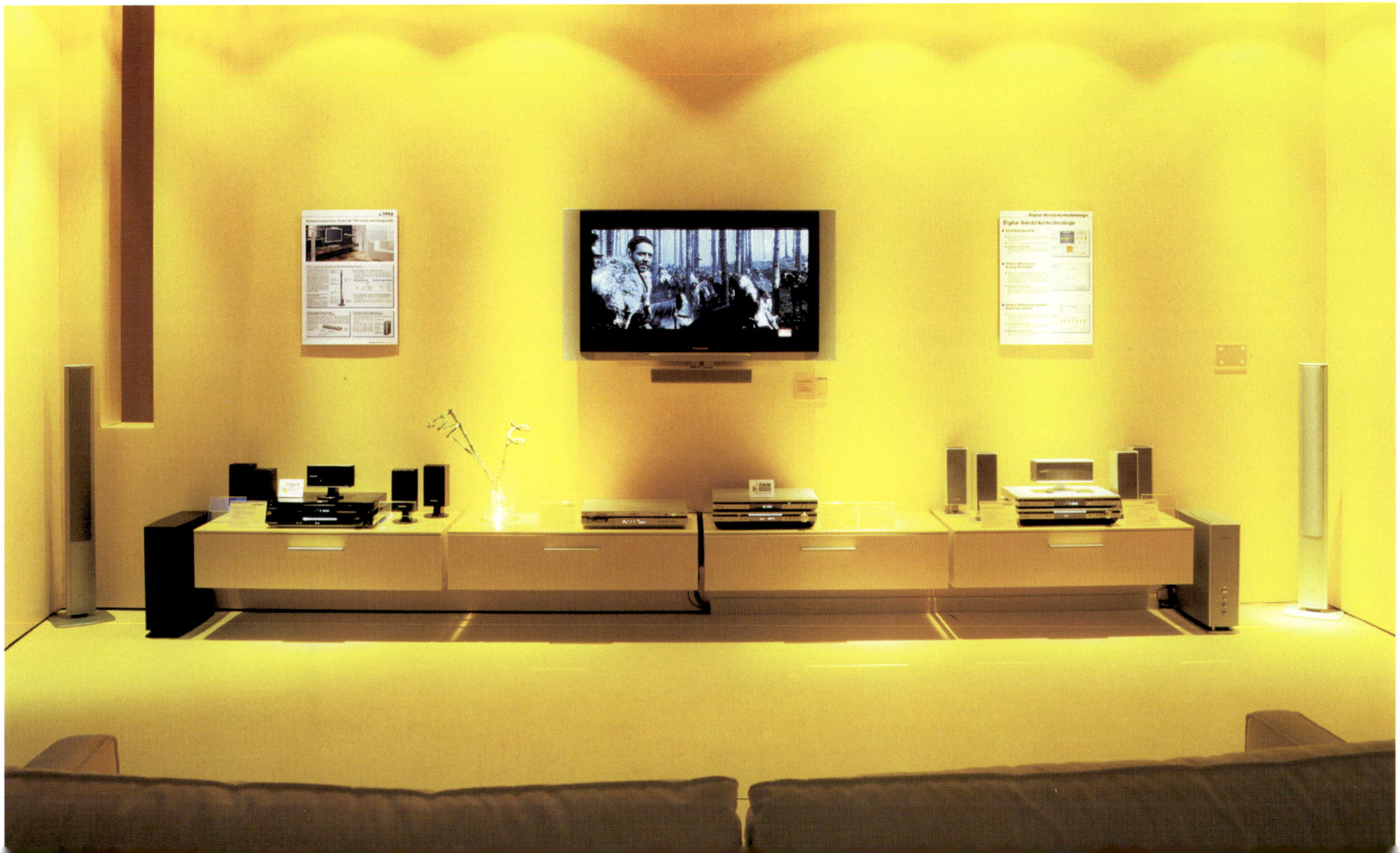

D'Art Design Gruppe

mono

Mono is a family-owned firm known for its elegance and idiosyncratic approach to design. Innovative, high-quality designs have made the company trendsetters in the areas of tableware and lifestyle products. The aim of the new trade fair stand was to allow visitors to experience this philosophy first hand.

The design concept was based on a triangular floor plan. A central space containing a small office and product display area divided the exhibition into three functional zones. Free-standing black walls defined the stand and were also used to display different product groups in back-lit recesses. Other items were displayed on free-standing elements in the center of the room, to complement the corridor displays. Like the company, the design reflected a timeless elegance.

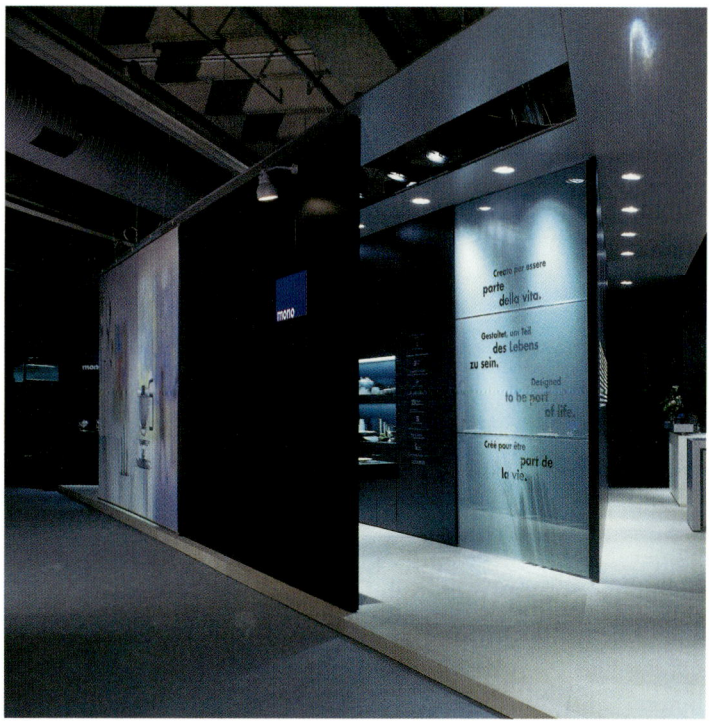

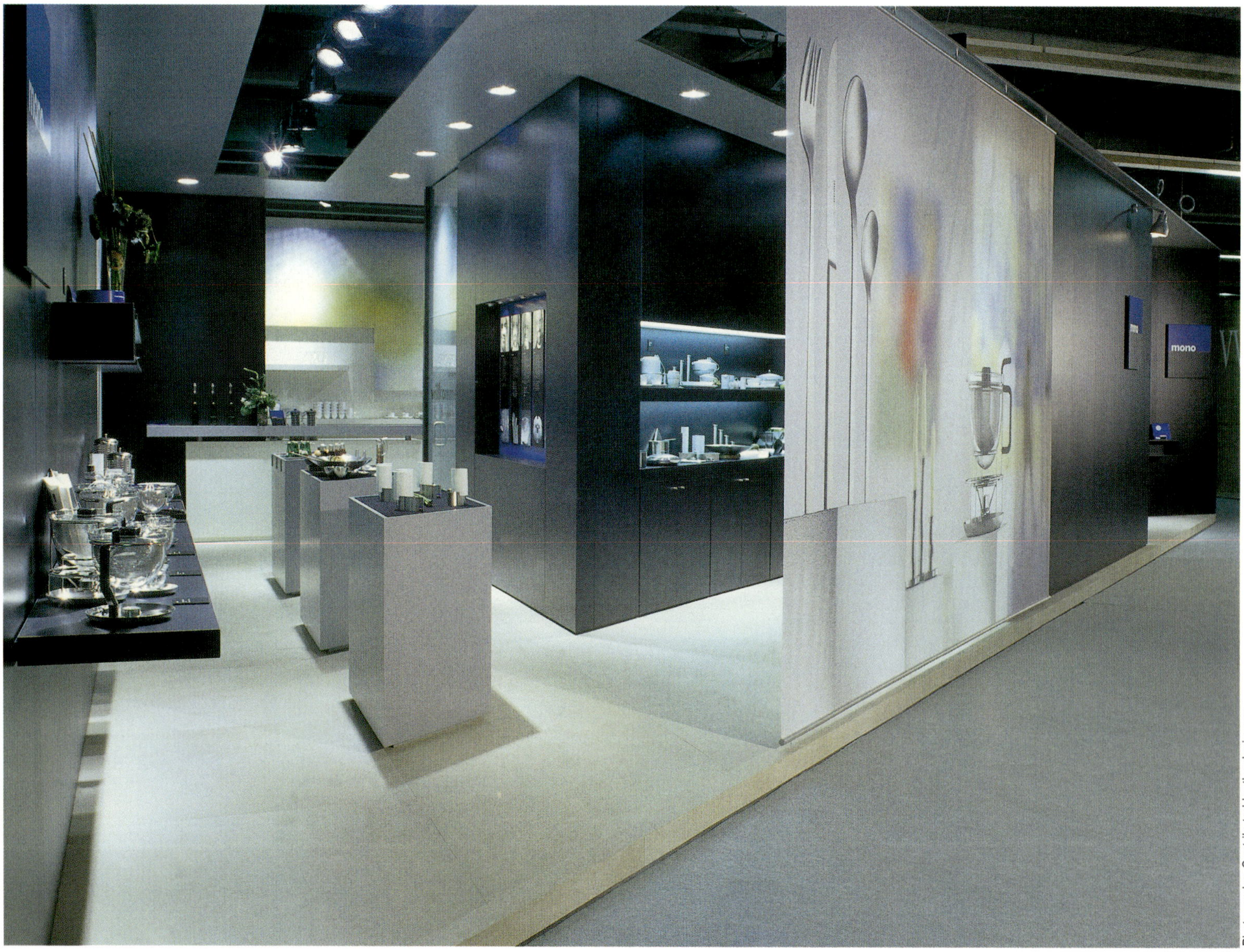

Photographs: Contributed by the designers

The stand included portraits and texts with information about how the products were conceived and developed. Limited forms and materials were used so that the products themselves became the main focus.

Peter Maly
ligne roset + cor

As he does each year, designer Peter Maly designed an elaborate stand for furniture manufacturers Ligne Roset and Cor at the Cologne Furniture Fair. His approach is to create understated and expressive interiors within the exhibition hall in order to showcase the furniture collections by various European designers, often including Peter Maly himself. The Cor stand consisted of a clearly defined expo architecture covering 286 m² for multiple use at several international fairs. A minimal design and simple materials became a neutral background that highlighted the furniture pieces, an effect heightened by the use of bold lighting.

The Ligne Roset stand featured lavish exhibition architecture on two levels, with a total area of 820 m². A generous ambience was created, with open areas flowing into one another offering the visitor a complete architectural concept doing true justice to the Ligne Roset "style de vie".

Photographs: Contributed by the designer

The designer's understated approach to design was evident in these stands, which were like simple stage sets that focused attention on the products. The simple, spacious stands and dramatic lighting were the perfect backdrop for carefully placed, stylish designer pieces. The overall effect enhanced the pieces and expressed a very modern, stylish feeling.

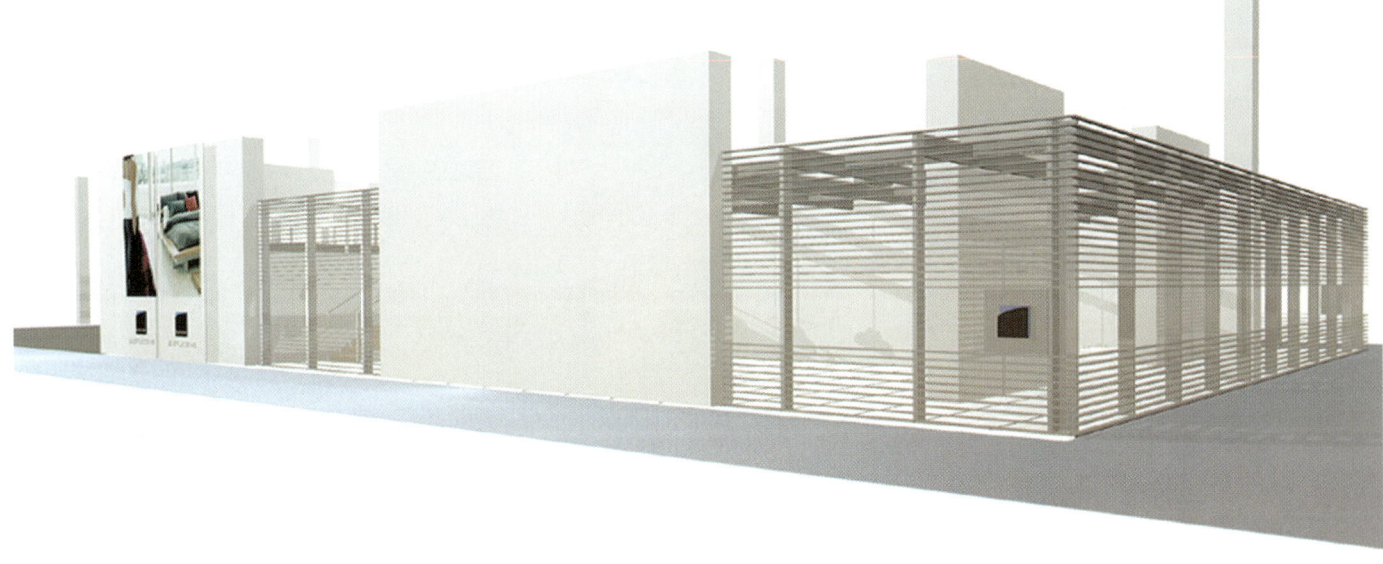

ANSICHT / SCHNITT QUER LINKS   BLICK RICHTUNG TEAM 7

ANSICHT / SCHNITT QUER MITTIG   TREPPE - GALERIE   BLICK RICHTUNG EGO FORM (EHEMALS GIORGETTI)

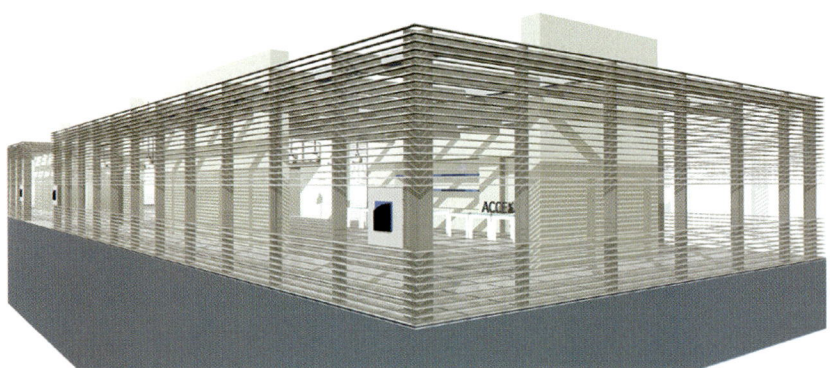

The Ligne Roset stand was based on an open plan design, with a series of interiors flowing into one another. A circulating semi-transparent slot construction enclosed wall discs in visible concrete, and structured the space without breaking it up into separate rooms. The second level, which functions as a discussion and hospitality area for visitors and potential customers, was a demountable steel construction.

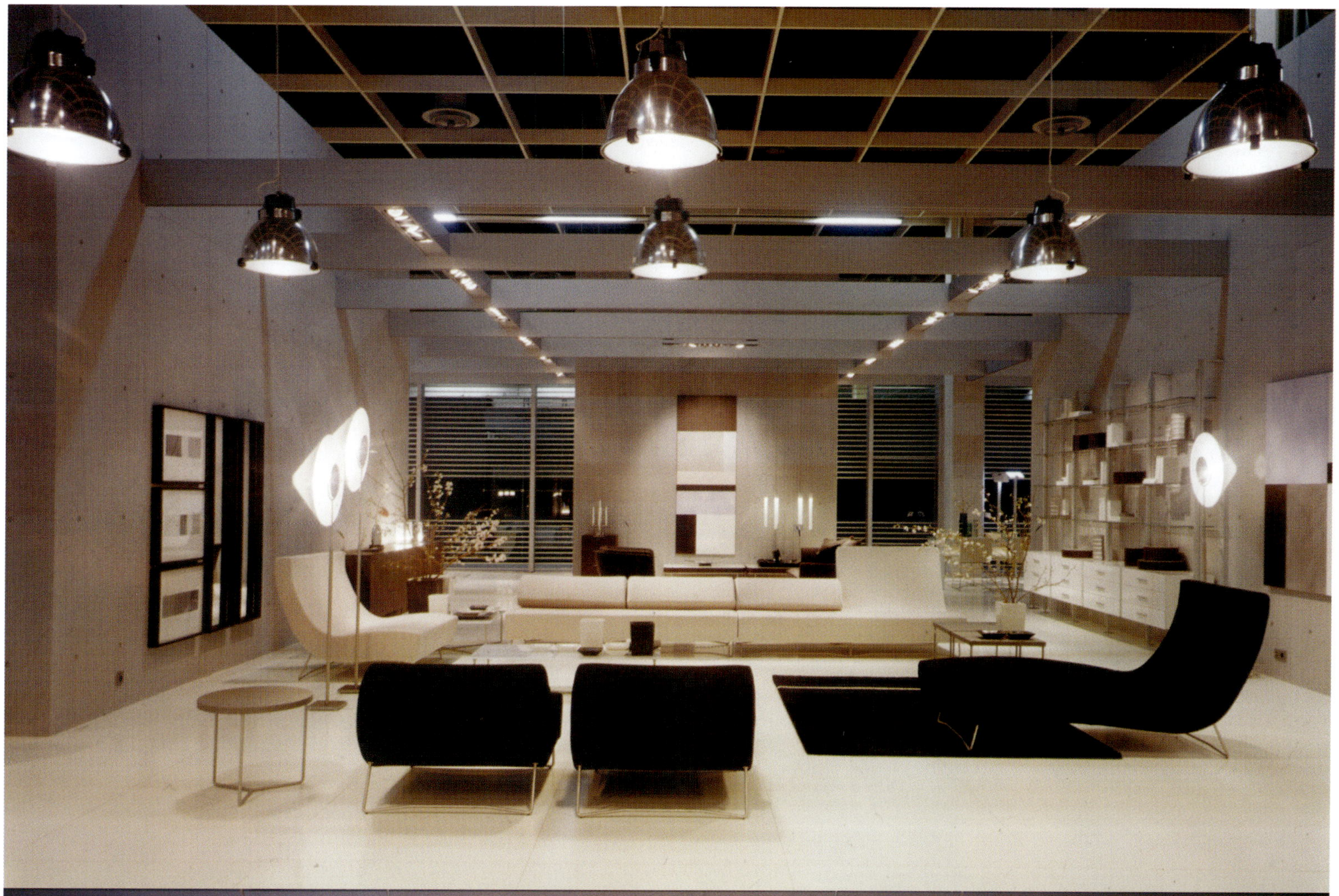

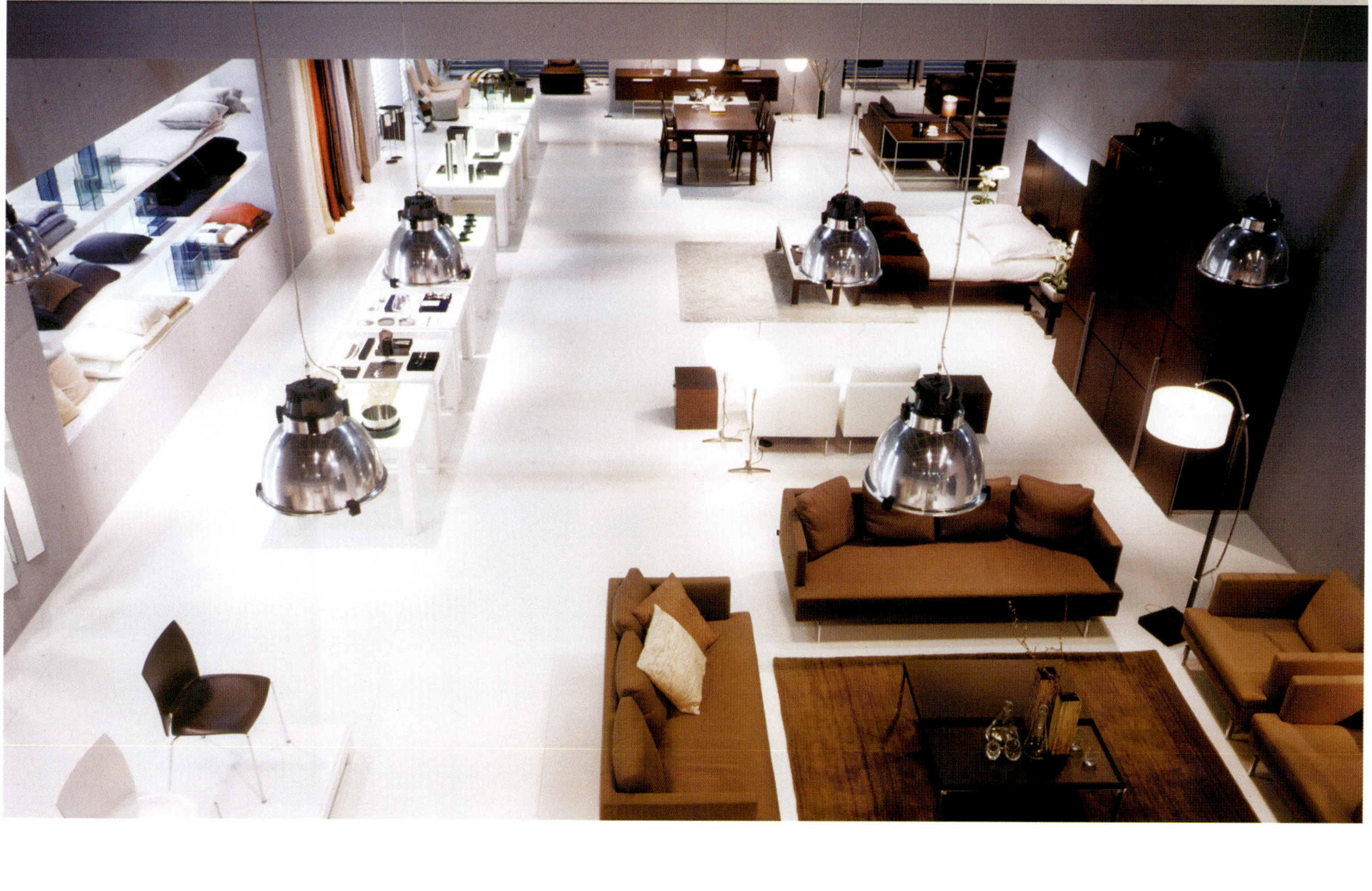

Arno Design
hoechst marion

Arno Design was asked by Hoechst Marion Roussel to create a display for a cardiology congress in Birmingham. The theme was taken quite literally by the designers, who used a playful and illustrative representation of different heart diseases as the decorative elements of the display. The striking sculptural pieces were created in the shape of hearts representing various heart diseases.

Different materials and special lighting were used to create the large sculptural elements: a huge inflated heart for hypertension, an iron-grid heart with flickering electric bulbs for heart attack and thin, shimmering steel tube hearts for cardiac insuffency. The attention-grabbing elements contained texts from exhibiting companies and other relevant information so that the display was both decorative and informative. Styling of the elements was carried out by Gaby Krauss / DesignPlus, Stuttgart for Arno Design.

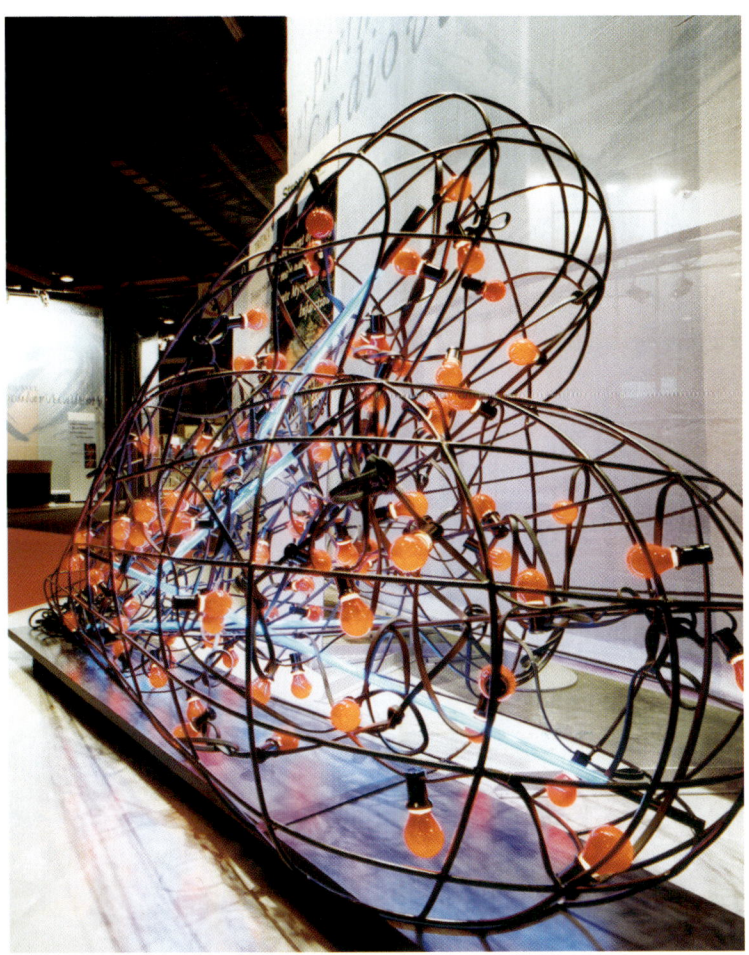

Photographs: Contributed by the designers

Mariona Benaín, Patricia de Muga & Laura García Hintze

cemex-españa

The design for this Cemex stand for the Construmat 2003 trade fair in Barcelona was based on a series of five metal porticos. These structures were repeated in a parallel formation, progressively becoming unaligned in plan and gradually increasing in height. The porticos covered the entire site (192 m²) in a diagonal floor plan, creating a space with progressively higher ceilings and sight lines that gave visitors a sense of perspective and depth that is unusual in a trade fair stand.

The stand was divided into two ground floor spaces for the general public that were interconnected but different in size and atmosphere, and a bar and VIP area on a mezzanine terrace three meters off the ground. All vertical and horizontal surface coverings were made from 50x200 cm white pieces that screwed into or simply rested on the steel structure. These pieces were made from different materials and varied in width according to their use within the space: GRC for walls and roofing, polished terrazzo for the ground floor pavement, and framework elements painted white for the mezzanine and staircase. The monochromatic nature of these elements focused visitors' attention on the advertising posters and lighting. The design simply provided a white background and created a space of varying heights which could then be filled with color, light and activity.

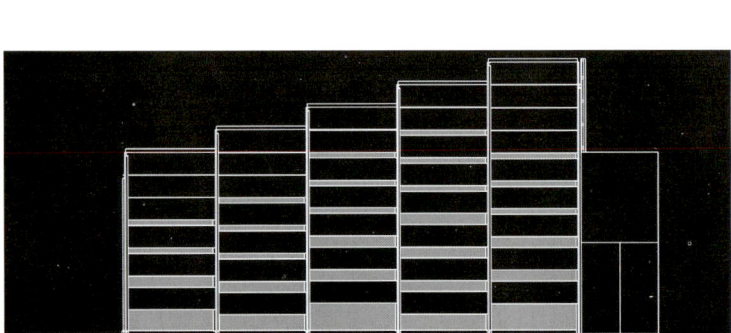

Photographs: Contributed by the architects

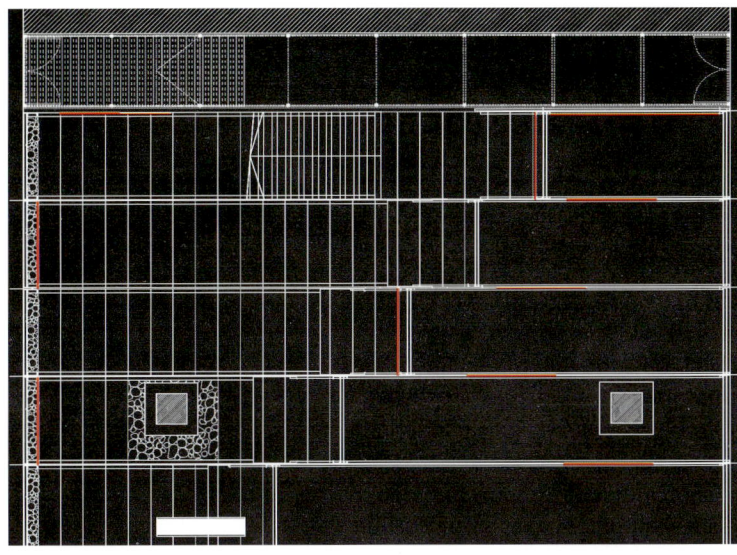

This project didn't reflect the usual ephemeral nature of stand design because it covered the entire site and because the building materials included stone and metal. But the structural elements, the pre-welded joining pieces, the anchoring elements and the modeling of all the external surface coverings were very carefully designed to allow the stand to be set up and dismantled as quickly and efficiently as possible.

Traast & Gruson
droog design

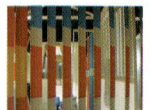

Droog Design had to express the ambivalence in Europe between collective and a specific (country) traditions. To illustrate this ambivalence, Traast & Gruson decided to use a kinetic effect (where the view changes constantly as visitors walk along the installation space). They created a house-like structure to display a range of Droog Design products, within different rooms and functional areas. From the structure of the "house", the designers hung vertical blinds decorated with motifs from the flags of different European countries. By changing the angles of the blinds, visitors could glimpse different views of "Europe", sometimes mixed with a fragmented view of the contents of the room.

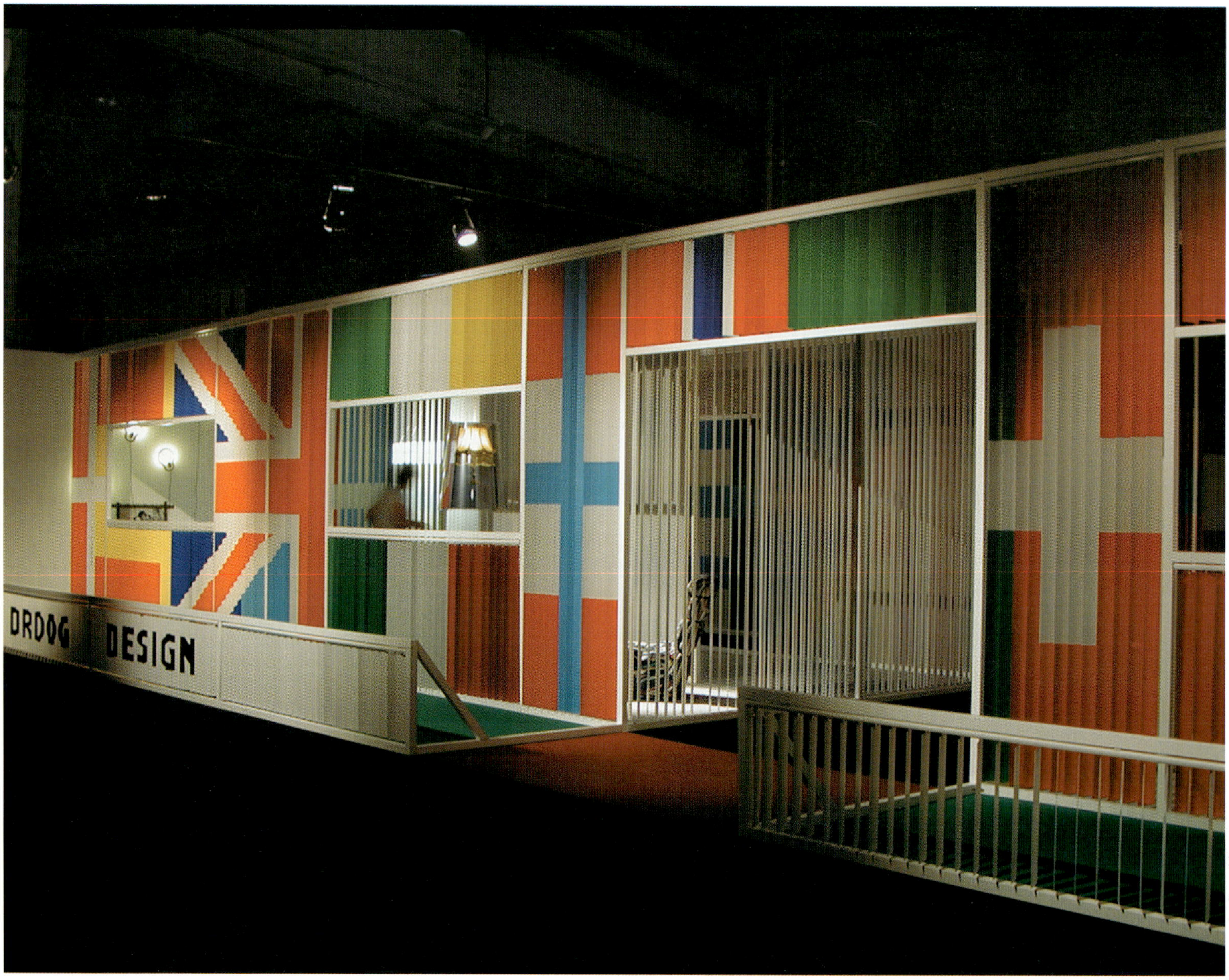

Photographs: Ewoud Traast

Dieter Thiel
ansorg

This twin-storey fair stand with its sociable central piazza offered all kinds of glimpses into and around the realm of light. Innovative lighting engineering and smart control work combined to bring out a broad spectrum of spell-binding coloured light. Cubes within cubes provided a spatial context for the new products. Internally open-ended, they flaunted their treasures far and wide, bathing the entire stand in richly varied light in the process.

The lower area was given over to the fascination of colour, serving as a launch pad for Brick, a new collection of fittings boasting a variety of light systems and resultant colour effects. In the adjacent cube, light from Cube LED light boxes - already prize-winners - changed colour at electronically governed intervals. A decorative effect was added by Cone, a fusion of white light and coloured enclosures.

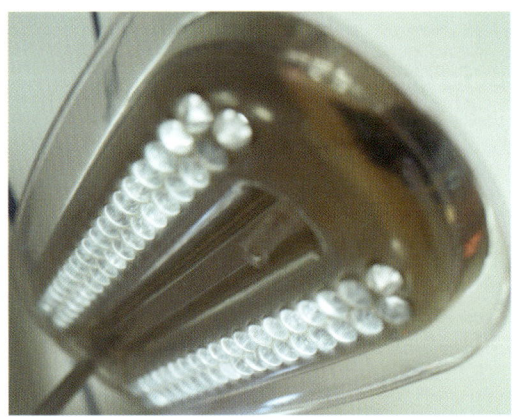

Photographs: Hans-Georg Esch, Hennef/Sieg

A mural comprising constantly changing shades of colour dispensed light to all parts of the stand from the upper storey. LED fittings from the new Lumis programme guided visitors unerringly towards the latest additions to the successful Cardo range.

Multipurpose in light.
Leuchtende Szenarien. Aus der Quelle in der Decke.
Präzise Helligkeit im Raum.
Ansorg. Think Light.

Multipurpose in light.
Illuminated scenarios. From the source in the ceiling.
Precision brightness to surround you.
Ansorg. Think Light.

Gert M. Mayr-Keber

perlen pöll

GMMK were asked to design a multi-use stand that could adapt to different contexts, initially at the first Annual International Jewelry Trade Fair Inhorgenta in Munich, and then at the World Fair for Watches and Jewelry in Bale and other future trade fairs. The designers created a series of separate geometrical units that can be used to form a variety of different stand configurations, simply by putting the parts together differently or using more or less parts each time. The units include a V-shaped show case and a geometrical light-wall, conference-cylinder and storage box, as well as decorative elements such as glass cases, lightscreens and mirrors, all of which can be mixed and matched as required. Some of the elements correspond to specific situations, due to the width required for a large space.

In order to ensure that the stand was inviting and easily accessible, it was designed to open out towards the public like a shop. The detailing was also very important for spatial definition, creating a special atmosphere that separated the stand from the surroundings of the large exhibition hall. The furnishings were created from high quality materials, and the careful detailing made reference to the exclusive nature of the products displayed. The materials used for the stand were highly polished chrome-nickel steel, beech wood, white-coated plates and screens, together with opal and luminescent glass and mirrors to achieve an illusion of space.

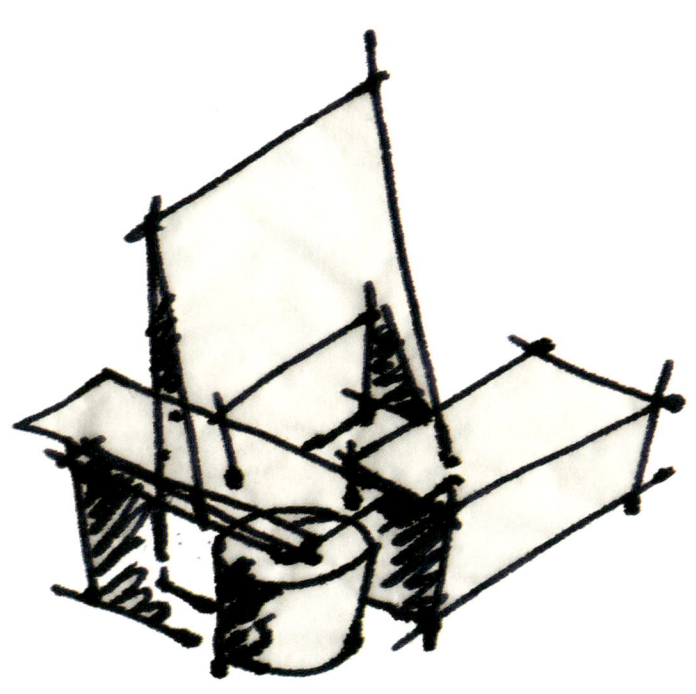

FOR YOU
MY PEARL
FROM NATURE

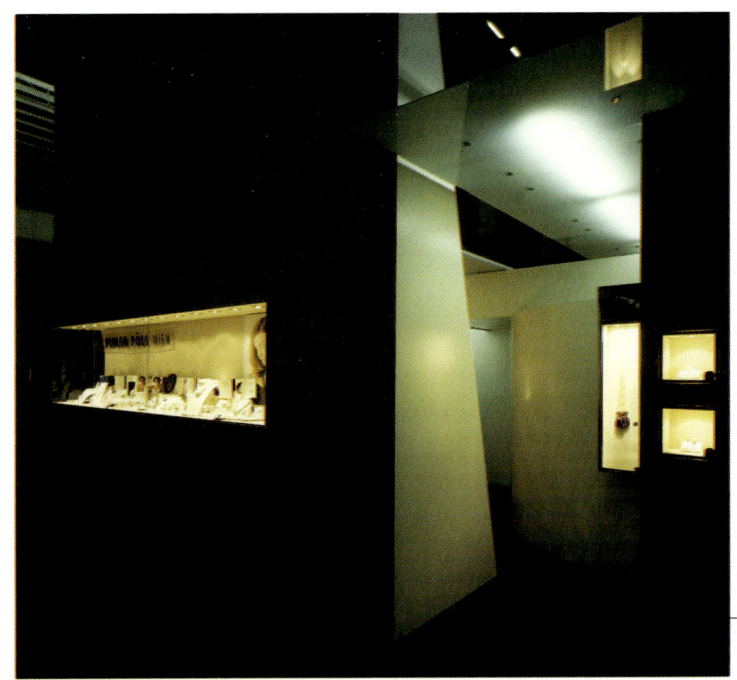

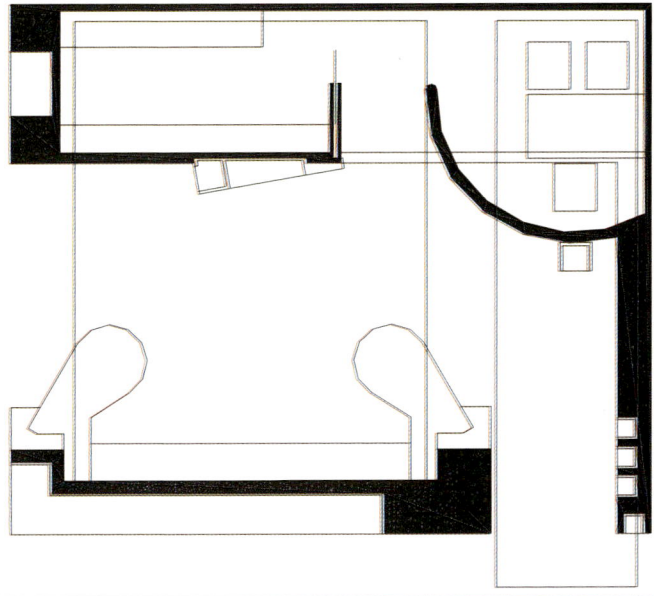

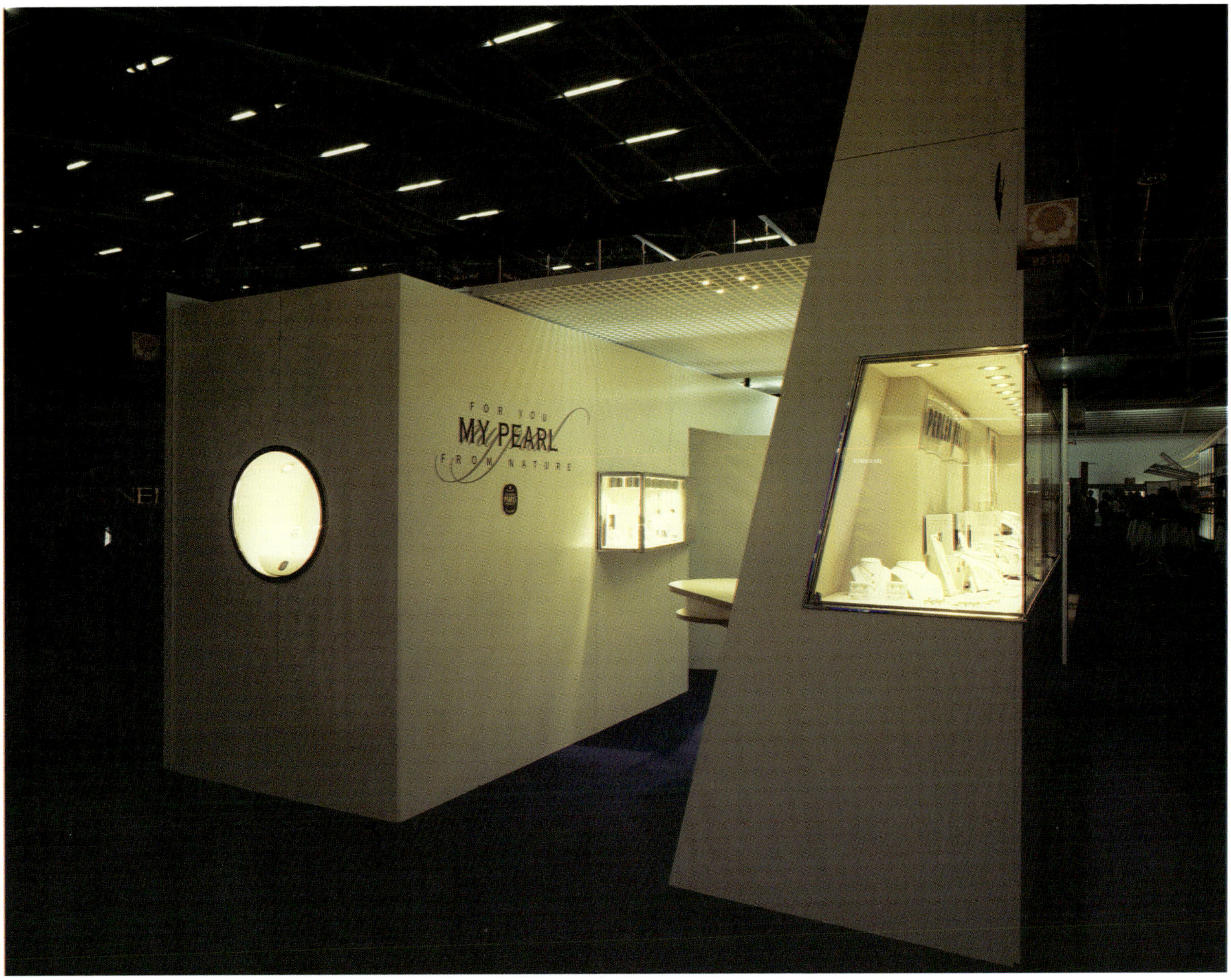

Zeeh Bahls & Partner Design
siemens

This stand is the result of a close collaboration between automation industry market leaders Siemens AG Automation & Drives, the advertising agency Publicis, architects Zeeh Bahls & Partner Design and multimedia designers Luxoom, resulting in an innovative and pioneering exhibition space.

The requirement was to create three levels with large, open areas in order to present the exhibition's three main concepts (Sectors, Solutions and Products). From the exterior, visitors were attracted towards the three colorful, dynamic elements and found themselves entering into a spectacular stage. Cloud-like shapes appeared to float over the stand, creating a magical and relaxing atmosphere. Moving through a "journey of the senses" of lights, moving images and projected texts, visitors were emotionally submerged in the Siemens world. Each of the three "clouds" was lit separately, and the play of colors in the entry level harmonized with those of the solutions and products levels. The colors and movement of lights, text and images created a rich and harmonious multimedia tapestry that defined the different areas while creating playful resonances and unifying the stand.

A completely different atmosphere was created in the VIP area, which was accessed through sliding translucent doors. In this area, soft shapes and backlit panels in various colors enclosed the space, creating a calm and distinctive space in which to relax and exchange information.

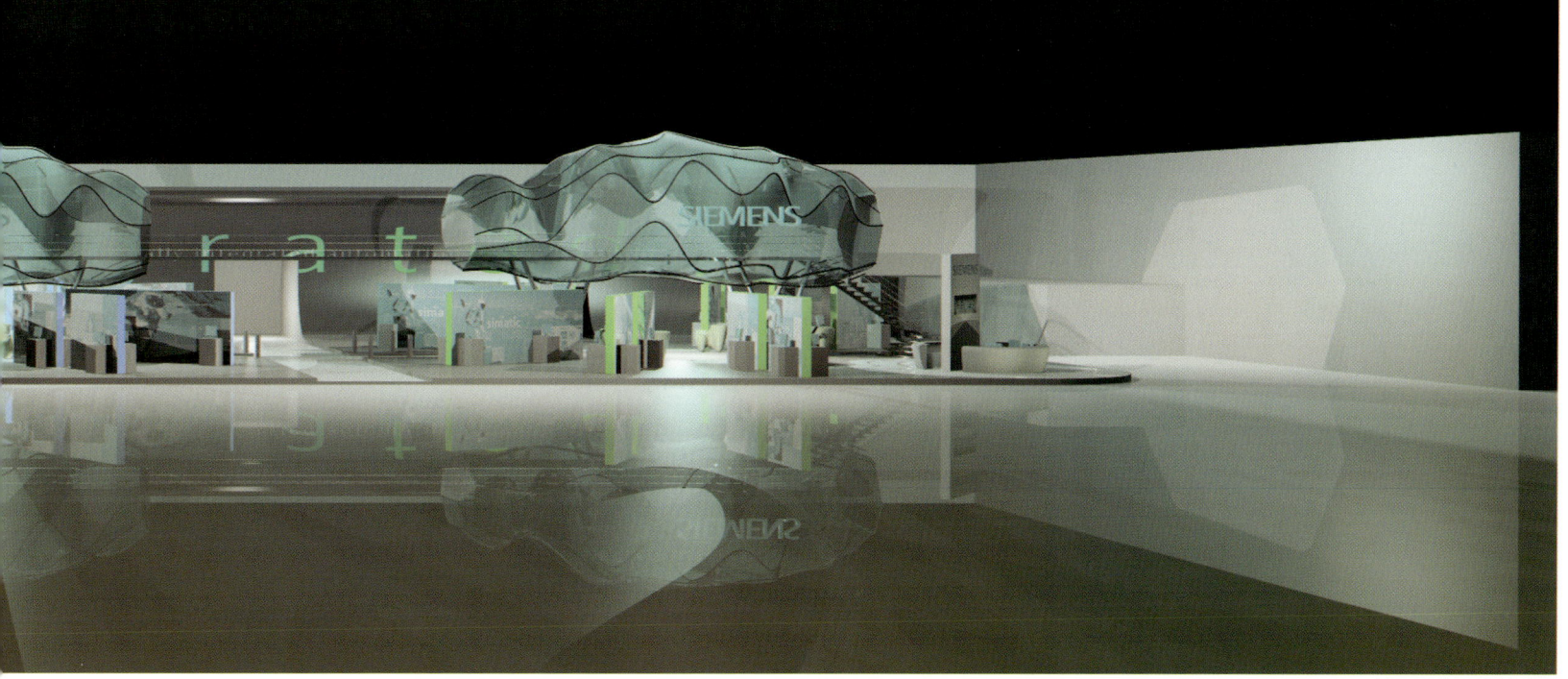

SIEMENS
power
automation

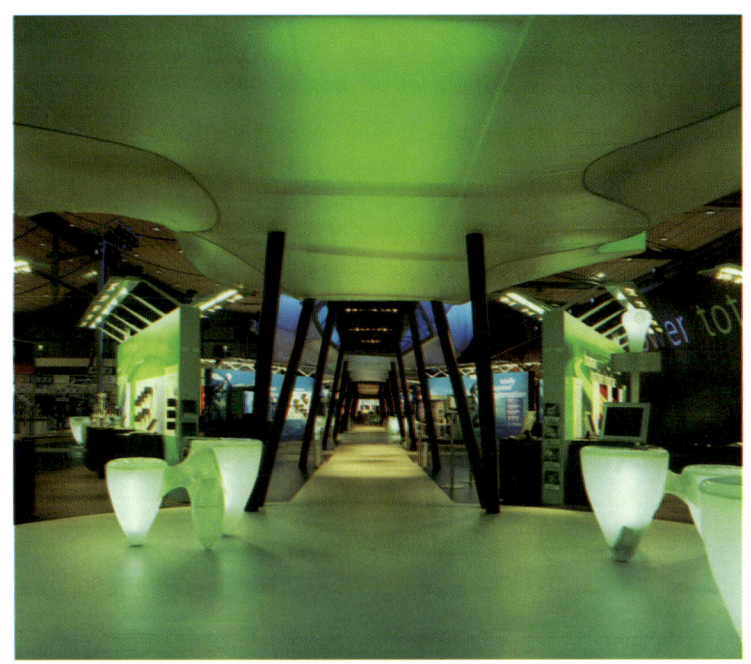

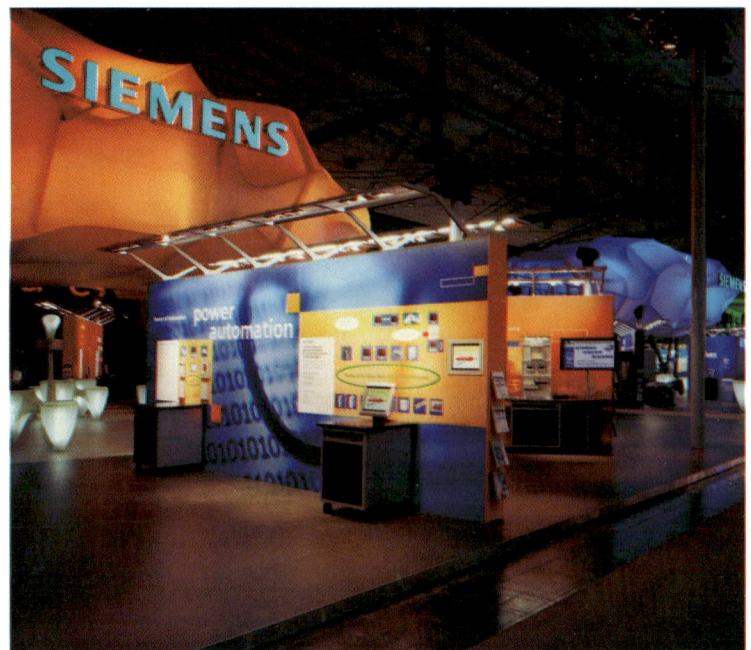

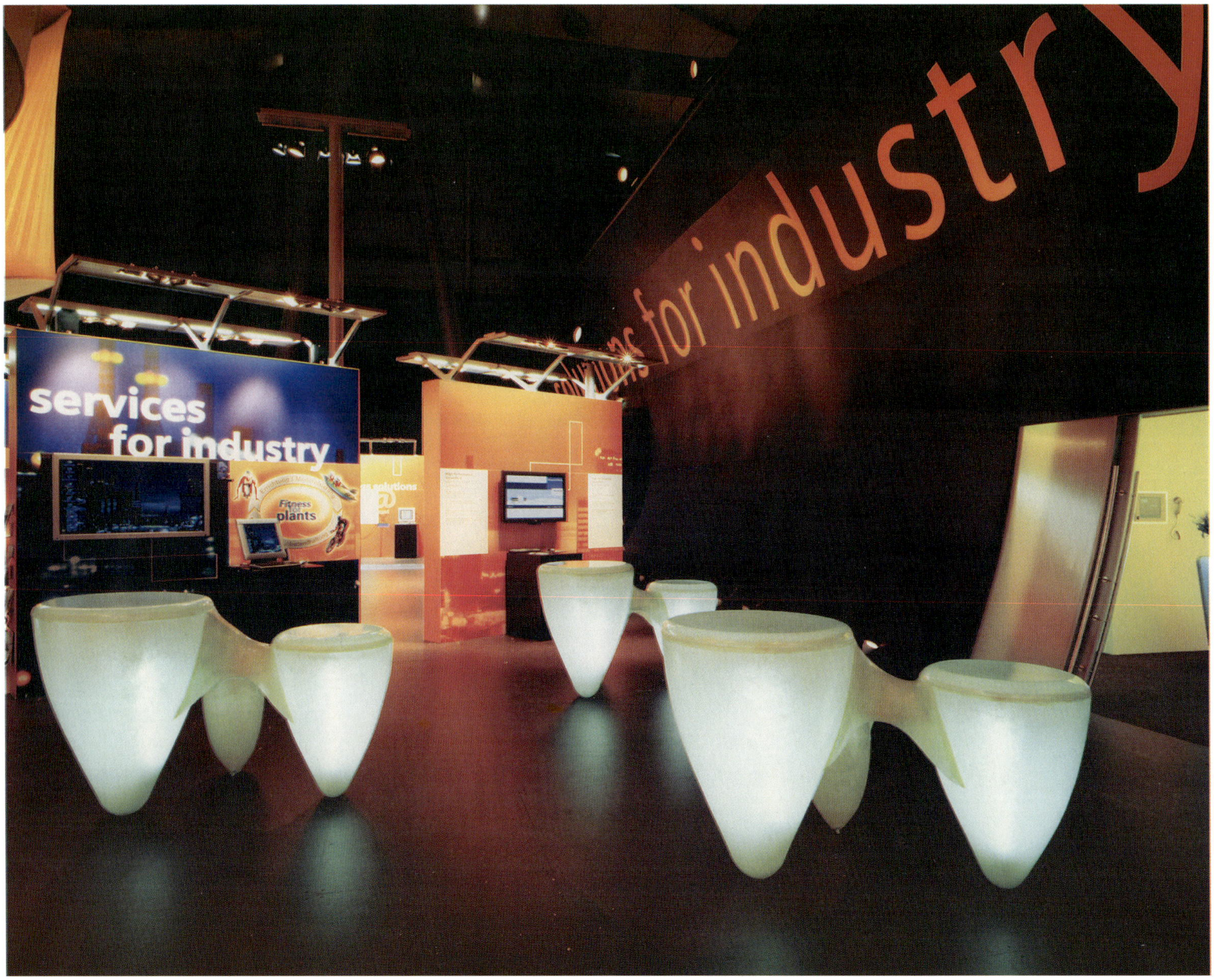
for industry
services
for industry
Fitness
plants

The "Solutions route" on the lower level connected three areas through a star-shaped design. The main Solutions areas, "Solution for Industry and Energy", "Totally Integrated Power" and "Totally Integrated Automation", were explained in detail on both sides of the connecting path. These led to the Product level, with its own color code of orange, apple green and blue allowing visitors to easily navigate through the spaces and enter the "Product streets" that radiated in all directions and contained individual product information. A communications area for information exchange between company representatives and visitors was easily identifiable by individually lighted organic-shaped counters that encouraged conversation, while touch screens in this area provided information about e-commerce.

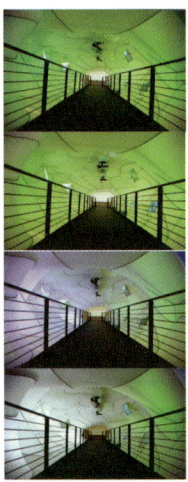

Clearly defined pathways and color-coding allowed visitors to navigate easily through the stand and learn about the products. Projected texts and displays provided information, while the abstract elements created a memorable sensual experience.

The curved internal and external surfaces of the "clouds" and the projection techniques were radically innovative elements that required intensive research and three-dimensional computer modeling. The constantly changing, stimulating projections had to precisely follow the irregular convex surfaces of the clouds in order to create an optimum effect, forcing the designers to create pioneering techniques. The immersive multimedia environment completely surrounded by a complex lightweight structure was designed to evoke the dynamism and spirit of the Siemens brand. The stand was a magnificent example of the integrated use of architecture, graphic design and multimedia elements.

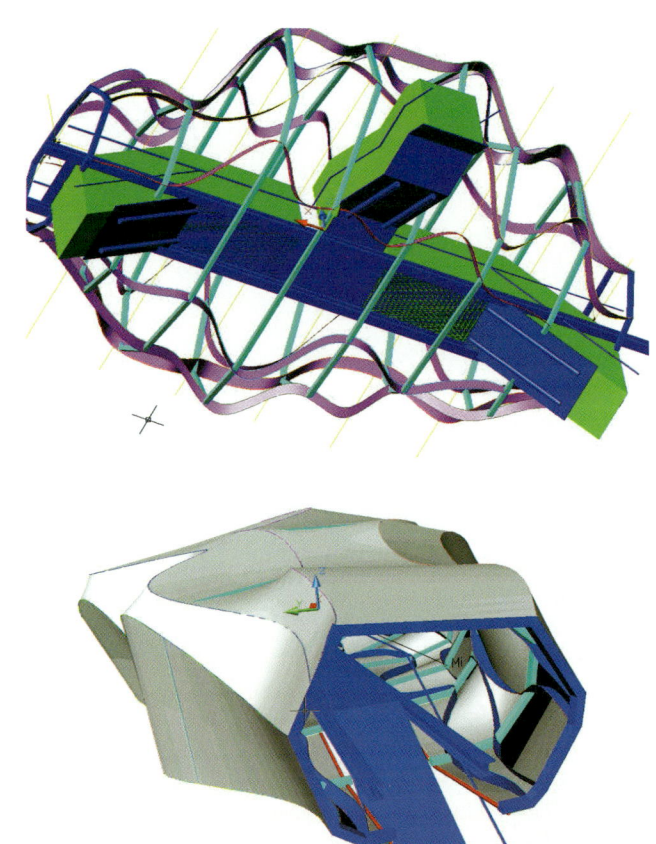

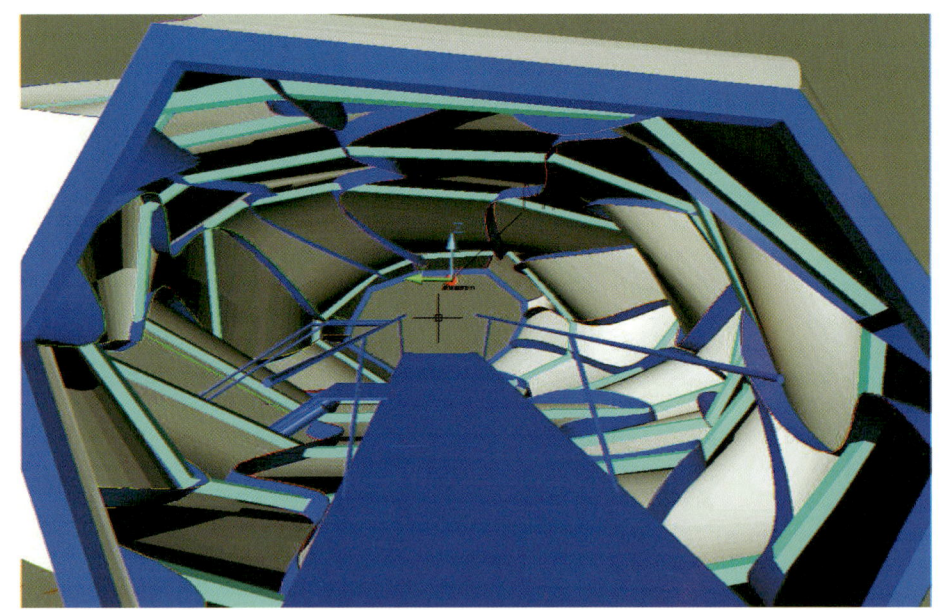

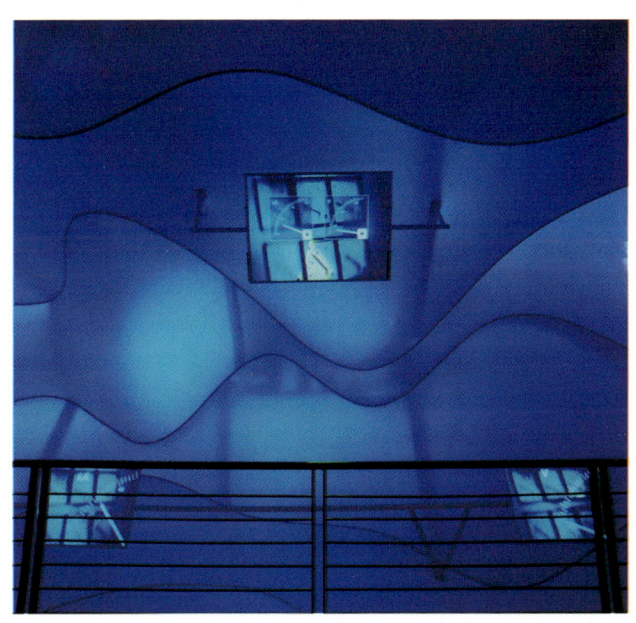

KMS / Schmidhuber + Partner

lamborghini

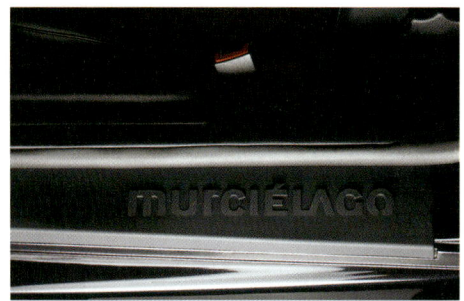

Ferruccio Lamborghini's decision to build the world's fastest automobile led him not only to create amazing cars, but also to develop the radical attitude that quickly turned Lamborghini into a myth recognized all over the world. Since their first project for Automobili Lamborghini in 1998, Schmidhuber + Partner and KMS have sought to develop a clearly defined brand concept that expresses the special nature of the company and can be applied to everything from showrooms to the company's manuals and font styles.

In keeping with the uncompromising nature of the brand, the Lamborghini stand for IAA 2001 was designed to evoke a sacred space. Within this context, the vehicles had the status of objects to be worshipped. The exhibition area was fenced off and the meeting rooms were in the inner area, shielded from the outside. The structural elements were sharp-edged square blocks made from brushed steel sheets, arranged at right angles throughout the space. Their size and shape made them appear compact and powerful and suggested mysterious megalithic objects. Throughout the stand, the predominant color was black, creating an overall impression of an ancient and important cultural space that radiated both superiority and seclusion. The exhibition area was also made from steel, and consisted simply of two vehicles and an engine block displayed in an empty, sober space. The designers decided to use only the colors yellow and black, derived from the company's coat of arms. About three meters above the vehicles there hung an aluminum-plated box that seemed to be a mold of the vehicles, a negative version of the contours of the car. This "absent form" was strongly lit, allowing visitors to contemplate it from below - the symbolic birth of the new Lamborghini "Murcielago". The area had been cordoned off by a glass fence, and could not be accessed by the general public.

Two columns, each supporting an illuminated coat of arms, reinforced the idea of a place of cultural importance. Three sheet steel blocks formed the rear section, and the meeting rooms were situated in the space beyond them. This meeting area was shielded from the outside, and it was impossible to look into it other than from the connecting rooms that served as a passage. The stand was designed in modules, allowing it be used at other trade fairs or even as an autonomous permanent construction, such as a Lamborghini showroom. The materials used, attention to detail and severity of the space provoked a respectful attitude in visitors, who were made aware that they were in an exceptional space and contemplating exceptional vehicles.

Photographs: Stefan Müller-Naumann

178

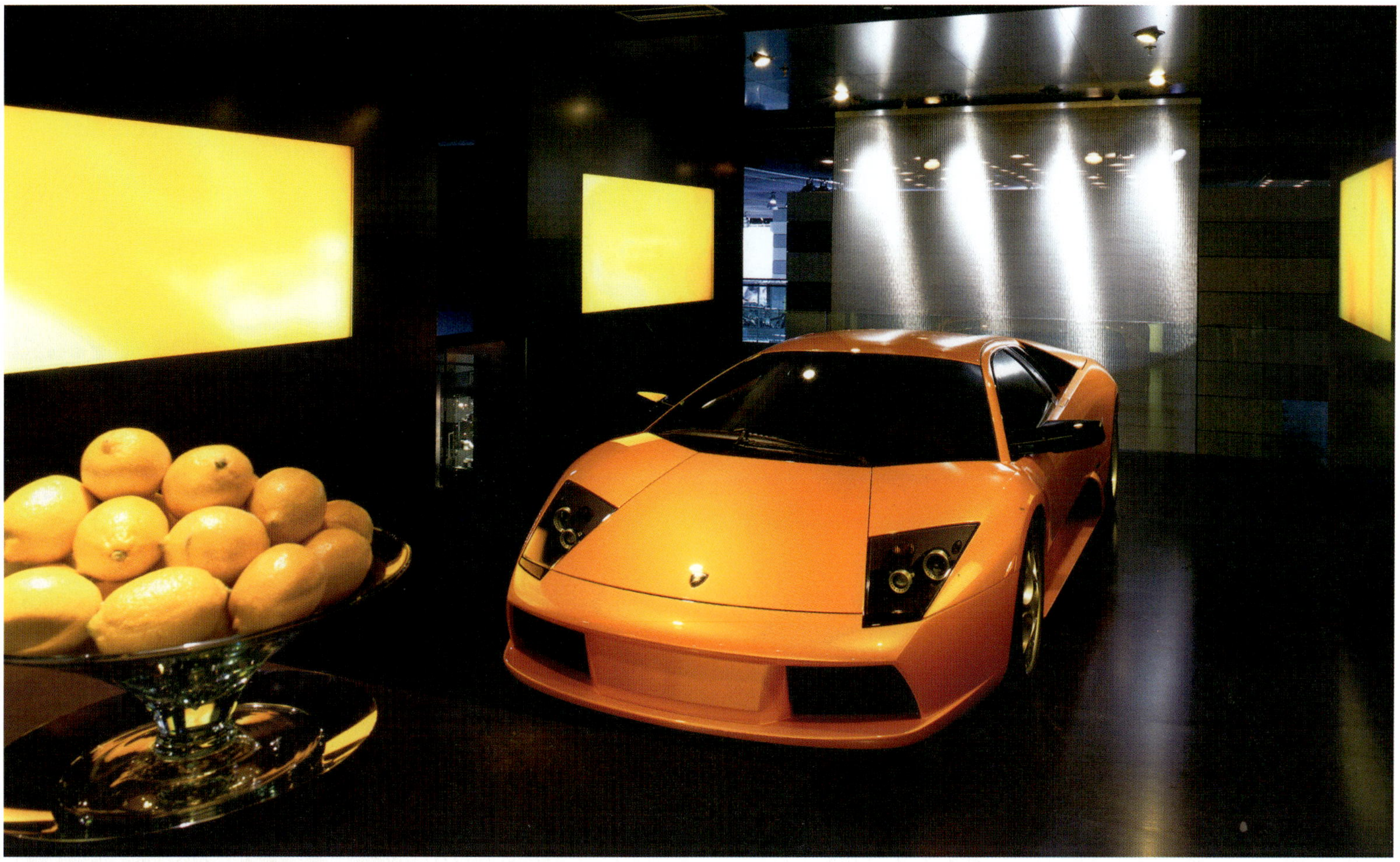

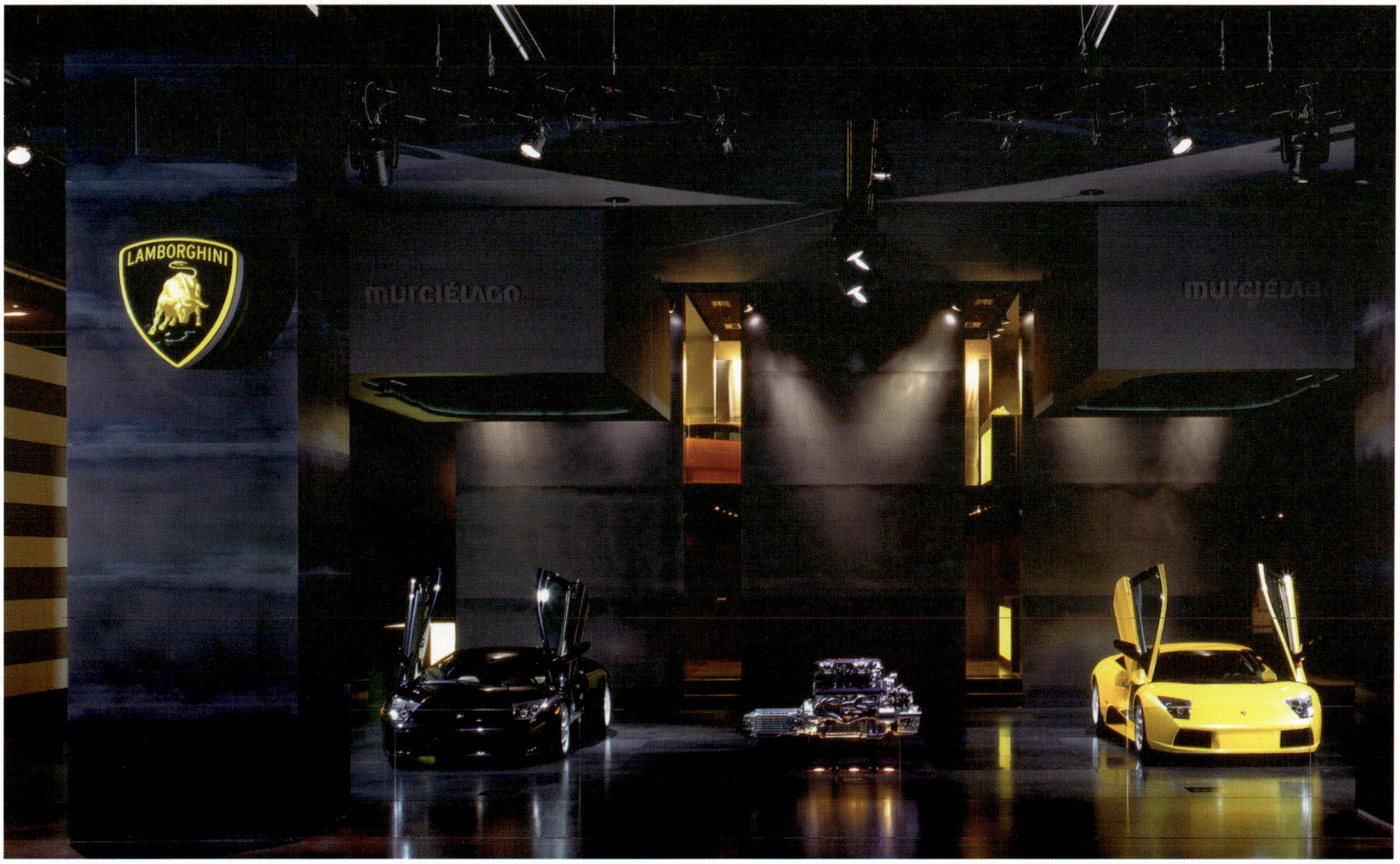
LAMBORGHINI
murciélago